Sams'
Teach
Yourself

AMERICA
ONLINE® 4.0

in 24 Hours

Sams'
Teach Yourself

AMERICA
ONLINE® 4.0

in 24 Hours

Bob Temple

SAMS
PUBLISHING

201 West 103rd Street
Indianapolis, Indiana 46290

Copyright © 1998 by Sams Publishing

FIRST EDITION

International Standard Book Number: 1-57521-327-3

Library of Congress Catalog Card Number: 97-66680

01 00 99 98   4 3 2

Interpretation of the printing code: the rightmost double-digit number is the year of the book's printing; the rightmost single-digit, the number of the book's printing. For example, a printing code of 98-1 shows that the first printing of the book occurred in 1998.

Composed in AGaramond and MCPdigital by Macmillan Computer Publishing

Printed in the United States of America

Publisher John Pierce
Director of Editorial Services Carla Hall
Executive Editor Angela Wethington
Managing Editor Tom Hayes
Senior Indexer Ginny Bess

Acquisitions Editors
Patty Guyer
Stephanie J. McComb

Development Editor
Henly Wolin

Production Editor
Heather E. Butler

Copy Editor
Julie McNamee

Indexer
Chris Wilcox

Technical Reviewers
Mark Hall
John Purdum

Editorial Coordinator
Mandie Rowell

Cover Designer
Aren Howell

Book Designer
Gary Adair

Production Team Supervisor
Victor Peterson

Production
Darlena Murray
Pamela Woolf

Overview

Contents

Dedication

Shortly before I began work on this project, my mother was diagnosed with brain cancer. I dedicate this book to her, and to the hundreds of lives she's touched.

Acknowledgments

I'd like to thank everyone who helped bring this book to fruition, but I did the whole thing by myself and I owe nothing to anyone.

Just kidding.

Seriously, there are many people whose help at various points along the way helped get this sucker to print, most notably Randi Roger of Sams and Brad Schepp of America Online.

(Many thanks, Randi, for getting me that secret decoder ring.)

Thanks also to Barb Melchior, for Sundays (and Saturdays); Ron Lesko, the schedule-juggler; Dan Clay, my computer guru; and Bev Eppink, who found me in the first place.

Primarily though, I'd like to thank my wife, for doing all the little things (and the big ones, too) that make it easy for me to handle a big project like this one. She also deserves recognition for keeping her sanity these past 11 years, and for helping me keep mine.

To Emily Temple, age 7, I say thanks for being my special lunch date, and try not to grow up so darn fast.

To Robby Temple, age 4, I say thanks for the smiles that brighten my day and try to remember that it hurts daddy when you jump on his kidneys.

To Sammy Temple, age 4, I say thanks for the alley-oop passes and try to remember that punching me in the stomach is a foul.

Finally, I want to express my appreciation to two people who had nothing to do with this book at all: My sister, Susan Kesselring, for the innumerable tasks she's undertaken and burdens she has borne on behalf of our family; and Pastor Gary Langness, for always being there for this family for as long as I can remember.

About the Author

Bob Temple

Bob Temple, a journalist by trade is currently General Manager/Director of Web Services of a group of weekly newspapers in the suburbs of Minneapolis-St. Paul. His first book, *Sports on the Net*, a guide to sports information on the Internet, was published by Macmillan in 1995. He has been a contributing author on three other Internet-related titles, and served as development editor for Sams' *The Internet Unleashed 1997*. He covers the Minnesota Timberwolves on a freelance basis for the Associated Press, and has covered all the major professional sports at one time or another in the past ten years. His other freelance work includes numerous articles for magazines and newspapers across the U.S. He can be reached at his Internet address: btemple@summitpoint.com.

Introduction

I can remember my first online communication, though it was almost 11 years ago now. Following a hockey game I covered for the Associated Press, I sent my story off from Minneapolis to New York, where the main computer greeted me first with

CONNECT

Then, after the file had been sent, the remote computer returned to my screen the following message:

"File Stored."

Somehow, through a maze of computer hardware and software, telephone lines, modems, and jacks, 500 words of outstanding prose had flown from Minneapolis to New York. From there, it would be distributed to the rest of the world.

I was impressed.

A couple of months later, I sent an article I wrote to the magazine that had requested it. This time, the computer at the other end of this digital transaction was being manned. After the file was sent, the following message appeared on my screen:

"Don't hang up, Bob."

I was completely freaked out. I knew this was a one-to-one computer connection, but it surprised me that the remote computer had spoken to me by name. I sat there and waited.

"Thanks, Bob. Good article. Thanks for meeting the deadline, Dave."

It was the guy on the other computer, somehow magically typing on his keyboard and making it appear on mine. I responded, and it worked.

I was hooked.

Although the above story doesn't reflect today's online communications very completely, it does foreshadow a little of what is going on in today's online world.

These days, things are a lot more complex. Services such as America Online are as technically complex as they are easy to use. It seems that for every new techno-geek advance that is made in the online world, the result is an easier-to-use product for the average Joe.

Thank goodness for that.

America Online's new version, 4.0, is every bit as easy to use as it is complex. The good news for you is that you don't have to worry about or even understand much of the complex stuff.

If you're new to America Online, or to online stuff in general, you'll find that the new version of the software feels like you're just using a great computer program. There's nothing spooky about being online at all—just a lot of opportunity.

If you're experienced with America Online, you'll find the new version packed with enhancements, some of which you might have suggested to the technical folks at AOL.

What This Book Is

The title of the book explains it all, I think: It's a 24-hour guide to learning the basics, and some not-so-basic stuff, about America Online and the Internet connection it contains.

To make it easier, we've divided the topic into 24 chapters, each of which should take you about an hour to complete (an approximation, not a guarantee). The 24 chapters are divided into six parts comprised of four chapters each. A seventh part comprises three appendixes that provide valuable information.

The parts are divided as follows:

☐ Part I, "The Basics," takes you through the start-up stuff you need to do and know in order to get you going. Included are how to install the software and get your membership set up, some discussion of what America Online is all about, some of the basics of using the service, and a complete chapter on email.

☐ Part II, "Getting Comfortable with AOL," takes you to the next level, as you discover how to download files, how to run FlashSessions, how to chat with other AOL members, and how to use AOL's channels.

☐ Part III, "Getting Started on the Internet," moves you outside of AOL to the larger Internet. Along with some Internet basics, you learn about newsgroups and mailing lists, file transfers and Gopher, and how to use the World Wide Web.

☐ Part IV, "Personalizing and Customizing AOL," teaches you how to set up your own home page, how to set up your own navigational tools, how to set preferences, and how to take your AOL membership on the road with you.

☐ Part V, "Getting Information Online," covers how and where to find news, entertainment, and personal finance and sports information on America Online.

☐ Part VI, "Your Family and AOL," teaches you about parental controls, getting your kids involved, how to use educational tools within AOL, and how to plan travel, including the family vacation, with AOL.

☐ Part VII, "Appendixes," provides you with two important topics and a fun one. You learn which physical, system requirements you need in order to install AOL 4.0 on a Macintosh-compatible computer, and then you are walked through the installation process. The second appendix shares invaluable troubleshooting tips, and advises where you should turn when you can't resolve the problem yourself. The third appendix demonstrates how you can incorporate fun emoticons and sounds while you chat online.

Have fun!

Using the *Sams' Teach Yourself in 24 Hours* Series

Welcome to the *Sams' Teach Yourself in 24 Hours* series! You're probably thinking, "What? They want me to stay up all night and learn this stuff?" Well, no, not exactly. This series introduces a new way to teach you about exciting new products: 24 one-hour lessons, designed to keep your interest and keep you learning. Because the learning process is broken into small units, you will not be overwhelmed by the complexity of some of the new technologies that are emerging in today's market. Each hourly lesson has a number of special items—some old, some new—to help you along.

Minutes

The first 10 minutes of each hour lists the topics and skills about which you will learn by the time you finish the hour. You will know exactly what the hour will bring, with no surprises.

Minutes

Twenty minutes into the lesson, you will have been introduced to many of the newest features of the software application. In the constantly evolving computer arena, knowing everything a program can do will aid you enormously now and in the future.

Minutes

Before 30 minutes have passed, you will have learned at least one useful task. Many of these tasks take advantage of the newest features of the application. These tasks use a hands-on approach, telling you exactly the menus and commands that you need to use to accomplish the goal. This approach is found in each lesson of the *24 Hours* series.

40 Minutes

You will see after 40 minutes that many of the tools you have come to expect from the *Sams' Teach Yourself* series are found in the *24 Hours* series as well. Notes and Tips offer special tricks of the trade to make your work faster and more productive. Cautions help you avoid those nasty time-consuming errors.

50 Minutes

By the time you're 50 minutes in, you'll probably run across terms you haven't seen before. Never before has technology thrown so many new words and acronyms into the language, and the New Term elements found in this series will carefully explain each one.

60 Minutes

At the end of the hour, you may still have questions that need answered. You know the kind—questions on skills or tasks that come up every day for you, but that weren't directly addressed during the lesson. That's where the Q&A section can help. By answering the most frequently asked questions about the topics discussed in the hour, Q&A not only answers your specific question, but it also provides a succinct review of all that you have learned in the hour.

Tell Us What You Think!

As a reader, you are the most important critic and commentator of our books. We value your opinion and want to know what we're doing right, what we could do better, what areas you'd like to see us publish in, and any other words of wisdom you're willing to pass our way. You can help us make strong books that meet your needs and give you the computer guidance you require.

Do you have access to the World Wide Web? Then check out our site at `samspublishing.com`.

COFFEE BREAK

> If you have a technical question about this book, call the technical support line at 317-581-3833, or send email to `support@mcp.com`.

As the team leader of the group that created this book, I welcome your comments. You can fax, email, or write me directly to let me know what you did or didn't like about this book—as well as what we can do to make our books stronger. Here's the information:

Fax: 317-581-4669

Email: `awethington@mcp.com`

Mail: Angela Wethington
          Comments Department
          Sams Publishing
          201 W. 103rd Street
          Indianapolis, IN 46290

PART

I

The Basics

Hour

Hour 1

Installing America Online and Signing Up

Congratulations! You might not realize it, but you've just taken the first step of a big adventure—traveling into cyberspace with America Online 4.0.

Before any of that can happen, you need to install the America Online software.

In this hour you'll walk through the first basic steps of getting set up on America Online (AOL). You'll learn

☐ How to install AOL 4.0 for Windows 95

☐ How to sign on to the service

☐ What the various billing options are

☐ How to pick a screen name and password

☐ How to sign off from the service

Without a doubt, this hour is the easiest and most necessary hour in the book. If things aren't set up properly in the first place, you'll never be able to enjoy the service.

Where Can I Find AOL Software?

AOL 4.0 software is available *everywhere*; you can find it in magazines, by phone, in your mailbox, and even on AOL itself. You may have the software already—they aren't exactly shy about mailing copies to strangers.

If you haven't already found a copy, give the AOL Customer Service line a call at 1-800-827-6364. They'll be more than happy to send you a copy of the software, either on a CD-ROM or on disk.

CAUTION

To Use the AOL software you'll need the following minimum requirements:

4.0 for Win 95 (32-bit) and Win 98 System Requirements

16MB of RAM, Pentium PC, 30MB of hard disk, 640×480, 256 colors, 14.4 or faster modem. 4.0 for Windows 3.1 (16-bit) System Requirements

16MB of RAM, 486 PC or better, 30MB of hard disk, 640×480, 256 colors, 14.4 or faster modem.

Installing AOL 4.0 for Windows

After you have the software and you've made sure your system is up to the task of running it, you're ready to install AOL 4.0 for Windows. Installing the software is fairly easy and there's step-by-step instructions onscreen as you go.

TIME SAVER

This section covers installing the software on a Windows-based computer. Although installing the Macintosh version is similar, there are a few differences. Appendix A, "Installing AOL 4.0 on a Macintosh-Compatible Computer," covers installing the software on a Mac.

Assuming that your computer is up and running, and you have the AOL CD (or disk) in hand, you're ready to go. There are a couple of "If" steps here that apply only to folks upgrading from a previous version of AOL. If you're not upgrading, you can blithely pass them by.

Installing AOL 4.0

To Do

1. Put the disk (or disc) into the appropriate drive on your computer.

2. Start the setup routine. For Windows 95, that means: click the Start button, then click Run on the Start menu. In Windows 3.*x*, select File | Run from the Program Manager menu.

3. When the Run dialog box opens, type **E:\SETUP** (this assumes that E is the drive letter assigned to your CD-ROM drive, if that's incorrect, substitute the letter of the drive in which you've put the AOL disk). If it's simpler for you, click the Browse button, then navigate to the Setup.exe program on the disk, and double-click it. You'll go back to the Run dialog box. Click the OK button in the Run dialog box and Setup will start and present you with the dialog box shown in Figure 1.1.

Figure 1.1.

The first installation dialog box—they're all similar to each other.

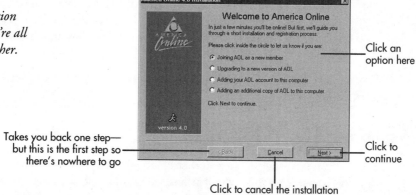

Click an option here

Takes you back one step— but this is the first step so there's nowhere to go

Click to cancel the installation

Click to continue

4. When the setup routine begins, it first asks you to explain yourself—not in any Zen meaning of life sort of way, but just whether you're a new AOL member, upgrading from a previous version of AOL, or adding AOL to another computer. Click the appropriate description, then click the Next button.

5. If you're upgrading from a previous version of AOL, Setup looks for an installed copy of the old software, and asks you to click on the software copy (if you have more than one installed) to upgrade from. Click the old version of AOL, then click the Next button.

6. Setup asks where you want the software installed. The default location is on your C:\ drive. Unless you want it put elsewhere on your hard drive, simply click Next. Otherwise, click Choose Directory and select a new destination for the software, *then* click Next.

7. If you're upgrading from a previous version, AOL asks what you want it to do with any files you've downloaded and left in your Download folder. You can choose to move them to the new version, copy them to the new version, or just ignore them. Click the option you want, then click Next.

8. Setup then asks if you want to automatically start the AOL software when you start your computer. If you do, just click Next. If you don't, click the check mark in the box labeled Start AOL when You Start Your Computer to deselect it, then click Next.

9. AOL is ready to install itself on your computer. You can review the available disk space (AOL 4.0 takes up about 30MB of space during the installation, dropping down to about 16MB after all the copying and installing of files is done). Click Next to install the software. You can take a short break while Setup does all the work.

10. When the installation is nearly complete, Setup asks if you'd like to print a copy of the Quick Reference Guide. If you do, click the Print button. If not, click the Finish button and AOL wraps up the installation.

11. When the installation is complete, a dialog box appears to notify you. Click OK. You'll return to your Windows desktop with either an AOL 4.0 program group in the Program Manager (in Windows 3.*x*) or a shortcut on the desktop and a little AOL logo on the taskbar near the clock (in Windows 95).

You can take five now, if you'd like. Otherwise, we'll move on to setting up your newly installed software.

Setting Up AOL 4.0

Your software is installed, but you're still not quite ready to sign on and use the service. To function properly, the AOL software needs some information about your computer and your phone line. AOL also needs a telephone number or two to use to actually connect you to AOL. You'll set all that up now. It's a simple process, like installation, that holds your hand every step of the way.

TIME SAVER

Before you begin, take a minute to make sure the phone line is connected to your modem, your modem is turned on (if it's an external model), and no one is using the phone. Also, grab the card that came with your AOL software (or the envelope the CD came in). The card has two bits of information you'll need: a registration number and a temporary password. If your card is missing or has been used by someone else to set up *their* account, call AOL Customer Service at 1-800-827-6364. They'll be happy to give you a new number and password over the phone.

CAUTION

If you are upgrading from a previous version and you performed the optional steps in the installation section, you're ready to roll. You don't need to do any of this—the setup program copied all your information from your old version of AOL.

Setting Up Your AOL Software

1. To begin, double-click the AOL 4.0 icon (the blue, triangular one), either on your Windows 95 desktop or your Windows 3.1 AOL Program Group. The software starts and you'll be presented with the Welcome to America Online dialog box shown in Figure 1.2. Read the information on the dialog box. You're given the option to start automatic setup, or go to custom setup. Most users will want to use automatic setup (you really need to know what you're doing to use custom). To use automatic setup, just click the Next arrow.

Figure 1.2.

Welcome to America Online. You're ready to set up your software.

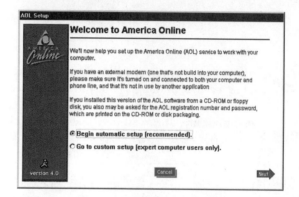

2. The software then checks your computer for a way to connect you to the service—either a modem, network, or Internet connection. It may take a minute or two. When it's done, the Select Your Connection dialog box appears (see Figure 1.3).

CAUTION

> If Setup mis-identifies your modem, you can click the Change Connection button and select the correct modem from a list of all the modems AOL knows how to use. Then click OK.
>
> If AOL doesn't recognize that you have a modem at all don't panic. Leave the setup routine alone, flip to Appendix B, "When Things Go Wrong," and call AOL's technical support line for help.

3. Click the connection you want to use (in most cases, your modem), then click the Next arrow.

4. You'll need to select a local access number. Your computer dials this number to connect to AOL. A dialog box appears asking you to select your country from a drop-down menu (United States is the default, unless you have an international version of the software), and to enter your area code in small text box. When you've done both, click the Next arrow.

Figure 1.3.

Select your connection here. Most users will only have one, a modem.

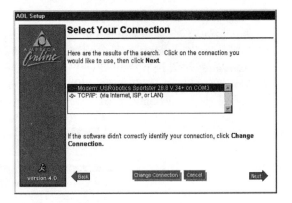

5. Before the software can call AOL and get the list of access numbers, it needs to know a couple of things about your phone (see Figure 1.4). AOL assumes you have a touch-tone phone line and that you don't need to dial a 9 or other number to get an outside line. It also assumes that you don't have call waiting. If any of these assumptions is incorrect, change them now. When you're done, click Next.

TIME SAVER

Call waiting is great for regular phone use, but bad when you're online. The beep that alerts you to an incoming call will probably disconnect you from America Online. If you have call waiting, make sure to click the check box that says Dial *70 to disable call waiting, and call waiting will be turned off during your online sessions.

If you obtain (or remove) call waiting at a later date, you can change this setting later by way of the Setup button on the Sign On dialog box. Hour 16, "AOL Away from Home," explains how.

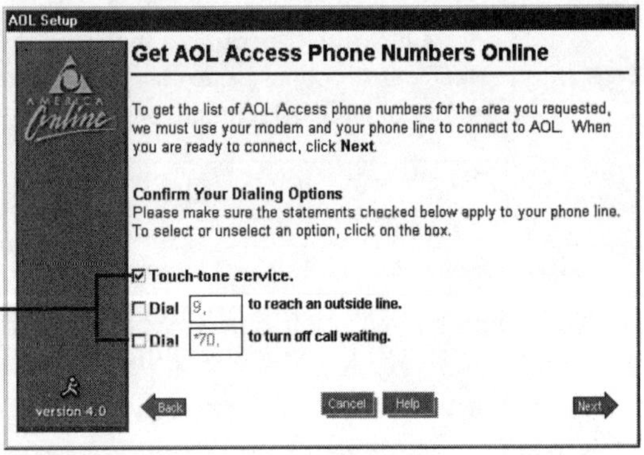

Figure 1.4.

Check your dialing options.

Change your dialing options here, if necessary

6. Setup then dials an 800 number and the Select AOL Access Phone Numbers dialog box appears as shown in Figure 1.5. The list box on the left shows all the access numbers in your area code. Each entry shows the city name, the speed at which you can connect with the number, and the number itself. Click on one that matches your modem speed and is *not* a long-distance call. Click the Add arrow in the center of the dialog box.

Figure 1.5.
Select at least two local access numbers.

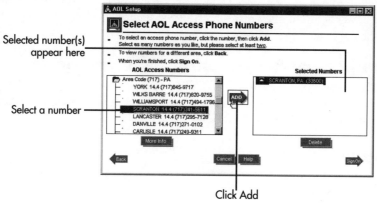

Click Add

JUST A MINUTE

If the only local phone numbers available are at modem speeds slower than your modem's top speed, go ahead and select one of them anyway. It's better than making a long-distance call. Also, if you can't find any suitable numbers in your area code, click the Back arrow. This takes you back to the area code dialog box. You can enter the area code of an adjacent area, and try again. You'll wind up paying long-distance charges in addition to your AOL membership fees.

7. When you click Add, a confirmation box appears showing you the number that will be dialed. If it's okay as is, click OK. If you need to change it (add an area code for a long-distance number, for instance), click Edit and make your changes.

8. Repeat steps 6 and 7 for at least one additional access number (you can select as many as you like, however).

9. After you've selected your access numbers, click Sign On. You're ready to connect to AOL and create your account. If you need a break, you can take one at this point—just leave the software running and you can pick up right where you left off.

Becoming a Member of AOL

You've logged on to the system and gone through some initial setup, but you're still not a full-fledged member of America Online. All America Online knows about you so far is what area code you live in.

It's time to get personal. To create your AOL account, have your temporary password and registration number handy. Then, click the Sign On arrow on the bottom of the Select AOL Access Phone Numbers dialog box (refer to Figure 1.5). Your computer dials in to AOL and the registration process begins.

Temporary Registration Information

When you connect to AOL, you'll see a window as shown in Figure 1.6. You need to enter those cryptic registration numbers and your temporary password that came with your AOL software.

Figure 1.6.
Enter the codes that come with the CD-ROM or disk.

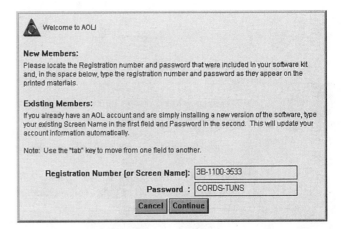

If you're signing up for a new membership, enter the certificate number in the first field and the password in the second. Both of these are found on the card that accompanies the CD-ROM or disk.

When you've entered your information, click the Continue button. As shown in Figure 1.7, a dialog box appears that you use to provide your personal information. Enter it carefully, and press the Tab key to move from field to field. When you're done, click Continue.

Getting the Billing Set Up

America Online doesn't send out bills to any of its customers. Instead, it automatically charges your credit card or makes an automatic deduction from your checking account.

You select the billing method in the dialog box shown in Figure 1.8.

1

Figure 1.7.

Tab to move to the next field and type your information carefully.

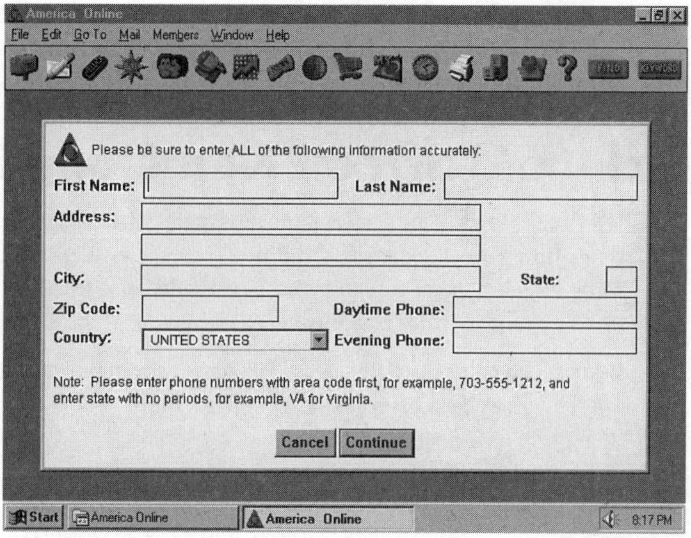

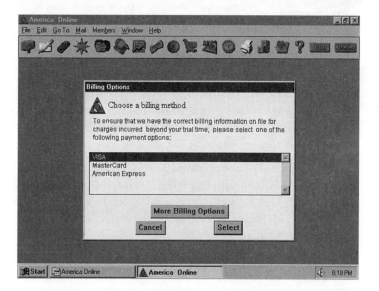

Figure 1.8.

Click the credit card you want to use for your AOL account; then click Select.

If you want to use your checking account or a different credit card, click More Billing Options. Otherwise, click the name of the credit card you want to use, and then click Select.

You are then prompted to enter your card number, expiration date, and the name that appears on the card. Enter the credit card number without spaces or dashes. If the name on your credit card has a middle initial, enter it with your first name in First Name field, like this: (first name)(space)(initial). When you're done, click Continue.

Next you are asked to select a billing plan. The default option is $21.95 per month for unlimited access to both America Online content and the Internet. You may, of course, select any plan you want. When you've chosen your plan, click Continue.

Picking a Screen Name and Password

It's time to pick your screen name and password. Your screen name is important because that's how you are identified online. Your screen name is also your email address. Select something that suits you and your personality, and that you won't be embarrassed to say in front of your mom or to a business associate.

Your screen name must be at least 3 characters (letters, numbers, or spaces), and no more than 10. The first character must be a capital letter.

TIME SAVER

The first screen name you choose might already be in use. There are more than eight million AOL subscribers. Have a couple of variations on the name you want, and maybe even a couple of alternative selections in reserve, just in case.

Type your screen name in the text box, then click Continue. If that name is already in use, you are prompted to try again.

Next comes selecting a password. The screen provides some helpful advice: The password should be easy for you to remember, but hard for other people to guess. In other words, don't use your spouse's name, your kid's birthday, and so on. Be creative.

You won't see your password as you type it, you'll see asterisks (****) instead, so type it carefully. You need to enter it twice, just to make sure that you typed it correctly. Make a note of your password somewhere secure (like the place where you keep your PIN numbers for credit cards and ATM cards), and don't share it with anyone, unless he or she is authorized to use your account.

Click Select Password. You'll be notified when you're done, and must sign off before you can use your new account. Click OK, and you'll be disconnected from the service. You're ready to sign on with your new screen name.

If you aren't going to sign on immediately, you can shut down your AOL software. Just click the File menu, and select Exit (or Quit on a Mac).

Signing On, Signing Off

To sign on to AOL, launch the software as you did earlier. When the program starts, you'll see the Sign On dialog box shown in Figure 1.9. Just type your password in the Enter Password text box, click Sign On, and you'll connect to the service.

Figure 1.9.

The AOL Sign On dialog box.

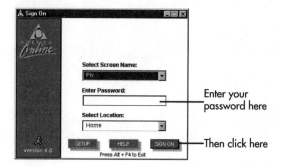

Enter your password here

Then click here

Poke around online and have fun. When you're done, you can sign off and leave your AOL software running—just click the Sign Off menu, and select Sign Off. You can also select Exit from the File menu—that signs you off AOL, and shuts down the program. The choice is yours.

Summary

In this hour you've installed the software, set it up, and created your AOL account. Now you're ready to explore AOL, and get on to the Internet.

Workshop

Use the following workshop to make sure that you're ready to explore America Online.

Q&A

Q I gave a credit card number for billing purposes, but I felt funny typing it in online. Is it safe?

A Yes, it's safe. When you enter that information, you have a "secure" connection to AOL. That is, the data you transmit should not be able to be observed by outsiders. The numbers are kept on a computer that is not part of the AOL network.

Q **For my password, I used the birth dates of my wife and both of my kids. Pretty clever, huh?**

A No. Remember, some people have nothing better to do than to figure out how to use other people's AOL accounts. Birth dates are one of the first things they try as passwords. Change that password as soon as possible. Hour 14, "Navigating Through America Online *Your* Way," explains how.

Quiz

Take the following quiz to test your knowledge of setting up AOL.

Questions

1. Which of the following will help you prevent sudden disconnection from AOL?
   a. Disabling call waiting
   b. Taking the phone off the hook
   c. Turning your answering machine on

2. Which of the following modem speeds is the fastest?
   a. 14,400
   b. 2,400
   c. 28.8

3. Which of the following is the best password to have?
   a. The last name of your favorite sports star
   b. Your mother's maiden aunt's middle name
   c. Your license plate number backwards
   d. None of the above

Answers

1. **a.**
2. **c.**
3. **d.** As obscure as the first three answers are, your password should be even *more* obscure.

Activity

Practice, practice, practice. Explore AOL on your own, or sign on and play along with the To Do exercises and examples in the upcoming hours.

Hour 2

Uses for America Online

America Online (AOL) has all kinds of uses, for all kinds of people. You can use AOL for education, entertainment, staying current on world events, and even getting the scoop on some juicy gossip. AOL has something for everyone. With time and experience (and this book, of course), you'll find your own set of areas and features you just can't live without.

This hour gives an overview of America Online. We'll look at the service in broad strokes, focusing on some of the more popular things you can do online. Later, we'll look at these areas (and lots of others) in more detail. This hour includes

☐ How to check for mail

☐ Where to look for software

☐ How to get the news of the world

☐ Entertainment areas on America Online

☐ Some places for the kids to check out

☐ For entrepreneurs, business and financial resources online

Beginning Your AOL Experience

Naturally, to experience AOL, you need to connect to AOL. That means starting your computer, launching the program, and signing on as described in Hour 1, "Installing AOL and Signing Up."

When you connect to the service (if your computer is equipped for sound), a friendly voice greets you with a hearty, "Welcome!" A Welcome screen appears as shown in Figure 2.1.

Figure 2.1.

The AOL Welcome screen greets you by name when you sign on.

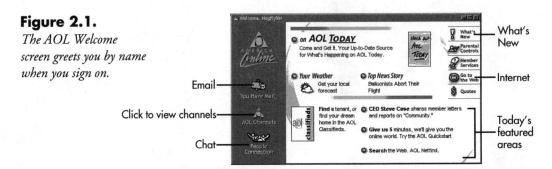

The Welcome screen has buttons you can use to jump right into different areas online—just click and go. The buttons at the bottom of the screen are featured areas that change from day to day. Check here for special events, seasonal topics, and the latest news.

The AOL Channels button on the left, takes you to AOL's main topics screen (you'll get a look at that in a moment). The What's New button, in the upper-right corner, showcases the latest, greatest stuff online.

Three buttons you'll probably use often are the You Have Mail button; the People Connection button for access to chat; and the Internet button, which is labeled Go to the Web.

The Channels window opens behind the Welcome screen. To see all the Channels, click the Channels button on the Welcome screen. It will pop right to the front—you can see it in Figure 2.2.

The Channels display gives you easy access to AOL's 19 different content areas. To visit an area, click its bar on the Channels display, and you're off. Try it with the Entertainment button. Click its button on the Channels window as shown in Figure 2.2.

2

TIME SAVER

Any time you want to switch Channels, you can save some time by using the Channels menu on the AOL toolbar. It gives you access to all the same Channels as the Channels window. To use it, just click the Channels button, and then click the Channel you want on the drop-down menu.

Figure 2.2.

Click the Entertainment button on the Channels screen.

Actually, *that's* entertainment

AOL thinks about it for a moment, and then the Entertainment Channel's main screen appears.

That's Entertainment

The Entertainment Channel, as shown in Figure 2.3, provides information on all things entertaining—from music and musicians, to movies, television, and books. Every day, you'll find a couple of entertainment items in the spotlight (like *The Women of Rock* in Figure 2.3), as well as buttons for the Channel's main departments.

The Entertainment Channel departments are Movies, TV Today, Music, Word of Mouth, Books, and Search and Explore. Each covers what the name implies…well, except for Word of Mouth. Word of Mouth is actually entertainment news and information, the stuff people are talking about (including gossip).

You'll also notice, along the left side of the window, a set of buttons for *all* of AOL's Channels—a new feature in AOL 4.0. It makes it much easier to navigate your way through the service. When you're done in one Channel, you can just click-and-go to visit another.

Figure 2.3.

The Entertainment Channel's main screen— explore at will.

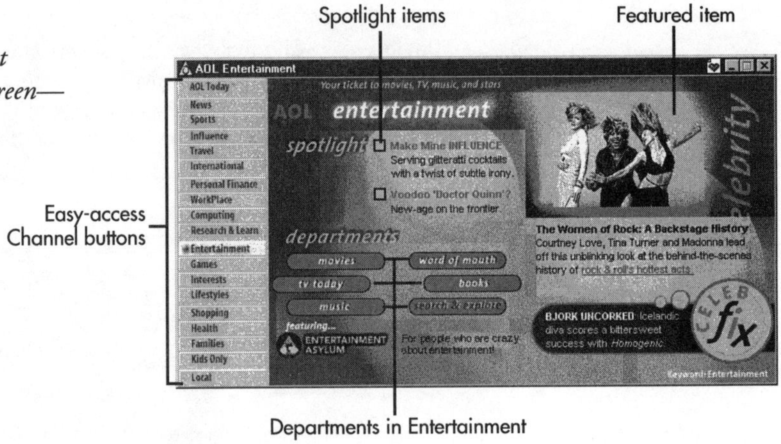

Spotlight items

Featured item

Easy-access Channel buttons

Departments in Entertainment

Speaking of clicking and going, go ahead and explore the Entertainment Channel. Don't be shy—click a department button or check out a spotlight item. Poke around and have some fun. It is the *Entertainment Channel*, after all. Pick a topic that interests you and go nuts.

CAUTION

This new Channel screen, with buttons for each of AOL's Channels, *can't be closed*. You can minimize it, but you can't close it. Don't let it throw you.

When you're done exploring Entertainment, close all the intermediate windows you've opened, until you're back at the Entertainment main screen, shown in Figure 2.3. You'll be ready to move on with the rest of the hour. Take your time, we'll wait.

Kids Only

AOL is a great place for kids—there's lots for them to see and do, and there are other kids online with whom they can share their thoughts and ideas. The Kids Only Channel (shown in Figure 2.4) is like a mini-AOL that pre-teen kids have all to themselves.

JUST A MINUTE

America Online is a family-oriented service, but there are areas online you might not want your kids to visit. You can control which areas your children visit, even whether they can communicate with other members online, using AOL's *Parental Controls*. Parental Controls are explained later in Hour 21, "Keeping Parental Control."

The Kids Only Channel is a collection of fun, entertainment, and education just for kids. Adults can visit, but may not participate online. Your children can chat with some online friends, play a game, or even get help with their homework.

To get to Kids Only, just click the Kids Only button on the left side of the Entertainment main screen. The Entertainment information is replaced with the Kids Only screen, shown in Figure 2.4. (If you're picking up where you left off from a previous online session, you can also click the Kids Only button on the AOL's Channel screen to get to the Kids Only main screen.)

Figure 2.4.

Kids Only—it really is just for kids.

You are here

As you saw with the Entertainment Channel's main screen, the Kids Only screen gives you a few highlights of what's going on online for kids today, plus buttons with which you can access the Kids Only departments.

The departments include

- ☐ **Central**—The main area where you access individual areas of Kids Only.
- ☐ **Games**—This department is fairly self-explanatory.
- ☐ **Create**—Here kids can create their own artwork and other projects.
- ☐ **Chat**—Chat rooms for kids.
- ☐ **Homework Help**—Help from *real* teachers no less.
- ☐ **Web**—With kid appropriate web pages and kid-sized browser.
- ☐ **Shows & Stars**—For TV fans.
- ☐ **Find It**—A Kids Only search tool.

A typical Kids Only area, Nickelodeon Online, is shown in Figure 2.5. The Nickelodeon Online area features a chat room (called *The Blabbatorium*), seasonal events (such as *The Gromble's Click of Horrors* for Halloween), Yuk of the Day, and other fun stuff.

Figure 2.5.
Nickelodeon Online—I'll meet you in the Brain Asylum.

Some of the best areas within Kids Only are those that stress creativity (where you can fiendishly inspire your youngsters to learn without their knowing it). Blackberry Creek allows kids to share their artwork with each other, and Hatrack Creek provides a way for them to experience a virtual village set in the 1800s.

Kids Only is covered in depth in Hour 22, "Letting the Kids in on the Fun."

Personal Finance and Business

After the kids are done playing and learning on America Online, you might want to hop online yourself to see if you'll be able to send them to college someday…yikes.

To get to the Personal Finance Channel's main screen (shown in Figure 2.6), click the Personal Finance button on the side of the Kids Only screen, or on AOL's main Channels window.

Figure 2.6.
The Personal Finance Channel—if you can't play the market for real, you can at least pretend.

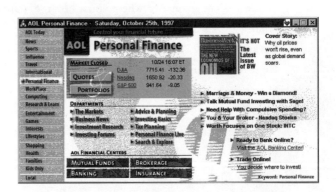

The main Personal Finance screen offers all manner of financial resources, including the latest market reports, stock quotes, mutual fund information, stock and insurance brokers, banking, and a vast array of advice and financial services. You'll also find lots of news you can use, and featured articles from the current issue of *Business Week* magazine.

Did you ever play the stock market game when you were in school? In the Portfolios area, you can build a portfolio of investments for yourself and track their progress. Lots of people use it to track their *real* investments, but it's not a bad idea to try it out with some fake ones first to see if you have any talent in that area. If you're really serious, however, America Online offers a brokerage service through which you can invest real money.

Whether you're tracking real investments, testing the waters, or just playing around, it's a good idea to get some solid information on any company in which you plan to invest your hard-earned dollars. The Company Research area can save you a lot of time in that information search (see Figure 2.7). To get there, click the Investment Research button on the main Personal Finance screen.

Figure 2.7.

*Use Company Research
to "look before you leap"
into investing.*

Complete stock reports, company financial statements, earnings and estimates, message boards, and more are available on the Company Research screen.

CAUTION

The Personal Finance Channel has some excellent sources of financial information. However, there may also be some shady characters hanging out online. Always play it safe online: Do your own research, and a lot of it, before making any investment. A hot tip from a stranger online could be as crooked as some of the pyramid, real estate, and other schemes you've heard about offline. There *are* people who will try to rip you off online, as well as in the real world.

For the entrepreneur in you, the Your Business area promotes the entrepreneurial community. Among other things, it's an area where you can share ideas, experiences, and advice with others. You'll also find links to government and business resources that can help you get started in business, or keep you going if you're already in business.

Personal Finance is covered in more detail in Hour 19, "Personal Finance."

Computing

The Computing Channel, shown in Figure 2.8, is a mecca for moderns. It's the source of all sorts of computer news, information, and even software. Whether you're an old hand with computers or just learning your way around one, the Computing Channel has something for you.

To get to the Computing Channel, you can click the Computing button on the left side of the Personal Finance screen, from the last section. You can also use the Channels display or the Channels menu on the AOL toolbar.

NEW TERM   **Newbie**—A slang word for someone who is new to the Internet, America Online, or any online service.

Figure 2.8.

The Computing area has software and information for new and experienced computer users.

As with the other Channels we've seen so far, the Computing main screen features a breakdown of the Channel's departments as well as highlights of popular areas. The departments include Download Software (where you can search for, and copy to your computer, actual software you can use), Help Desk, Companies, the Online Classroom (where you can take computer courses), Newsstand (for computer-related publications), Buyer's Guide, Classifieds, Chat & Messages, On the Net, and the usual Search & Explore.

For me, it is by far the coolest Channel online. I use it to get updates and fixes for software I've purchased; to get help with cranky computer components; and to stay current with what my favorite computer companies are doing. I also download tons and tons of software.

Download—The process of transferring a file from a remote computer (such as AOL's computer) to your own. When you do the same thing, but in the other direction (from your computer to another), that's called an *upload*.

Looking for cool software online is covered in detail in Hour 5, "Downloading Files and Searching Databases."

Keeping Up with the News

A lot is happening in the world, but most people have little time to keep up with it—unless there's some *major* calamity, or hot news topic, the major media reduce everything to 8-second sound bites. If you want news with a little more depth, you can find it on AOL. Nearly every Channel offers a News button or index: entertainment news, software news, kids' news, Internet news, weather news…you get the idea.

An entire News Channel is also available, shown in Figure 2.9, which you can flip through rather like a newspaper (there are even cartoons on the Back Page). To get to it, click the News button on the Computing Channel main screen, or AOL's Channels window. You can also select News from the Channels menu on the toolbar.

Figure 2.9.

Today's News acts a little like your local newspaper.

From the News main window, you can access the hour's headlines, news by department: U.S. and World, Business, Sports, Politics, Life, Weather, Local, Newsstand (for magazines and newspapers), Classifieds (just like in your local paper). Each of the sections also contains a list of current headlines. To read the full story, double-click a headline.

The Newsstand gives you access to hundreds of today's top publications, including luminaries like the *New York Times*, the *Chicago Tribune*, and the *Atlantic Monthly* magazine. You can often read the online version of your favorite publications hours, or even *days*, before they hit your mailbox or local newsstand.

News sources are covered more fully in Hour 17, "Your Computer as a News Source."

You've Got Mail!

Call me sneaky and underhanded, but I've saved the best for last: email and chat.

Email is perhaps the most often-used feature of America Online, or any online service, for that matter—although it might be neck and neck with chat (more about that in a moment).

COFFEE BREAK

> Email has helped thousands of people keep in touch long-distance without having to pay for long-distance phone calls. I use it to keep in touch with long-distance friends who, if left to high-priced phone calls, I might not call for weeks at a time. With email, I can be in daily contact, if I like.

Email is the online equivalent of regular postal mail—it even uses much of the same vocabulary. If you've ever written a thank-you note and dropped it in a mail box, you already have the basic concept of email under your belt. Really. Trust me.

America Online announces when you've got mail by saying, "You've got mail!" through your computer's sound card and speakers. It also lets you know you've got mail by way of the mail button on the Welcome screen (refer to Figure 2.1). Normally, this button has an envelope for its icon. When you have mail, however, it turns into a mailbox. You can see it in Figure 2.10.

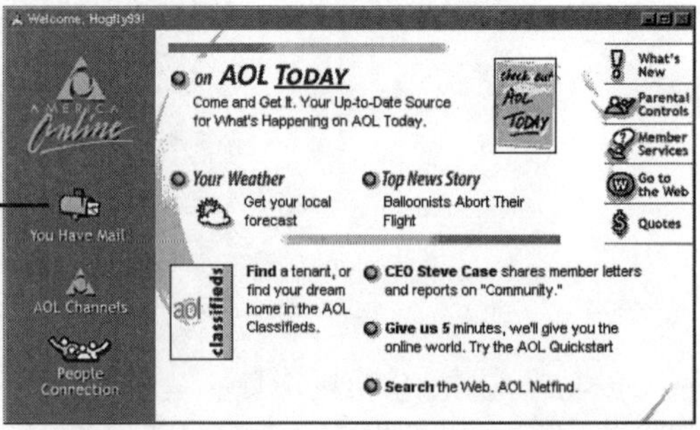

Figure 2.10.

You'll know when you sign on if you have mail.

You have mail! ——

You can also tell if you have mail by looking at the first button on the AOL toolbar. If the mailbox icon is open with a letter in it, you have mail. If it's closed, you don't.

If you do have mail, click either mailbox icon and the New Mail window opens. You'll see a list of the messages waiting for you. Just double-click one of the messages to read it.

Email is explained in Hour 4, "Using Email" (although I prefer to think of it as *Everything You Wanted To Know About Email But Were Afraid To Ask*).

Chatting in the People Connection

I'm usually not one for statistics, but someone somewhere told me that as much as 70 percent of the time people spend online is spent in chat rooms. Who knew?

Chatting is much the same as having a face to face chat, or even one by phone. The only difference is that, because you're online, you must type what you want to say and read the other person's response.

On AOL, you can zap yourself into a chat room in the People Connection and find yourself in conversation with people from across the country and around the world. That's pretty cool.

To get into a chat room, click the People Connection button on the Channels display, or select it from the People menu on the AOL toolbar. You'll land in a lobby, such as the one shown in Figure 2.11. You can stay there a while and chat, or you can move on to another chat room.

Figure 2.11.

Chatting in the People Connection—Lobby 375, to be precise.

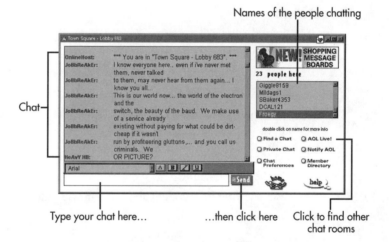

You can jump into chat with both feet, right now, if you care to. However, I suggest you check out Hour 7, "Chatting on America Online," before you take the plunge.

Summary

In this hour, you learned a bit about some of the many areas on AOL. These, and more, are covered in detail in later hours.

Workshop

Use the following workshop to help you discover the many features of America Online.

Q&A

Q How do I go to another channel, after I've explored a channel?

A You can close all the intermediate windows you've opened in that channel until you reach the main Channel window—the one with the Channel buttons down the left side. Then, simply click on the button for the next channel you want to visit. You can also select the channel from the Channels drop-down menu on the AOL toolbar.

Q Why do so many of these channels have a What's Hot or What's New button?

A America Online is constantly changing, adding new features, services, and areas. It uses the What's Hot and What's New buttons to give you easy access to these new items online.

Quiz

Take the following quiz to test what you've learned this hour.

Questions

1. To find out if you have new mail, you need to
    a. Type in a special Mail password.
    b. Look at the mailbox on the Welcome screen or toolbar.
    c. Go to the Mail Channel.

2. Where can you find a weather forecast?
    a. On the News Channel
    b. On the Radar Channel
    c. On the Hub Channel

3. Where can you find information about the movie industry?
    a. On the Movie Channel
    b. On the Entertainment Channel
    c. On the Hub Channel

Answers

1. **b.**
2. **a.**
3. **b.**

Activity

Get online and explore! Take some time now and poke around in some of the Channels we *didn't* look at in this hour. Keep this book handy, in case you get lost, or need some help.

2

Hour 3

Exploring America Online

In the first two hours, you installed America Online, registered with the service, and then spent some time taking an introductory look at some of the more popular areas online. Still, we've only scratched the surface of AOL, and learned how to use the various Channel buttons to move from area to area. That's all well and good, but it doesn't get you to the topic area that may be buried several layers deep in that Channel.

There are lots of ways to navigate through AOL, most of which take you to the exact spot you want to visit—without having to go through a lot of intermediate windows and lots of button clicking. These speedy shortcuts were designed to save you time online. They hearken back to the days of pay-by-the-hour access time, when every minute counted, literally.

Of course, that's less of a concern now, with the availability of flat rate subscription plans. With a flat rate plan, whether you spend two hours or two minutes online, you pay the same $21.95 per month (unless you've chosen one of the alternative subscription plans).

Still, even with that concern removed, it never seems like there are enough hours in the day. Who needs to spend an extra ten minutes clicking around trying to find a favorite area online? This hour takes a look at some shortcuts you can use to zip around the service, including

☐ How to use keywords to go right to an area online

☐ How to use your Favorite Places menu to find your way back, whenever you want

☐ How to find new features and services as they become available

☐ How to keep track of your time online and your bill

☐ How to use the Member Directory to find folks with interests similar to your own

These important concepts will help you begin to find your way around AOL, and back to areas you want to revisit. However, because it takes time to figure out which areas you want to visit regularly, we'll come back to these concepts in later hours, when you may actually *have* some places you'd like to get to quickly and with little fuss.

Using Keywords

Almost every area on AOL has a keyword that enables you to go directly to that area without passing GO, or collecting $200.

Say, for example, that you want to get to the Fidelity Investments area within America Online. You can go to the Channels window, click the Personal Finance button, click the Mutual Funds button (opening *another* window), and then use the list box on *that* window to find Fidelity Investments.

Or, you can use the keyword FIDELITY, and go there in one easy step.

Dual Access from the Toolbar

Using keywords couldn't get much easier. At the bottom of the AOL toolbar, you'll find the Type Keyword or Web Address Here and Click Go text box (see Figure 3.1). That's the navigation bar (you'll also be using it when you get on the World Wide Web in Hour 12, "The World Wide Web").

Figure 3.1.

Type a keyword in the text box, click Go, and you're gone.

Type a keyword here...   ...then click here

3

Click to place your cursor in the text box—if the text in it isn't automatically selected, you'll need to click-drag over it to select it all. Type your keyword and click the Go button. You'll be at the related area online in almost nothing flat.

Folks who are accustomed to an older version of AOL can use keywords the old-fashioned way. Click the Keyword button (it's to the left of the text box in Figure 3.1), and you'll get the old, familiar Keyword dialog box shown in Figure 3.2. You can also use the keyboard shortcut Ctrl+K (⌘+K on a Mac).

Figure 3.2.

The tried, true, and trusted Keyword dialog box.

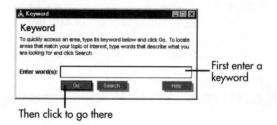

As with the navigation bar, you enter the keyword for the area you want to visit, then click the Go button. You're there.

How Do I Know What the Keyword Is?

It's all fine and dandy to know how to *use* a keyword, but where the heck do you find them? Well, they're *everywhere* online. If you flip back through Hour 2, "Uses for America Online," and look closely at the screen shots of the different areas we visited, you'll notice each of them has a keyword tucked into a corner of the window.

Kids Only, for example (shown in Figure 2.4 of Hour 2), has its keyword in the lower-right corner of the main window. Its keyword is KIDS ONLY. The Entertainment Channel's keyword is ENTERTAINMENT. Got the idea? Most of the keywords online are the names of the related area. Even if you only *think* you remember the name of an area, try it as a keyword. Most of the time, it will work.

If a keyword you try doesn't work, or if you enter one incorrectly, a message appears telling you that the keyword doesn't exist. You may, however, enter another keyword or click the Search button. AOL will offer you a list of functional keywords that might be the one you want.

When you're first starting out with AOL, you might find it handy to keep an AOL text document open on your screen, so you can type in the keywords for areas you think you may want to visit later. You can save it to your hard drive, or print it out. Then you'll have a list for easy reference, until you remember your favorite keywords.

If you want to begin keywording your way around AOL, you can also get a complete list of keywords by using the keyword KEYWORD. That takes you to an area online completely devoted to keywords. You can download the whole list and then print it out to keep by your computer. Downloading files from AOL is explained in Hour 5, "Downloading Files and Searching Databases."

Keeping Track of Your Favorite Places

After you've used AOL for a while, you'll find yourself returning to certain areas on a regular basis—a particular file library, perhaps, or even places that don't have keywords, such as a chat room. You can return to it with a couple of clicks of your mouse, whether it has an assigned keyword or not by using the Favorite Places menu.

You'll find the Favorite Places button in the middle of AOL's toolbar (refer to Figure 3.1). The picture on the Favorite Places button is a file folder decorated with a little heart.

You may have noticed the little heart icon at the top-right corner of most of the windows you've seen online (see Figure 3.3). That's the Favorite Places flag, and you can use it to add any area that's equipped with one to your Favorite Places menu.

Figure 3.3.

Click the heart to mark a site for later reference.

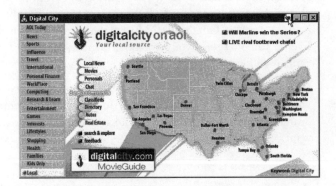

3

COFFEE BREAK

AOL has thoughtfully included some Favorite Places in your Favorite Places menu. You can use them to tour the service and visit some helpful, fun, and informative areas. Simply click the Favorite Places icon on the toolbar, then point at the category you want to explore. Click a Favorite Place from the category submenu that pops up.

Adding to the Favorite Places List

It's easy to add an area to your Favorite Places list. Simply follow these steps:

1. Find an area you like—one that you think you want to visit on a regular basis.

2. Locate the heart graphic at the top of the window and click it. (Remember, if the area doesn't have a heart logo, you can't add it to Favorite Places.)

3. The window shown in Figure 3.4 appears. It gives you the option of adding the area to your Favorite Places, or inserting the Favorite Place in an Instant Message, or email (these last two will be covered in Hour 4, "Using Email," and Hour 14, "Navigating Through America Online *Your* Way"). Click Add to Favorites.

Figure 3.4.

Click Add to Favorites and the selected area will appear in your Favorite Places menu.

Later, when you are ready to return to that area, click the Favorite Places icon on the toolbar, and then click on the name of the area on your Favorite Places menu.

You'll visit Favorite Places again in Hour 14. By then you'll have built up some Favorites of your own. Then, I'll show you how to organize and delete Favorites that have fallen out of favor.

Finding New Features and Services

America Online is constantly changing. Every time you turn around, there's something new to look at, explore, or play with online. How's a person supposed to keep up? You're not. AOL does all the "keeping up" for you.

Naturally, you'll find new areas online featured on the AOL Welcome screen (refer to Figure 2.1 in Hour 2). However, those change regularly, so you might *miss* something. (The horror, the horror!)

You can find out all about new areas, features, and services with the click of a button. On the Welcome screen, click the What's New button to go to the What's New On AOL screen shown in Figure 3.5.

Figure 3.5.

Click What's New on the Welcome screen to learn about the latest developments online.

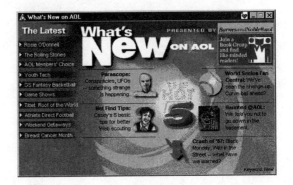

Down the left side of the What's New window, you'll find buttons that highlight recently added areas online. To visit a new area, just click and go. The rest of the window is taken up with the *really* new, just-hatched areas and features. You'll find seasonal areas that are gearing up (for holidays, Back to School, and so on), all-new areas, and even changes in billing or other need-to-know information for subscribers. I'd point out what they all are in Figure 3.5, but they'll most likely be different when you see them in person—things change fast in cyberspace.

You should drop in on the New Features area every once in awhile, just to make sure you're not missing out on anything. If you don't care for any of the new offerings online, you might want to check out what *everyone else* online is doing. You can do that by visiting the AOL Members' Choice area.

Members' Choice

Members' Choice, shown in Figure 3.6, is an area that gives you direct access to the 50 areas most often visited by AOL members. You can get to it by way of the What's New screen, or by using the keyword MEMBERS CHOICE.

The list box, at the center of the window, contains an alphabetical listing of the 50 most traveled areas online. This eclectic mix features areas as diverse as the Better Health & Medical forum and The Cartoon Network area.

You might want to check out a few of the Members' Choice areas. After all, over 9 million AOL users can't be wrong.

Figure 3.6.
*Members' Choice: the
people have spoken—
well, clicked.*

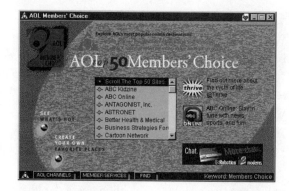

Managing Your Account

Even with the introduction of AOL's flat rate billing plan, you still may want to keep an eye
on your monthly bill. Anytime you succumb to the urge and click the Accept button on one
of those *"Buy now and save!"* offers that pop up at sign on, the cost of that purchase gets added
to your AOL bill. Or, if you've got kids (or you yourself) using the Premium Games area (at
an additional $1.99 per hour), your AOL could creep beyond that flat $21.95 a month pretty
quickly.

The keyword BILLING takes you to AOL's Accounts & Billing area shown in Figure 3.7. Here
you can change the name and address on your account if necessary, change your method of
payment or price plan, and check your current or previous month's bill.

Figure 3.7.
*Accounts & Billing gives
you access to your account
information.*

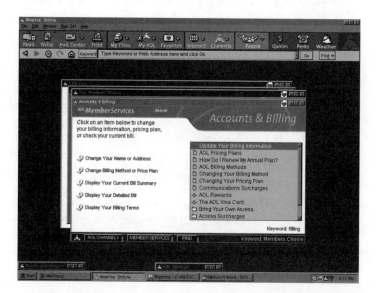

Checking Your Bill

You might want to check your current or previous bill for several reasons: You suspect there's been a mistake; you ordered something online and you want to know when it will hit your credit card; you think someone (such as a child, or spouse) may have ordered your birthday present online, and you want to know what it is…

Whatever the reason, you can check your bill easily enough. When you arrive at Accounts and Billing, click Display Your Detailed Bill. A dialog box opens asking if you want to view your current month's bill or your previous month's bill. Click the appropriate button.

Whichever button you choose, a window opens that details the amount of time you've spent online by screen name for the billing period, plus any additional charges incurred.

CAUTION

"Month," in this context, is misleading. Your billing period may not be a literal month, such as January or June. Your billing month begins with the date you joined AOL (say, on the 10th of the month), until the same date the following month.

You can even have a bill summary sent to your email account, so you can print it out for your records. You just click a button on the bottom of each billing summary screen to request an emailed copy.

Making Changes to Your Account

At some point during your America Online membership, you might move, you might want to change your pricing plan, and so on. These types of changes can also be made in the billing area.

To change your address, click the Change Your Name or Address button and make the necessary changes. If you want to go off the unlimited access plan or save a little money by paying for a year in advance, click the Change Billing Method or Price Plan button, and go in and make the changes.

CAUTION

You can only *change* information on your account (name, address, payment, or price plan) when you sign on to AOL using your *master account screen name*—that means the first screen name you created, back when you first set up your AOL account. Try it with any other screen name you may have created, and you'll be politely told to take a hike.

3

You can get information on terms by clicking the Display Your Billing Terms button, and you can also use the contents of the list box on the right side of the billing screen to answer other questions about your account or your bill. Simply double-click the relevant entry, and read the information.

Using the Member Directory

The Member Directory is a searching tool that enables you to search through all the Member Profiles AOL users have created. It gives you the chance to find people with interests similar to your own, or who live near you, or both.

To understand what a Profile is, and what sort of information it contains, why don't you create your own Member Profile?

Creating a Member Profile

Creating a Member Profile is a simple, yet important, part of getting into the swing of things online. It's strictly optional—no one will *make* you fill out one—but you might find it useful, and *some* people won't chat with someone who is without a completed profile.

Creating Your Member Profile

1. Click the My AOL icon on the toolbar.
2. Click My Member Profile on the My AOL menu to open a blank version of the screen, as shown in Figure 3.8.
3. Fill out as much (or as little) of the profile as you'd like. Remember that member profiles must conform with the Terms Of Service language guidelines.
4. Click the Update button.

Figure 3.8.

A completed Member Profile form.

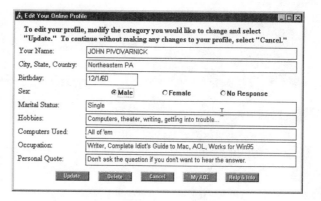

3

Completing the form makes your personal information available in the Member Directory. You might be surprised at what that can mean.

COFFEE BREAK

My career as an author of computer books began when someone searched an online member directory. A publisher was looking for someone to write a book about sports sites on the Internet. She searched for people with writing experience and knowledge of both sports and the Internet. I was among the names that came up. Long story short: I got the job. The rest, as they say, is history.

You'll also hear tales of people who met and fell in love by way of similar searches. You just never know what will happen.

Searching the Member Directory

Now that you're in the directory yourself, you might want to search for people with similar interests, professions, hobbies, or whatever, to your own. It's easy.

To search the Member Directory, click the People icon on the toolbar, and then click Search AOL Member Directory. You'll open a Member Directory screen with two tabbed forms. The Advanced Search form is shown in Figure 3.9. The Quick Search form only includes the first three text boxes for a faster, easier search. To switch forms, simply click on the tab for the search you want.

Figure 3.9.
Use the Member Directory to search for people with similar interests.

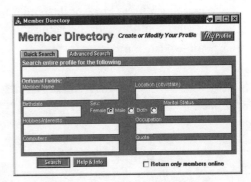

Enter a word or phrase typical of the kind of person you want to meet in the Search Entire Profile for the Following text box. The word or phrase can be a hobby, a favorite sports team, or whatever.

You can then provide any, or all, of the optional information: a name (if you want to see if a relative is on AOL, for example), a city and state (to find folks nearby), gender, birth date, marital status, and more.

If you want to be sure that the people who match are online, click the Return Only Members Online check box at the bottom of the screen. That way, you can chat immediately, if you care to.

When you're done, click Search, and you might be surprised at the number of other America Online members who match the criteria.

Pick one of the names and double-click it to see the person's complete Member Profile. What the heck, why not drop him or her an email message? Just remember that the Profile information (like your own) was provided by the member—there's no guarantee that he or she didn't just make the whole thing up.

Summary

In this hour, you've learned some ways to help you get around America Online a little more quickly, and return to your favorite areas even *more* quickly. You also learned how to check your bill, and how to scope out other AOL members with interests similar to your own.

Workshop

Use the following workshop to help you solidify the skills you've learned in this hour.

Q&A

Q Keywords are great. How can I find more of them?

A You can use the keyword KEYWORD to find lists of just about every keyword known.

Q I see these What's New buttons all over the place, not just on the What's New window. What's up with that?

A A lot of different areas have their own What's New (sometimes What's Hot) buttons to highlight new areas within that Channel or forum.

Quiz

Find out just how much you've learned by taking the following quiz.

Questions

1. If a window doesn't have a little heart graphic, it means you can't

    a. Print the content of the page.

    b. Add it to your Favorite Places menu.

    c. Use a keyword to get there in the future.

2. What's the fastest way to find an area when you don't know the keyword?

    a. Guess at the keyword and then, if necessary, search the keyword list.

    b. Click a Channel that sounds right and keep clicking until you find it.

    c. Go to the What's New page.

3. Filling out your Member Profile is a good idea because

    a. You'll get to write a book like this one.

    b. It helps other members find you.

    c. You'll lose your membership if you don't.

Answers

1. **b.** You can't add a page to your Favorite Places unless the heart logo is present.

2. **a.** Trying a keyword that might be close will keep your search of the keyword list brief.

3. **b.** However, the possibility of writing a book is there, if the right people discover you.

Activities

1. Now that you've seen a few places on the service, take some time to add the ones you like most to your Favorite Places list.

2. Do a quick search of the Member Directory to see how many people you can find who share your hobbies, or live in your hometown.

Hour 4

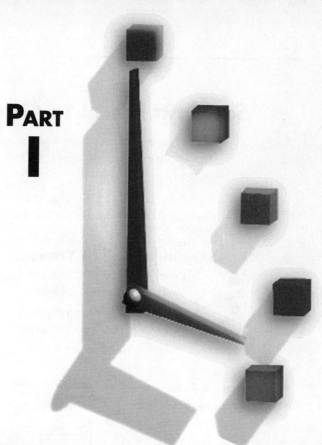

Using Email

Electronic mail, or email for short, is probably the most-often–used feature of AOL. Even the folks with only the barest, most basic Internet access use email frequently—it may even be the *only* thing they do with their Internet accounts.

As techno-geeky as it sounds, email is easy to master. Anyone who has ever written and mailed a regular postal letter has the basic concepts down. Trust me, you'll be sending and receiving email in no time flat.

In this hour, you'll learn all about email, including

- ☐ How to send email to other America Online members
- ☐ How to send mail to folks on the Internet and other online services
- ☐ How to read your mail
- ☐ How to save mail on your computer
- ☐ How to attach files to your email
- ☐ How to use files that people send to you
- ☐ How to set up and use your AOL Address Book

It sounds like a lot to learn, but really, it's easy.

Sending Email to Other AOL Members

Sending email is such a simple affair, it really is best explained by just doing it. So, let's start with a simple exercise that gives you the basic steps for composing and sending email—to yourself.

You might think it's a little crazy to send mail to yourself, but that way you'll learn how to read your incoming mail as well. For the sake of this exercise, sign on to AOL before you begin.

Sending Email to Yourself

1. Open the Write Mail window (see Figure 4.1) by clicking the Write button on the toolbar, or by pressing Ctrl+M (⌘+M on a Mac).

2. Click to place your cursor in the Send To text box. Type just your screen name. (When you send email to someone else, you'll type in his or her screen name.)

Figure 4.1.

Composing email with America Online.

Secondary addressee(s) here (optional)

Click to send now

Save mail to send later

Open your Address Book

Click to send a "postcard"

Help with email

Main addressee goes here

Click to attach a file to your mail

Subject of your note   Message text here

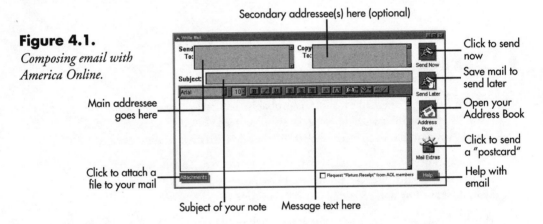

3. In the Subject field, type a subject—something like Trying it out or A message to myself.

4. In the message box (the big one at the bottom of the form), type a message to yourself. Type anything—but you have to type something there.

5. Click the Send Now button.

After a moment, you'll see an alert that says Your mail has been sent. You'll also hear, "You've got mail!" and the mail icons on the AOL toolbar and Welcome screen will change—all signs that you have mail.

That's all it takes to send email to another AOL member. You can also send email to anyone, anywhere, as long as they have access to email through the Internet or another online service. The process is the same, but the addresses are a little different.

Go ahead and take a moment to read your mail (even though you already *know* what it says). Opening new mail was explained previously in Hour 2, "Uses for America Online." If you've forgotten how, or are skipping around, just click the Read button on the toolbar, then double-click the letter on the New tab of your mailbox. When you're done, carry on reading, and you'll learn how to send mail beyond the boundaries of AOL.

Sending Email to Other Online Services and the Internet

Even if this is your first experience with the online world, you've probably seen or heard email addresses before—they're in commercials on television, in magazine ads, and on business cards. It probably sounded something like this: Name-at-gobbledygook-dot-com.

It probably looked even worse, such as `coworker@technophobe.com`.

Don't be scared. It's actually simple, after you break it down to the component parts.

Understanding Email Addresses

Everyone who has an email address belongs to some service—whether that's AOL, Prodigy, or an Internet service provider. When you send mail from your AOL account to another AOL account, you don't have to identify the service.

When you send a message, you have to address it, just as you put an address on an envelope in conventional mail (often referred to as snail mail by online users because it's so comparatively slow).

The first part of the address identifies the person (just like the first line of a postal address). Typically, it's the screen name they use on their service. The *at* symbol (@) connects the name to the rest of the address. The next part of the address identifies the service that the addressee uses (it's like the rest of a postal address).

When you send mail to a friend on Prodigy, for example, the address would look something like `mypal@prodigy.com`.

When your friend replies to your message, it would arrive with *your* address looking like `screenname@aol.com`.

4

(You *never* have to add that @aol.com when you're sending mail to another AOL member, just their screen name is enough.)

Some email addresses are worse. For example, CompuServe's screen names are a string of numbers and commas: 75212,607. To address email to a friend on CompuServe, replace the comma in their ID number with a period, then follow the regular addressing steps, like 75212.607@compuserve.com.

Folks with Internet accounts have similar addresses, but there are a lot of Internet service providers, so the portion after the @ symbol varies widely. Figure 4.2 shows an AOL email form addressed to a fictitious Internet account.

Figure 4.2.
Use the full address to send email to a service other than AOL.

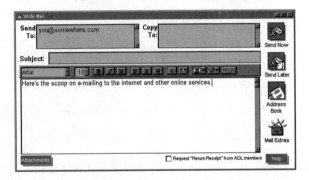

CAUTION

Be careful when typing email addresses. They must be typed *exactly* or they won't be delivered—or, worse, they will be delivered to the wrong person. How embarrassing.

As a general rule, addresses for mail being sent outside the boundaries of AOL should be typed with all lowercase letters and no blank spaces in the address.

Sending to Multiple People

You can easily send the same email message to several people. You can even CC: (carbon copy) messages to people.

NEW TERM   **CC (Carbon Copy)**—A term borrowed from business correspondence. When you need to send a copy of a letter to someone other than the addressee, you'd send them a carbon copy of the original letter, with the notation: CC: My Lawyer. You might send a copy of an email to a supervisor who needs to know what progress you're making on a project.

4

To send a message to more than one person, simply enter all the screen names and Internet addresses in the Send To box. Be sure to separate each name with a comma and a space, such as ScreenName, ScreenName, jblow@zephyr.com.

To send carbon copies of a message, simply type the additional recipient's name in the Copy To field.

What's the difference? Well, an example is this: If you write to three people and want them all to respond, you'd put all three addresses in the Send To box. If you just wanted someone to see what you wrote to someone else, you'd use the Copy To field.

Using the Send Later Button

The Send Later button is a wonderful tool (refer to Figure 4.1). It gives you the power to compose email offline (that is, not connected to America Online), which you can deliver later using Automatic AOL.

Whether you're sending mail to someone on AOL or another service, address and compose the message as described previously. When you're done, however, click the Send Later button. You'll receive a message that says, "Your mail has been saved for later delivery." Click OK to make the message go away. Compose any other mail you need to write, clicking Send Later for each.

When you're done, check out Hour 6, "Automatic AOL," for details on sending out your saved mail.

Coping with Your Mail

After you've been online awhile, you may run into the nightmare of having *so* much mail stored in your mailbox, that you can't receive any more (that's a lot of mail—over 100 messages). You may also want to reread old mail, pass along a message you've received to someone else, or take back a poison pen letter you've already sent. Your AOL mailbox gives you an assortment of tools to help you do all this and more.

Checking Mail You've Sent

Email is a lot faster than postal mail—that is, it gets where it's going faster. However, there's no guarantee that it will be read or answered any faster. You can find out if your message has been read by the addressee. Click the Mail Center button on the toolbar. Then, click Sent Mail on the Mail Center menu to open your online mailbox with the Sent Mail tab foremost (see Figure 4.3).

Figure 4.3.

Checking mail you've sent with the Sent Mail tab of your Online Mailbox.

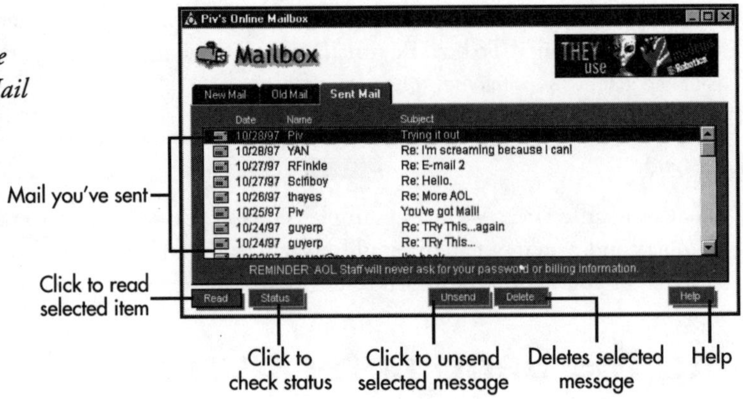

To reread any mail you've sent, double-click its name in the list or click once on the name, and then click the Read button. The message will open in a standard mail form.

To delete a message, click its name, and then click the Delete button. Deleting messages will prevent that ugly mailbox build-up that keeps you from receiving new mail.

TIME SAVER

> If you don't receive hundreds of pieces of email in a week, you don't have to worry about deleting mail from your Online Mailbox. AOL automatically deletes messages you've sent, and those you've read, after about 5–7 days.

To find out if mail you've sent has been read by the addressee, click the mail in your list, and then click the Status button. A summary window appears that tells you when you sent the message, the screen name of the addressee, and the date and time the message was read (*if* it was read). If the message hasn't been read, it will read Not yet read.

You can only check the status of mail that's been sent to other AOL members. If you try to check mail sent to an Internet account, or another online service, the status line will read Not Applicable.

If you've sent a piece of mail that you shouldn't have sent (it happens, I know, because I've done it), you can use the Unsend button to delete it from the recipient's mailbox—but there are some conditions here, too. The mail has to have been sent to another AOL member, and the addressee can't have already read the message.

When you unsend an email, not only is the recipient's copy deleted, but so is your own. Click the offending letter in your Sent Mail list, then click the Unsend button. You'll be warned that no copy will remain in your mailbox. Click OK, and the message is history. Pretty cool, huh?

Checking Mail You've Read

After you read a message and close your Mailbox, AOL moves read messages from your New Mail list to the Old Mail list (see Figure 4.4).

Figure 4.4.
The Old Mail tab of your Online Mailbox.

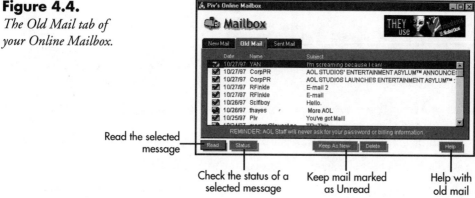

Read the selected message

Check the status of a selected message

Keep mail marked as Unread

Help with old mail

The Old Mail tab works much the same as your Sent Mail tab: You can reread a message; check its status (although you should already know if you've read it or not); or delete mail you no longer want to keep on hand.

You can also mark a message as unread: Click the message in the list box, and then click the Keep As New button. The message will reappear on the New Mail tab as if you'd never read it.

Why keep a message as new? In case you need to answer an important piece of mail, but don't have time right now—you can reread and reply to it the next time you sign on. And, mail you've read is automatically deleted from your Online Mailbox after about five days. Mail can be kept "as New" for a maximum of 30 days—so if you don't want to lose a piece of mail that soon, mark it as unread.

To Print or to Save?

Want to take an email message with you? You can print it out or save it to disk.

To print a piece of mail, open the message you want to print. While it's open, click the Print icon on the AOL toolbar. Your regular Windows printing screen opens, enabling you to print the message for later reference.

Alternatively, you can save a message to your Personal Filing Cabinet. With the mail message open, click the My Files icon on the toolbar. Then, click Save to Personal Filing Cabinet.

TIME SAVER

You can set your AOL Preferences so copies of all the mail you read and send are *automatically* saved to your Personal Filing Cabinet for future reference. Hour 15, "Setting Preferences," explains how.

Attaching Files to Email

Say that you're at home creating a business proposal for work. You need the folks at your office downtown to approve it before you give it to the customer. What do you do?

Well, you could hop in the car and drive to the office to get approval in person, but an easier solution would be to email the file to your supervisor. Then, you just call and tell her the file is waiting in her mailbox. That way, you don't even have to change out of your bunny slippers.

You can easily attach just about any kind of file to an email message.

On the Compose Mail window next to the Copy To text box, there's an Attachments button (refer to Figure 4.1). When you're done composing your message, click Attachments, and the Attachments dialog box, shown in Figure 4.5, opens.

Figure 4.5.

The Attachments dialog box enables you to attach one or more files to your message.

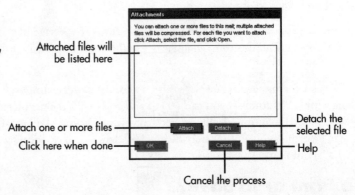

Click the Attach button on the Attachments dialog box. A standard Open-type dialog box appears. Use the dialog box to navigate to the file you want to send. Click the file's name to select it, then click Open. The selected file (and its location on your hard drive) appear in the Attachment's list box. You can repeat the process as necessary to attach all the files you'd like to your message. When you're done attaching files, click OK. You'll return to the email form.

When you send the message, it will take a little (or a lot) longer depending on the size of the attachment. The file must be uploaded from your computer to AOL. You will see a File Transfer window with a bar graph that shows the progress of the file you sent.

Reading Attached Files

Continuing with the idea of getting your proposal approved, say your supervisor makes some changes to your proposal, and sends the file back to you attached to an email message. How do you get your hands on the attached file?

When you read a message that has a file attached (such as the one in Figure 4.6), it will have two lines of text that tell you the filename, size, and the approximate download time.

Figure 4.6.

An email message with a file attachment.

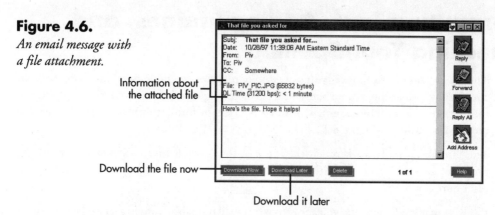

At the bottom of the window are two buttons: Download Now and Download Later. These work exactly the same as in file libraries online (those are explained in Hour 5, "Downloading Files and Searching Databases").

CAUTION

Never, ever, ever download a program file (with an .exe file extension) from people you don't know. Computer viruses are often spread by programs attached to email and a virus can scramble your entire hard drive. Trojan Horse programs exist that also try to capture your screen name and password information, so some geek can use your AOL account for free. Document files are usually okay, although some can contain viruses.

If a stranger sends you a mail message with an .exe file attached, be suspicious. Better yet, just delete that bad boy. Or you can forward it to the address `tosemail1`, for appropriate action.

To retrieve the attached file, click the Download File button, and a Save-type dialog box opens. If you care to, you can use the Save dialog box to rename the file (but you don't have to), or change the location where it will be stored on your hard drive. Unless you change it, AOL saves downloaded files to the Download folder in your AOL folder (c:\ao140\download). Otherwise, click Save and the transfer commences.

When the transfer is complete, you can open the file whenever you're ready.

If you'd rather, you can click Download Later and use AOL's Download Manager to retrieve the file for you. The Download Manager is explained in Hour 5.

Formatting Text, Adding Images, and Checking Your Spelling

The new version of AOL gives you some funky tools for prettying up your email. You can apply fancy formatting to your message text (including colors, fonts, and font sizing) using the formatting toolbar on the email form. You can see the formatting tools above the message box, shown earlier in Figure 4.1.

The formatting tools work much the same as those you'll find in any word processing program, so I won't bore you with details. Besides, it's more fun to *play* with them, and you can't hurt anything.

Be aware that any formatting you apply to your email probably won't travel well when you're sending mail to Internet accounts or to other online services. They'll only work in messages sent to other AOL members.

You can also insert photographic images and your Favorite Places into a message to share with friends. To insert an image, click the button with the camera on it, to the right of the text formatting tools. An Open-type dialog box appears that you can use to select the image file.

To insert a Favorite Place, click the button with the heart icon, also to the right of the formatting tools. A menu of your Favorite Places pops up. Just select the one you want to mail to your friend. It will appear in the message body as colored and underlined text. When your friend clicks the text, they'll be taken to your Favorite Place.

Before you send your mail, click the formatting button (icon with ABC and a check mark). AOL checks the spelling of your message for you. No more embarrassing typos. It works the same as the spell checkers built into most word processors. You won't have any trouble figuring it out.

Using the Address Book

AOL's Address Book acts just like your personal telephone directory. It stores often used email addresses (even those hard to type Internet addresses) so you can address your mail with

4

just a few clicks of the mouse. That simplifies keeping in touch with your family, members of your club, business clients, or whomever you correspond with regularly.

The easiest way to add someone to your Address Book is to open a piece of mail from him or her, then click the Add Address button. A New Person form, such as the one shown in Figure 4.7, opens with the screen name already entered in the First Name and Email Address text boxes. You can then edit and add whatever information you care to add. When you're done, click OK.

Figure 4.7.

Adding a new person to your Address Book.

You can even add a picture!

To manually add a new person, click the Mail Center icon on the AOL toolbar, then select Address Book from the drop-down menu. When your Address Book opens (you can see mine in Figure 4.8), click the New Person button. A blank form such as the one shown previously in Figure 4.7 appears. Enter the appropriate information, then click OK.

Figure 4.8.

The AOL Address Book.

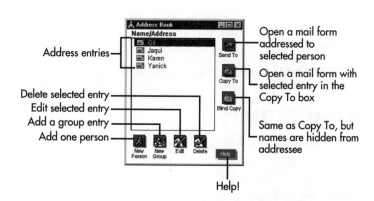

Address entries

Delete selected entry
Edit selected entry
Add a group entry
Add one person

Open a mail form addressed to selected person

Open a mail form with selected entry in the Copy To box

Same as Copy To, but names are hidden from addressee

Help!

Blind Copy—A Blind Copy works the same as a regular Copy To:, however, the addresses are hidden from the recipients—they don't know who else you've sent the message to. It's practical where confidentiality is concerned (for, say, an Alcoholics Anonymous email list). However, for everyday use, Blind Copies are considered rude.

If you regularly send the same message to a number of different people (for a club, perhaps), you can create a *group* entry in Address Book that will automatically address a message to all the members of that group. In the Address Book window, click New Group. A New Group form appears, such as the one shown in Figure 4.9. Enter a name for the group (like SciFi Club, or Clients, or whatever you want) in the Group Name text box.

Figure 4.9.

Adding a whole group to your Address Book as a single entry.

In the Addresses box, enter the email addresses for all the members of your group separated by commas and spaces, like this: `yourname, hername, him@theother.com`.

When you are ready to use the Address Book to send a message, open the Compose Mail window. Click the Address Book button on the left side to open your Address Book. Then, click on the name or group to whom you want to send a message, and click the Send To button. The name(s) will automatically be added to the Send To field in the Compose Mail window. You can do the same for the Copy To text box.

The Address Book is a wonderful tool to streamline the process of addressing your email.

Summary

In this hour, you've learned how to use America Online's email system. You're officially ready to email the world.

Workshop

This workshop contains some of the more commonly asked questions and answers about email.

Q&A

Q **I received a message in my mailbox that was called "Returned Mail." It was a message that I tried to send to one of my buddies, but it came back marked "user unknown." Did he send it back to me?**

A No. *User Unknown* mail usually comes back because the address you gave for the recipient was incorrect—either you entered it incorrectly, or the addressee has deleted that screen name. Check the address and try to send the message again. Mail sent to the Internet or another online service may be returned because of a mail handling error between AOL and the destination. You may need to send it again.

Q **Someone sent me mail with a document file attached. I downloaded the file just fine, but when I tried to open it, it didn't work. What happened?**

A To open a file attached to email, you need to have the same application that created the file (such as WordPerfect, to open a WordPerfect document), or you need an application that is capable of opening that sort of document. AOL can open common graphic files and text files. For other documents, you may need other software.

Quiz

Use the following quiz to check your knowledge of the lessons in this hour.

Questions

1. I am a member of CompuServe, and my username is `75212,607`. How would you send me email from America Online?

    a. `CompuServe@75212.607.com`

    b. `75212@607.compuserve.com`

    c. `75212.607@compuserve.com`

2. Regular email messages are readable on all computers because they come as

    a. Microsoft Word documents

    b. WordPad documents

    c. Plain text

3. True or False: America Online enables you to take back a message erroneously sent to another AOL member.

    a. True

    b. False

4. True or False: You can only attach one file to an email message.

    a. True

    b. False

Answers

1. **c.** This is a little bit of a trick question. CompuServe is somewhat confusing because it uses numbers instead of screen names. The entire number, including punctuation, is the user's name. Because you can't use commas in an address, the comma becomes a period, and the whole number set comes before the `@compuserve.com`.

2. **c.**

3. **a.** True, but you *cannot* take back messages that have been read or messages that were sent to an Internet address.

4. **b.** False. AOL 4.0 allows multiple file attachments.

Activity

Get the email addresses of some of your friends and enter them into your Address Book. Then drop them a line—maybe send them a file or two.

PART
II

Getting Comfortable with AOL

Hour

Hour 5

Downloading Files and Searching Databases

There are plenty of good reasons for you to have joined America Online—but I bet the ability to download files and software was *not* one of your reasons.

Most people join America Online for other reasons: to chat online, to email their friends and family, or to use as an educational resource. Many, however, soon find that the ability to download is one of their favorite parts of life online.

If you don't know what downloading is, you'll soon learn what all the hubbub is about. In this hour, you'll learn

- [ ] What downloading is
- [ ] Why you might want to download something
- [ ] Where you can find downloadable files
- [ ] How to go about downloading
- [ ] How the Download Manager works
- [ ] How to compress/decompress files
- [ ] How to upload a file

What Is Downloading?

You've probably heard the word before, perhaps in one of the *Star Trek* series—"Captain, we're downloading the Romulan ship's log now"—but you may not have fully understood its meaning. Reduced to its most basic elements, *downloading* is the process of transferring a file from one computer to another.

When you copy a file from a remote computer (from America Online's or a Romulan ship's) into your own, it is called *downloading*. When you transfer a file from your computer to another one, it is called *uploading*. Once you upload a file to America Online, you'll be able to download it into your computer.

What's So Great About Downloading?

America Online offers thousands, maybe even *millions* of files that you can download. But why would you even want them?

Well, there's a lot of great stuff available—software programs, text files, graphics, and much, much more. If you take the time to look around, you might find some that you like and others that you can't live without. And you know the best part of the whole downloading thing? A lot of the software and other files you can download are *free*. That's right! You can get software that might be helpful or entertaining, and a lot of it is free. Of course, that implies that some of it isn't.

In some areas online—online software and computer stores—you can pay for and download commercial products that you would normally have to buy in a store or from a mail order catalog. More often, however, you'll find file libraries full of software and other files that are there for downloading. In these libraries, you'll generally find two kinds of file (at least as far as *money* is concerned): freeware and shareware.

Freeware

Freeware, as the name implies, is free software. Many of the programs you'll find on AOL are freeware. Go ahead, download and use them. Heck, you can even make copies of this software and pass them along to a buddy or two. These programs, for whatever reason, are offered by their creators free of charge.

Shareware

Many programs found online are *shareware*—software that you can download and try out. If you don't find a program useful, you can delete it off your computer without paying for it. If you do like it and use it, you need to register your copy with the program's author and pay the registration fee (it's usually priced much lower than the stuff you find in stores). Shareware authors offer their creations this way to avoid the added expense of selling it through distributors and retailers who mark up the price to make their own profit. Therefore, shareware is generally less expensive to buy.

Unfortunately, most people who use shareware never pay for it. Not only does this keep shareware authors from creating new programs (why take all that time to write software if you don't make any money from it?), but it's also stealing. Pay your shareware fees.

Finding Files to Download

Many of the forums within America Online's channels have some type of software library or document area that is full of things you can download. The problem is, where do you look for the kind of file you want?

You could spend a lot of time poking around in every file library online, looking for that perfect download—but if you *sort* of know what kind of file you want, you can cut to the chase and do a software search. Let AOL do the looking for you.

Software Search

Let's say that you have a vague idea of what kind of program you'd like to download. Let's assume you're in the mood to play a new game, an adventure game. With only that notion, you can do a software search and sift through any or all the file libraries on AOL to find the games that might suit your needs.

To begin your quest, click the Find button on the toolbar (see Figure 5.1), and then click Software on the drop-down menu.

Figure 5.1.
Click Software on the toolbar's Find menu to get started.

The Software Search window, shown in Figure 5.2, will open. You can use it to limit your search to files posted in the past month or week. You don't have to limit your search by date; choose All Dates. To narrow the search further, you can choose one or more file categories that are appropriate to the file you want. In this case, you would select Games. Why have AOL search the list of telecommunications programs when it probably won't find many games there?

Figure 5.2.

The Software Search window helps you narrow your search.

Select a date

Click a category or two

Enter a keyword or phrase

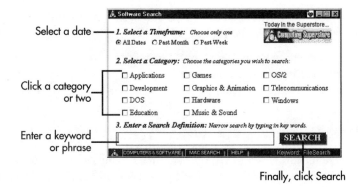

Finally, click Search

Because you've told AOL to look only in the Games libraries, you can now type a word or phrase in the text box at the bottom of the Search window to describe the kind of game you want. For a swashbuckling adventure, for instance, you might enter *adventure*. The results of your search might look like the ones found in Figure 5.3.

TIME SAVER

You can further narrow your search by using several words connected by *and* or *or*. For example, you could enter adventure and role playing as the search phrase. AOL will only list games that fall into both categories. If you use adventure or role playing, you'll get a list of games that fit *both* categories.

Figure 5.3.

Adventure games found by our search.

List of games that matched our criteria

Click to see more files in list, if necessary

Displays description of the selected file

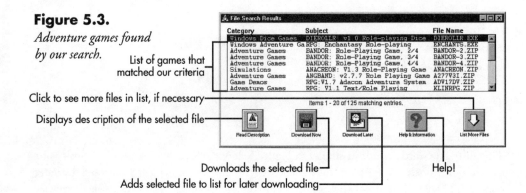

Downloads the selected file

Adds selected file to list for later downloading

Help!

Our search netted 125 games that matched our search criteria. To learn more about any of the listed files, click the filename to select it, then click the Read Description button. Alternatively, you can just double-click the filename. Either way works.

You can see a typical file description in Figure 5.4. It's important that you *read* the file description before you download a file. The description tells you what hardware and software you must have to use the file—if you don't have the right equipment, you're wasting your time downloading the file.

Figure 5.4.

A typical file description.

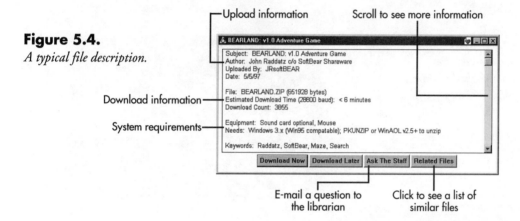

All the files you'll find online have a similar description attached. You can see who created the file, who uploaded it, and when. There's also information about how long it will take you to download the file and how many people have already downloaded it.

The bottom of the description window also gives you a few buttons you can use to work with the file. You have the same Download Now and Download Later buttons that you saw on the Search Results window, and they work in the same way here. You also have an Ask The Staff button, which allows you to send a question by email to the librarian in charge of the file's library. The Related Files button opens a list of files that are similar to the one you're currently considering. If the file at hand doesn't seem *quite* what you're looking for, click Related Files and browse the list. You might find what you want there.

JUST A MINUTE

Now that you know how to perform a software search, why don't you take a minute and search for an antivirus utility. All the software on AOL is scanned for viruses before they are put in the file libraries. That isn't true for the files you'll download from the Internet. You should have an antivirus program installed on your computer before you get to Part III, "Getting Started on the Internet." Viruses are explained in more detail there.

Browsing for Files in Forum Libraries

In addition to searching for files, you can browse through individual libraries whenever and wherever you find them online. Most forums include libraries full of software, text, sounds, and other files that you may download.

Keeping with the previous example, let's try to turn up some adventure games by manually digging through a forum's file library. To begin, use the keyword PC GAMES to get you to the PC Games Forum, shown in Figure 5.5. (Keywords are explained in Hour 3, "Exploring America Online.")

Figure 5.5.
Click the Libraries button in the PC Games Forum to browse for files.

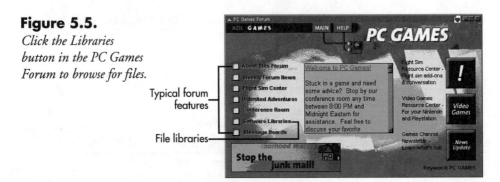

Typical forum features

File libraries

When you arrive at the PC Games Forum, click the Libraries button. You'll open a file library window that lists the different categories of games. Find the Adventure Games entry and double-click on it. You'll open a file listing like the one shown in Figure 5.6.

Figure 5.6.
The Adventure Games library.

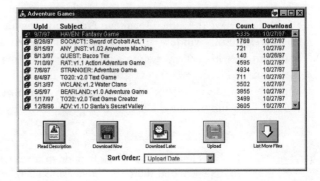

The libraries window looks, and works, much like the File Search Results window you saw back in Figure 5.3, but with some minor differences: Instead of a Help button, you have an Upload button, and at the bottom of the library window, you can select how the files are displayed from the Sort Order drop-down menu. You can view the files by Upload Date, Alphabetically by Subject, Download Count (how many folks downloaded the file), and Download Date (when was the file last downloaded).

As in the Search Results window, a simple double-click the filename will give you a description of the file. Once you find a file that interests you, you need to download it to your computer so you can install it and play.

Learning to Download

Now, you're ready to try a download.

Downloading a File/Program

To Do

1. Find a file you'd like to download, either by using a software search or by browsing a forum library. If you can't find anything that strikes your fancy, use one of the Adventure games you found earlier.

2. In the Search Results or Library window, double-click the filename. When the description opens, be sure to check the system requirements to be sure you can use the software.

3. Click Download Now.

4. A standard Windows Save-type dialog will open. Use it to navigate to where you want the file to be saved. Click Save.

5. A bar graph appears that shows you the progress of the download and estimates the amount of time remaining.

6. When the download is complete, a window pops up to inform you that the file has been transferred. Click OK to make it disappear.

Your download is complete. Good job!

CAUTION

Be aware that *most* of the software (and some of the other file types) you'll download from AOL will be compressed so they take up less space and less time to transfer between computers. You'll have to decompress most downloads before you can install and use the software. That's all explained later in this hour in the section, "Compressing and Decompressing Files."

5

Using the Download Manager

Earlier, when we were looking at the various file listings, we glossed over the Download Later button. While the Download Now button transfers the selected file immediately to your computer, the Download Later button passes the file on to AOL's Download Manager.

The Download Manager does just that: manages all the files you want to download. Instead of roaming around, randomly downloading single files (which, to be blunt, is not particularly exciting, in and of itself), you can instead click the Download Later button and download one or more files in a group before you sign off. You don't even have to sit there and baby-sit the computer—you can walk away, and the Download Manager will disconnect you from AOL when it's done transferring the files.

Once you've clicked Download Later for a couple of files, open the Download Manager by clicking the My Files icon on the AOL toolbar, then clicking Download Manager on the My Files drop-down menu. The Download Manager will open, looking something like mine, shown in Figure 5.7.

Figure 5.7.
The Download Manager.

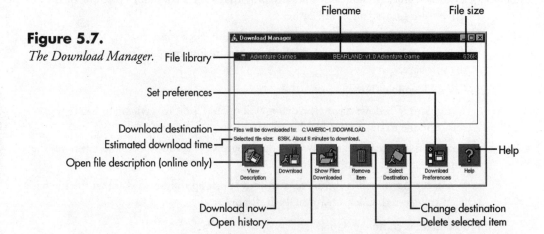

At this point, you can still back out of downloading any or all the files. Click the filename to select it, then click Remove Item button. You can also review your selections, while signed on to AOL, by selecting a file, then clicking the Read Description button. It will open a file description, like the one shown in Figure 5.4, so you can make sure you *really* want to download the file.

To start downloading your files, click the Start Download button. The Download Manager will now download the files for you, one at a time. If you have a large number of files and they will take quite a while to download, you may want to click the Sign Off After Transfer check

5

box in the File Transfer status window. Then, you can walk away without having to remember to come back to the computer and disconnect from AOL.

You also can run a completely unattended download of files by using a FlashSession as described in Hour 6, "Automatic AOL." FlashSessions are very cool and very handy. Definitely check them out.

TIME SAVER

> While downloading files individually or with the Download Manager, you may continue using AOL. You may also minimize AOL and work with another program while the download is in progress. The download will continue in the background. Be warned, however: Download time may increase considerably, and/or your computer's performance may get noticeably sluggish while downloading in the background.
>
> Sometimes it's just better to take a coffee break while downloading.

Compressing and Decompressing Files

Many of the files you will download will have been compacted with a compression utility. For Windows, PKZip is the industry standard for compression and PKUnZip is for decompression. Zip files have .zip at the end of the filename. For Macintosh computers, the compression standard is StuffIt. StuffIt files have the .sit extension at the end of their filenames.

Still other files are self-decompressing, which means you don't need any outside software to decompress them. On the Windows side, self-decompressing filenames end with the .exe extension. For the Mac, they end with the .sea extension.

Your America Online software can decompress files; it will even do it automatically when you sign off of AOL. You just need to tell your software to do so by way of your Download Preferences. To learn more, see Hour 15, "Setting Preferences."

If you really get into the whole file compression thing, you might want to search for and download a compression utility that streamlines and simplifies the process. WinZip is an excellent shareware product, but there are others, both shareware and freeware, available online. Mac users might want to find a copy of StuffIt Lite, also available online.

Uploading a File

After you've bounced around AOL for a while—joined a few discussions, visited some forums and message boards, and read and downloaded files by other folks—you might want to contribute a file of your own. You most certainly can.

CAUTION

America Online takes great care to make sure that anything it has available for download is free of viruses, and you should do the same. Use your virus-scanning software to check anything you plan to upload before you do it.

If you don't have an antivirus program, there are a number available online. Use the keyword VIRUS to learn more.

To upload a file, first go to the forum library in which you want the file to appear. In the appropriate forum, open the file library and locate the Upload area. If you look back at Figure 5.5 for the PC Games Forum, you'll notice that the upload area is called Free Uploading; it's the last item in the Forum's list box at the right of the screen.

Open the Upload area. It will look like the file library shown in Figure 5.6, but the Upload button will be active (not dimmed, as in the figure). If you see a file called "Read Before Uploading" or something similar, make sure that you read it. Many areas have strict guidelines on what can and cannot be uploaded, or may even contain special uploading instructions.

Once you've made sure your upload is acceptable to the area, click the Upload button. You'll open a file uploading form like the one shown in Figure 5.8. You need to completely fill out the requested information—this is where file descriptions come from, so you know it's important to the folks who will consider downloading your work.

Figure 5.8.

The uploading form requires you to provide all the requested information.

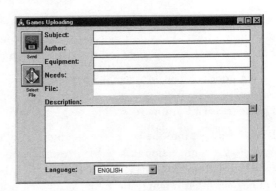

On the form, these are several areas you need to complete:

- ☐ **Subject**—Make sure that you describe the file accurately. Don't use catch phrases or other jargon that might be misunderstood. Be descriptive.
- ☐ **Author**—Type in your full name here.

5

☐ **Equipment**—List any special hardware that a user will need to use or view the file properly.

☐ **Needs**—Enter any additional software that is required. For example, if you upload a Microsoft Word document, the user will need Word to read it.

☐ **Description**—This larger field gives you the space to detail what your file is all about.

Once you've filled out the information, click the Select File button. Use the Open-type dialog it gives you to locate and select the file you're uploading, then click Open. You'll return to the Games Uploading window, and the filename will appear in the File text box of the form.

Finally, click Send and the upload will begin. It looks like a file download, but things are going in the opposite direction. After your file has uploaded, you'll get a message saying that your file has been received and will appear in the library after it has been reviewed for content and scanned for viruses by an AOL staff member. You're finished. Check back in a couple of days, and your file should be in the library.

Summary

In this hour you have learned everything you need to know about downloading and uploading files to America Online, both manually and via the Download Manager.

Workshop

Use the following workshop to solidify the skills you've learned in this hour.

Q&A

Q I uploaded a file, but it's not in the list of files that can be downloaded. Why?

A It usually takes a few days for any file that is uploaded to appear for others to download. Be patient.

Q I was in the middle of a download, and my computer froze. What do I do now?

A AOL offers the option of "resuming the download," but I don't recommend doing that. The portion of the file you've already received is often damaged. You're usually better off just starting over.

5

Quiz

Take the following quiz to see how much you've learned.

Questions

1. What is shareware?

    a. A free program you can download and use

    b. A program you can download, try, and pay for if you choose to keep it

    c. A software program you can buy at a computer store

2. A file with the extension .zip is

    a. Too large to be downloaded

    b. A file or files that are compressed

    c. A text-only file

3. The Download Manager allows you to

    a. Download multiple files at once

    b. Install and organize the files you've downloaded

    c. Change the extension of files you've downloaded

4. Using, but not registering, shareware programs is

    a. Illegal

    b. Immoral

    c. Fattening

    d. All of the above

Answers

1. **b.**
2. **b.**
3. **a.**
4. **d.**

Activity

Browse some file libraries in your favorite forums online. Download a few files or programs using the Download Now *and* the Download Later buttons. Use the Download Manager to get the files you've selected for later downloading.

Hour 6

Automatic AOL

For the sake of putting Automatic AOL in context, let's recap for a moment. In Hour 4, "Using Email," you learned how to use the Send Later button to save your email for later delivery. In Hour 5, "Downloading Files and Searching Databases," you learned how to click the Download Later button to add files to your Download Manager for later downloading. Well kids, it's later.

In this hour, you'll learn Automatic AOL, the AOL feature that allows to you to send and retrieve mail, and download files, with your eyes closed—while you're asleep, even. You'll learn

- ☐ What Automatic AOL is
- ☐ What Automatic AOL can do for you
- ☐ How to set up Automatic AOL
- ☐ Different ways to use Automatic AOL
- ☐ How to read email offline
- ☐ How to use Automatic AOL to retrieve the files listed in your Download Manager

This hour can really simplify your life, so let's get to it. If you didn't prepare any mail for later delivery, or select any files for downloading later (as described in Hours 4 and 5), you may want to do one, the other, or both before you begin.

What Is Automatic AOL?

Automatic AOL is an automated online session. Your computer and AOL software do all the work for you, so you can relax, read a book, or take a nap.

With Automatic AOL, you schedule a time for your computer to sign on to AOL and perform a set of specific tasks, including sending and receiving email and downloading files.

For Automatic AOL to do it's job, your computer needs to be on with your AOL software running.

Benefits of Automatic AOL

Back in the days when every minute of online time ran up your AOL bill, Automatic AOL sessions (then called FlashSessions) were an invaluable resource because you could preset activities for a session and minimize the amount of time spent online.

Flat rate pricing has, for the most part, eased the expense problem, but Automatic AOL can still be useful. For instance, Automatic AOL enables you to sign on to AOL at off-peak hours (say, in the wee-small hours of the morning), when it's less likely to tie up your phone, and when no one else needs time on the computer. Automatic AOL sessions that are run at off-peak hours generally go faster and more smoothly. In the morning, or whenever, all your incoming mail and other items are waiting for you.

You can use Automatic AOL whenever you happen to think of it, or you can schedule to run it whenever you like, so you don't *have* to think of it. You can schedule sessions for as often as you like—from every day at half-hour intervals, to once a day on specified days. All it takes is a little setting up.

Setting Up an Automatic AOL Session

You don't need to be connected to AOL to set up Automatic AOL on your computer, but your AOL software must be running. To begin the set up process, click the Mail Center icon on the AOL toolbar. Then, click Setup Automatic AOL (FlashSessions) on the Mail Center's drop-down menu. The Automatic AOL Walk-Through dialog box opens (see Figure 6.1).

JUST A MINUTE

Folks who are already familiar with using Automatic AOL or FlashSessions with previous versions of the AOL software may want to click the Expert Setup button. You'll bypass the question and answer screens described in the following paragraphs.

6

Figure 6.1.

The Automatic AOL Walk-Through dialog boxes simplify the set up process.

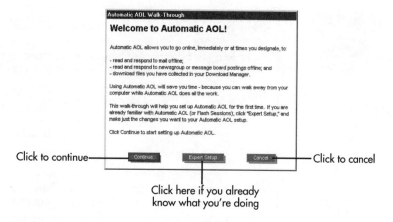

Click to continue

Click here if you already know what you're doing

Click to cancel

Click the Continue button, and AOL will ask you a series of yes or no questions about the jobs you want Automatic AOL to perform. The questions are, *Do you want Automatic AOL to*

- ☐ Retrieve unread mail?
- ☐ Download files attached to mail? (As mentioned in Hour 4, downloading files attached to email from strangers is a *bad* idea. You should probably click No here. After you've read the email, you can click Download Later to retrieve the attached file in a future session, should you decide you want it.)
- ☐ Send outgoing mail?
- ☐ Download files from the Download Manager?
- ☐ Retrieve unread newsgroup postings?
- ☐ Send outgoing newsgroup postings?

NEW TERM **Newsgroup**—A newsgroup is the Internet equivalent of the message boards you'll find on AOL. A newsgroup enables people to post messages, and read and reply to messages posted by others. Newsgroups are explained in Hour 10, "Newsgroups and Mailing Lists."

Next you'll be asked to select the screen names for which you want to run Automatic AOL sessions. Click the check boxes in front of the screen names you want to use, then carefully enter the password for each screen name in the Password text box beside the name. A screen name is selected when a check mark appears in the box beside it. To deselect a screen name, click the check mark to remove it.

6

CAUTION

Storing your password makes Automatic AOL possible—otherwise your AOL software couldn't connect to the service to do your bidding. Storing your password also makes it possible, however, for anyone who has access to your computer to run an Automatic AOL session for your account. If you use AOL in a work environment, or anywhere privacy is limited, you might want to think twice about storing your AOL passwords.

TIME SAVER

At this stage of the game, most readers will only have one screen name—the one you created when you first established your AOL account in Hour 1, "Installing America Online and Signing Up." You can create others—up to a total of five—for yourself, or other members of your household. Hour 14, "Navigating Through America Online *Your* Way," explains how.

When you're done, click Continue. You'll be asked if you want to schedule times for Automatic AOL to do it's stuff. Just for the sake of doing it, click Yes. You can come back and change these settings whenever you like, following these same steps.

Next you'll be asked to select the days of the week on which to run Automatic AOL sessions. The default selection is every day. If that's okay with you, click the Continue button. Otherwise, click on the check marks in front of the days on which you *don't* want to run Automatic sessions—that deselects them—before you click Continue.

After you've set the days, you'll be asked to select how *often* Automatic AOL should run on those days. You can select anything from every half-hour, to every eight hours, or to once a day. Click your selection, then click Continue.

Finally you'll be asked to select the start time—this is in Military time, where 1:00 p.m. is 13:00. Set the hour and the minute, then click Continue. You'll receive a little Congratulations screen because you're ready to run an Automatic AOL session.

Running an Automatic AOL Session

As mentioned earlier in the hour, you can manually start an Automatic AOL session whenever you like, or you can let the scheduler do all the work.

To let the scheduler handle all the Automatic AOL sessions, you don't have to do anything—except be sure your computer is turned on, and your AOL software is running for the scheduled sessions. An unattended session works much the same as the session you're about to begin, except you can be asleep and dreaming during a scheduled session, instead of sitting at your computer.

However, you should first manually start a session so you can see what happens.

Run Automatic AOL

1. Click the Mail Center icon on the AOL toolbar, then click Run Automatic AOL (FlashSession) Now. The Automatic AOL dialog box appears as shown in Figure 6.2.

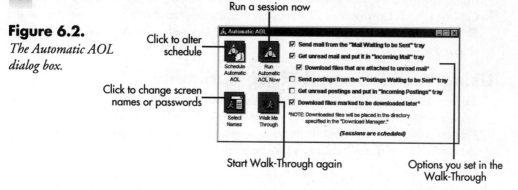

Figure 6.2.

The Automatic AOL dialog box.

2. Click the Run Automatic AOL Now button. AOL opens the Activate Automatic AOL Now dialog box asking if you *really* want to run a session (see Figure 6.3).

Figure 6.3.

Click the Begin button to start your Automatic AOL session.

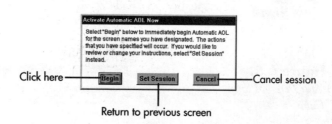

3. Click the Begin button.

Now you can just sit back and relax as your computer automatically connects to AOL for each of your screen names (if you have more than one), and completes the tasks you selected during the Automatic AOL Walk-Through.

You can watch what it's doing by reading the contents of the Automatic AOL Status window (see Figure 6.4).

6

Figure 6.4.

*The Automatic AOL
Status window tells you
what's happening, as it
happens.*

When the session is done, Automatic AOL disconnects you from the service. You'll be able to read any new mail that's come in, or deal with any files you've downloaded.

Automatic AOL deposits copies of your mail and newsgroup postings to your Personal Filing Cabinet (PFC). Downloaded files are stored in the download destination specified in the Download Manager—probably the Download folder inside your AOL folder, unless you changed it.

Using Your Personal Filing Cabinet

To read your incoming mail, you'll need to open your Personal Filing Cabinet. Click the My Files icon on the toolbar, then select Personal Filing Cabinet from the drop-down menu. The Personal Filing Cabinet window opens as shown in Figure 6.5. Figure 6.5 shows that the Personal Filing Cabinet has three organizing folders—Mail, Newsgroups, and Download Manager.

TIME SAVER

You can also jump right to a specific mail folder in your Personal Filing Cabinet. Click the Mail Center icon on the toolbar. On the Mail Center menu, point at Read Offline Mail, then click the type of mail you want to read on the Read Offline Mail submenu.

Figure 6.5.

*Your Personal Filing
Cabinet.*

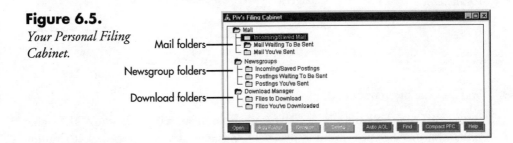

Mail folders

Newsgroup folders

Download folders

The Mail folder holds three folders—Incoming/Saved Mail (for mail you've received), and two folders for sent mail (Mail Waiting To Be Sent and Mail You've Sent).

The Newsgroup folder has three subfolders of its own (exactly the same as for Mail, but for newsgroup postings)—Incoming/Saved Postings, Postings Waiting To Be Sent, and Postings You've Sent.

6

The Download Manager folder only contains two folders. Files to Download contains a list of files for which you've clicked Download Later. Files You've Downloaded holds a list of the files you've already downloaded. Remember, it doesn't contain the actual files you've downloaded, only information about the files.

To open any of the folders in the PFC, double-click the folder. The folder opens, dropping down a list of its contents, as shown in Figure 6.6. To read an item in the list, double-click it.

Figure 6.6.

My list of saved mail.
Double-click an item
to read it.

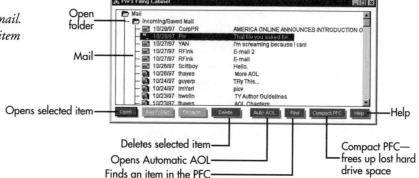

Open folder · Mail · Opens selected item · Deletes selected item · Opens Automatic AOL · Finds an item in the PFC · Compact PFC—frees up lost hard drive space · Help

You can then read, reply to, or delete any of the items in the Filing Cabinet. If you double-click one of the Download Manager entries, you'll open a description of the file you downloaded, or want to download—however, you must be online for it to work.

To delete an item from the PFC, click its name in the list, and then click the Delete button. If you care to, you can add subfolders to each of the main Filing Cabinet folders (Mail, Newsgroups, and Download Manager), to help you further sort and organize your cabinet. To do so, click the folder to which you want to add a subfolder, and then click the Add Folder button. AOL asks you to enter a name for the new folder. Enter the name, and then click OK. You may then click and drag items from any of the other folders into the new folder.

JUST A MINUTE

Every now and then, when you close your PFC, AOL puts up an alert saying that the PFC needs to be compacted. It's nothing to panic over. It means that from adding and deleting files in the PFC, some hard drive space is being wasted that could be used for other things. Compacting your PFC frees up that space. Click the Compact Now button and get on with your life.

6

Automatic AOL and Personal Filing Cabinet Tips

Just a few simple little tips are listed here to help you make the most of these handy tools:

- ☐ Instead of reading your email or newsgroups online, run an Automatic AOL session before you sign off. Then you can read and reply to your messages offline, and send those replies in another Automatic AOL session.

- ☐ You can change your Automatic AOL settings as often as you want. If you don't want to run a session for *all* your screen names, turn off the unwanted names before you run your session. Click the Select Names button on the Automatic AOL dialog box (refer to Figure 6.2).

- ☐ Keep up with your mail and newsgroup messages. Regularly read, reply, and delete old messages from your PFC—otherwise you're eating up hard drive space with a lot of old news. It's especially important if you use Automatic AOL to retrieve your newsgroup messages—you can get buried in them if you don't clean house on a regular basis.

- ☐ When you delete a lot of items from the PFC (say about 10 or more), click the Compact PFC button when you're done. You don't have to wait for the software to warn you that there's a lot of wasted space in there.

- ☐ Remember, when you store your passwords for use with Automatic AOL, anyone who has access to your computer can run a session and get at your mail.

COFFEE BREAK

If you like the whole idea of automatic AOL, and wish there was some way you could use it to download your favorite message boards and forums from AOL—and even your favorite web sites from the Internet—hold onto your hats. As of this writing, AOL is in the process of testing an AOL add-in that will do just that. It's called Driveway, and it sounds cool.

By the time you read this, Driveway should be available. Keep an eye out for messages online, announcing its release. Then download it and give it a try. If you like Automatic AOL, you'll *love* Driveway.

Summary

In this hour, you've learned how to set up and run Automatic AOL, both while you're at the computer, and while you're tucked in bed, fast asleep.

Workshop

Use the following workshop to strengthen the skills you learned in this hour.

6

Q&A

Q I ran Automatic AOL. When it was done, the computer signed right back on to America Online and ran another one. What gives?

A Check those screen names—you have more than one screen name checked in the Select Names window. AOL runs a session for each selected name.

Q I know I can use Automatic AOL just before I sign off AOL, but can I use one right after I sign on?

A Sure, you can. Just be aware that Automatic AOL will disconnect you from AOL when it's done with its assigned chores. A better idea might be to schedule a session for the early morning hours, so all your mail, and so on, is waiting for you when you're done with your morning coffee.

Quiz

Use the following quiz to gauge your knowledge of Automatic AOL.

Questions

1. Automatic AOL can start even if your computer is turned off.

    a. True

    b. False

2. You can schedule Automatic AOL to run as often as

    a. Every minute

    b. Every half-hour

    c. Once a month

3. Which of the following is Automatic AOL *not* able to do?

    a. Download files you've added to the Download Manager

    b. Send and receive email

    c. Enter a chat room

Answers

1. **b.** False. Your computer must be turned on, with your AOL software running.

2. **b.** Automatic AOL sessions can't be scheduled more than every half-hour.

3. **c.**

Activity

Now that you've got the basics, go ahead and use Automatic AOL, if only to send and receive email. You'll be surprised at how much it can simplify your life.

Hour 7

Chatting on America Online

Chatting is probably the most popular pastime on AOL. People are blathering away in chat rooms at all hours of the day and night—I know, because I'm there right along with them. This hour is all about chatting online, the wheres, the whys, and the hows.

In this hour, you will learn

☐ To find chat rooms that interest you

☐ The basics of chatting

☐ To use some special chatting features

☐ To chat privately

☐ To participate in AOL Live!

All About Chat

I could bring in a team of psychologists to tell you why chatting is so popular, but it's probably best explained by saying this: Chatting is popular for different reasons for different people.

The most common answer is that it gives shy people a chance to be a little more outgoing anonymously, without prejudices such as physical appearance, race, gender, and so on.

Chatting sometimes gets a bad rap because of the people who use it as a sort of dating service or adults-only 900-number (I'm Bambi, call me.). That does happen, but it's only a small part of the whole chat experience. A huge number of chat rooms are dedicated to a set topic, rooms that people regularly go to for serious (or not) discussions of subjects that interest them.

Chat grabs online users because it's live, uninhibited, and a lot of fun. To get in on the fun, of course, you have to get into a chat room.

CAUTION

If you've spent any time online since you've signed up, you've no doubt seen the warning that says: REMINDER: AOL staff will never ask for your password or billing information.

That's an important warning. You might find that you *are* asked to reveal your password—either in an Instant Message or email. If you learn nothing else in this hour, learn this: **Never, ever give out your password online**.

Finding Chat Rooms

Chat rooms are all over AOL. You'll find chat rooms in forums to discuss the forum's topic, or host a live event. You'll know a forum has a chat room when you see either a Chat button on the forum's screen, or a button for Events—events usually mean special guests in a chat room.

An Events button, however, usually takes you to a screen that tells you about upcoming events, rather than directly to a chat room. To enter a forum's event chat room, you usually need to do some more clicking. You can see the Computing Events dialog box in Figure 7.1.

Figure 7.1.

The Computing Events screen has easy chat room access.

Formerly was "Active Rooms"

Event rooms and start times

Click for a list of active chat rooms

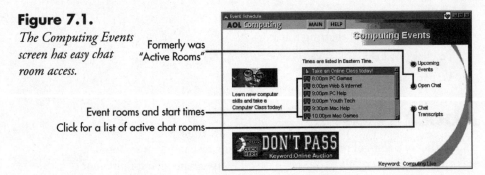

To get at the chat in Computing Events, you can either double-click a chat entry in the list box at the center of the screen, or click the Open Chat button to get a list of any Computing chat rooms that have people in them. You can then double-click an entry in the list to enter that chat room.

There's a simple way to see every single chat that's happening in the Channels other than the People Connection. You'll learn how a little later, in the section called "The Plaza."

As many chat rooms as there are in the Channel forums, you'll find many more in People Connection. The People Connection is abuzz with chat 24 hours a day, 7 days a week.

Getting into the People Connection

Chat rooms are so popular that there's a button for the People Connection on the Welcome window that greets you when you sign on. You can click that or select People Connection from the People menu on the toolbar.

The Town Square

When you click the People Connection button, you receive a People Connection dialog box. There are many options here; choose chat now and you're dropped into a lobby chat room in Town Square (see Figure 7.2). Town Square is the generic chat category online—there are others (you'll see them in a moment). A lobby is just that: a waiting room where you can chat, or move on to a room with a more defined topic of conversation.

Figure 7.2.
Your basic chat room—this one's a lobby.

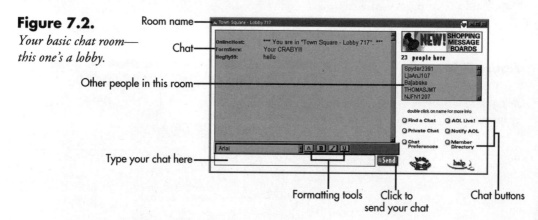

Room name

Chat

Other people in this room

Type your chat here

Formatting tools

Click to send your chat

Chat buttons

At any given moment, there can be *hundreds* of lobbies in the People Connection—the one shown in Figure 7.2 is Lobby 717, and that was during a *Friday evening*.

On the right side of the chat window you'll see a list of the people who are in the lobby with you (your screen name is there, too). You can find out a little something about the folks in your room by seeing if they have a Member Profile. To read a Member Profile, double-click a screen name from the room list, then click Get Info on the dialog box that appears.

JUST A MINUTE

If someone is getting on your nerves in a chat room, and you wish they'd just shut up, you can shut them up—as far as you're concerned at least. The same Info dialog box that lets you read another member's profile also has a little check box labeled Ignore. Click it so it's checked, and nothing that person says will appear on your screen. You're *ignoring* him, and he'll lose interest and go away.

When you first start out in a chat room, it's a good idea if you sit and read the chat scrolling up your screen. It will give you an idea of what's being talked about, who's doing the talking, and whether you want to join in. Just listening for a while also lets you get a handle on the slang and etiquette of chat rooms.

If you want to participate in a lobby chat, simply type what you want to say in the text box at the bottom of the window, and then press Enter (or click Send). Your chat will appear in the chat window, and you can carry on a conversation.

If there isn't much going on in the lobby, you may want to move to a room with a more specific chat theme.

Moving to Another Room

To see a list of the currently active chat rooms in the People Connection, click the Find a Chat button at the bottom of the chat window. A list of categories and chat rooms appears in the Find a Chat dialog box as shown in Figure 7.3.

Figure 7.3.

Chat room categories help you find rooms of interest.

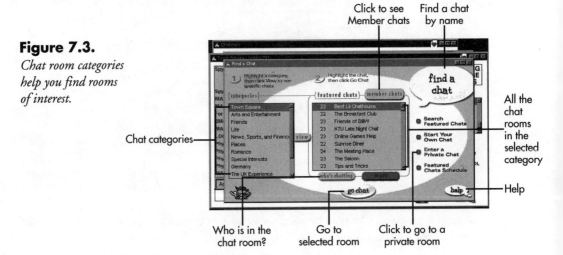

Chat categories

In the Find a Chat dialog box, you'll see a list of room categories in the box on the left side of the screen. Categories include Arts and Entertainment; News, Sports, and Finance;

7

Romance; and more. Several countries even have categories, including the U.K. and Canada. Each category contains a fleet of chat rooms.

When you double-click a category name, the list box on the right of the screen shows all the rooms that are available for that specific category. At peak chatting hours, you may need to click the More button a couple of times to see all the chat rooms in a given category.

To enter a room, double-click its name in the list. You can also peek in and see who's chatting in a room. Click on the room's name in the list, then click the Who's Chatting button. A list of the members in the room appears, much like the room list in an actual chat room. You can use it to see who's around before you drop in for a chat.

From a lobby, you'll only see lists of chat rooms that are opened by AOL. To see the rooms other AOL members have opened, click the Member Chats button. The list looks, and works, exactly the same as the one shown previously in Figure 7.3, but the rooms have all been created by AOL members.

You can create your *own* chat room from the list of Member Chats by clicking the Start Your Own Chat button. Enter a name in the Create Room dialog box and then click Create. You'll appear in your very own chat room. You may have to wait, alone, for a while before other members find your room and come in to talk. Be patient.

Caution

> These Member created rooms can be much wilder and woollier than the AOL sanctioned rooms—consider that a warning, or a piece of advice, depending on your mood.

The Plaza

The Plaza (shown in Figure 7.4) is like a big easy-access ramp to some of the most exciting stuff online. To get to it, click the Plaza button on the bottom of every chat room window, or use the keyword PLAZA.

Figure 7.4.

The Plaza is a gateway to much that's cool and interesting online.

The Plaza window can lead you to a number of interesting areas that you may want to explore. For the purpose of chat, however, one button you might find interesting is the Channel Chat button.

When you click the Channel Chat button, a list appears of every single forum chat room, in every Channel on AOL. How cool is that? You can see it in Figure 7.5.

Figure 7.5.

Use Channel Chat to find forum chat rooms.

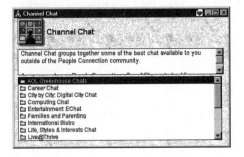

The lower pane of the window shows the list of all the forums with chat rooms. To visit a forum's chat area(s), double-click its name in the list to go directly there.

Channel Chat is useful because it helps you find chat rooms on a specific topic of interest to you. For example, if you want to chat about science-fiction movies, you can use Channel Chat to find an appropriate chat in the Entertainment Channel.

The Basics of Chatting

All the chat rooms on AOL work the same, and that simplifies your life. Take a minute to find one of interest to you, and pop in, or just refer back to Figure 7.2.

The largest part of any chat room is the window where all the chat appears. To the right of the chat window, you'll see the list of people in the room—the list you used earlier to read another member's profile.

Below the list of people are the four chat buttons: List Chats, Notify AOL, Plaza, and Member Directory. You've already used the List Chats and Plaza buttons. You'll see the Notify AOL button in action shortly. The Member Directory button enables you to search all the profiles for folks online for a word, phrase, or other information. Performing such a search was explained in Hour 3, "Exploring America Online," along with creating a Member Profile for yourself.

You type your chat messages in the text box at the bottom of the chat room window.

7

Adding Your Two Cents

When you have something to say in a chat room, click in the text box at the bottom of the window to put your cursor there, if it isn't already. Then, type your message and press Enter. Your message will scroll up in the chat box, preceded by your screen name, like this:

Me: Hi everyone!

That's the technical portion of chatting. There are some skills you'll need to develop to chat well with others. Here are some tips to get you started:

- ☐ **Keep up**—if you take too long to reply, or wait to see what others have to say, the current chat could veer in another direction completely. Folks will excuse a few typos for the sake of a speedy reply.

- ☐ **Direct your comments**—In a busy room with lots of chat going on, it will help everyone if you preface comments to a particular person with his or her screen name, like this: Piv—here's $2, go buy a clue! That way everyone knows for whom the chat tolls—it tolls for me.

- ☐ **Be polite**—Chat rooms are a public place, with folks of all ages present. Don't send anything into a chat room that you wouldn't be ashamed to say in front of your grandmother.

- ☐ **When in doubt, ask**—If someone says or does something you don't understand, ask them to explain. They will.

- ☐ **Learn the secret language of chat**—Flip to Appendix C, "Using Smileys, Short-hands, and Sounds," and learn how to use special language in a chat room.

Watch Your Language

As in everyday life, minor disagreements can escalate into heated arguments. In chat rooms with the blanket of online anonymity, these arguments can easily get out of hand. On the flip side of that coin, "intimate" discussions in "love connection" chat rooms can also get out of hand.

Rules of conduct exist in chat, just like there are rules in just about every aspect of life. The details on what is and isn't acceptable are available in the Terms Of Service, or TOS. You can read the TOS at the keyword TOS, but here's the short form:

Obscene, offensive, or abusive language is not allowed. Nor can you discuss illegal activities (such as taking or selling drugs) online. Disruptive behavior (such as monopolizing chat with irrelevant comments, or by drawing pictures on multiple lines of chat) is not allowed either. You can (and will) have your membership canceled if you lose control in a chat room.

If you're a witness to, or the recipient of, any abusive or obscene language online, you can report the offender to AOL by using the Notify AOL button on the bottom of the chat room window. When you click Notify AOL, the Notify AOL dialog box opens as shown in Figure 7.6.

7

Figure 7.6.

Let AOL know about inappropriate chat room behavior.

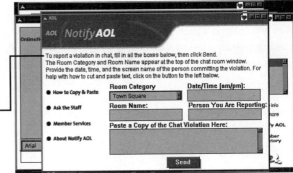

Follow these instructions—it's easy

The Notify AOL dialog box asks you to provide details of the incident. Just follow the simple instructions at the top of the window. You'll need to know the Time and Date of the incident, the Room Name in which it happened, the Screen Name of the Person You Are Reporting, and a sample of the offending chat or Instant Message (you can just copy and paste it from the chat room into Paste a Copy of the Chat Violation Here).

It's a powerful tool, and it should be used responsibly. Don't bog down this mechanism by reporting minor incidents and don't report someone just because you don't like him or her. A fake abuse report is a Terms Of Service violation in its own right.

JUST A MINUTE

In the chat rooms and lobbies, you'll run into a *Guide* from time to time. Guides are the online equivalent of park rangers: They patrol the People Connection, keeping things low-key, aboveboard, and within the TOS guidelines. You'll also see them in Help rooms, and playing host in some of the lobby rooms. You'll always know a Guide because their screen names are all Guide Something. Guides are good, fun folks, say "Hi" when you run into one.

Using AOL's Chatting Features

Chat is a fine, fun thing without any frills. You do, however, have a number of options at your disposal to jazz it up even more. You can style your text, chat in a private room, send and receive Instant Messages, and more.

Style Your Text

One of the newest features of America Online is the ability to use stylized text in chat rooms. Right above the chat text box you'll see a familiar looking toolbar. It's the same sort of toolbar you've used in your favorite word processor to change fonts, or to make text appear in a color, **bold**, *italicized*, or <u>underlined</u>.

Using the toolbar, you can also change the font—the actual typeface sent into the room—to any font you have installed on your computer.

It's a fun toy, but be smart about using it. The longer you take to send your message, the more likely it will be irrelevant when it hits the chat window. If you want to have a distinctive look for your chat, set it with your *first* chat, then let it be. You'll save yourself time and annoyance later in the chat session.

Private Rooms

Although it sounds like you're sneaking away to a seedy hotel room with your paramour, private rooms are not just for intimate online encounters. People regularly use them for business meetings or long-distance chat with family and friends without the distractions of a busy public chat room.

CAUTION

Online chat has played a major role in some frightening news stories. Use common sense when chatting with people you don't know.

☐ Don't give out *any* personal information to someone online.

☐ If you're tempted to arrange face-to-face meetings, schedule it during daylight hours, and in a public place.

Parents should be especially concerned about letting their children into chat rooms. Read Hour 21, "Keeping Parental Control," before you let your kids sign on.

Private rooms look and work exactly the same as public rooms, only their names don't appear on any of the List Chats room lists. You have to know the name to get into one. To *use* a private room, you have to *create* a private room.

TIME SAVER

The steps you take to *enter* a private room that already exists, are almost exactly the same as those for *creating* a private room, as described in the following section. The only difference is this: When you're asked to enter a name for the room, enter the name of the existing room, and you'll go right there. Enter it *exactly*, or you'll create a new room rather than enter the room you wanted.

Creating or Entering a Private Room

1. Enter a chat room—any chat room will do. Click the Find a Chat button.
2. In the room list window, click the Private Room button.

7

3. In the Private Room dialog box, type a name for the room. Make it a unique and unusual name so strangers won't accidentally wander in on you.

 4. Click OK.

You are now in a private room.

You'll need to make sure that whoever you're planning to meet in private knows the *exact* spelling of the room name. You can send it in an Instant Message, if you like...

Instant Messages

Instant Messages, or IMs, are private messages sent between folks online. They pop up instantly on the recipient's screen—unlike email, where they have to take the time to get and read their mail. You have to be online to send or receive an IM.

You're much more likely to receive an Instant Message when you're in a chat room, because folks can *see* you in a room; however, you can send or receive them anywhere online.

To send an Instant Message, click the People icon on the AOL toolbar, then select Instant Message from the menu. You can also use the keyboard shortcut Ctrl+I (⌘+I on a Mac). The Send Instant Message dialog box opens as shown in Figure 7.7.

Figure 7.7.
A blank IM form.

Recipient's screen name goes here

Formatting tools

Message here

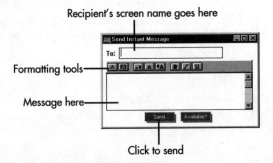

Click to send

TIME SAVER

The Available? button on the IM form enables you to check and see whether the addressee is online and able to receive IMs. A handy feature if you want to see whether a friend is online. Buddy Lists, explained later in this hour, are an even quicker way of spotting your pals online.

Type the recipient's screen name in the To text box (spell it right to be sure it goes through and doesn't fall into the wrong hands). Type your message in the large text box. Format with the formatting tools if you so desire, then click the Send button. Off it goes.

7

When Instant Messages arrive for you, a little bell will notify you and the message will pop to the front of your screen. To answer the message, click Reply, and type your response in the bottom text box. Click Send.

COFFEE BREAK

> Soon you'll be able to send pictures in IMs. On the IM's formatting bar, you'll click the Picture button (the one with the camera icon on it) to open a standard Open dialog box. Use it to locate the picture on your hard drive, click Open, and send the image on its way. It will take longer to send an Instant Image, but it sure will be fun!
>
> Instant Images will be added to AOL in an update soon after 4.0 is generally available. All sorts of announcements about it will be made online, so you won't miss it.

Buddy Lists

Buddy Lists let you know instantly if any of your friends are online. As soon as someone on your list signs on, their name appears in the Buddy List window to alert you to their presence—with sound effects, even. It's just too cool.

To create a Buddy List, use the keyword BUDDY. A Buddy List dialog box opens as shown in Figure 7.8.

Figure 7.8.

Create a Buddy List.

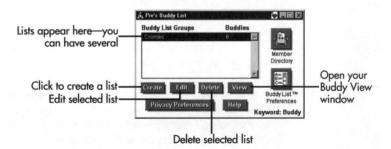

To create a Buddy List, click the Create button shown in Figure 7.8. You'll be asked to enter a name for your list. Call it whatever you like—I call mine *Cronies.* Click OK. You'll go to the Edit List dialog box shown in Figure 7.9.

To add a buddy, click to place your cursor in the Enter a Screen Name text box. Carefully type your friend's screen name. Click Add Buddy. Your buddy's name will appear in the Buddies in Group list box. Repeat as necessary to add all your buds to the list. When you're done, click Save. If you don't save the list, all the names you've entered will disappear in a puff of digital smoke, and you'll have to reenter them.

7

Figure 7.9.

Adding buddies to your list.

Enter a screen name here ——
Click here to add buddy to list ——

Click to save list ——

Removes selected name from list

After you have a list saved, you'll see a Buddies Online dialog box when you sign on (or you can open it whenever you like with the keyword BUDDYVIEW). When a buddy signs on, his or her name will appear in the list. You can then click their name, and use one of the buttons on the bottom of the window to:

- [ ] **Locate**—Find out where your friend is online.
- [ ] **IM**—Open an Instant Message form that's already addressed to your buddy.
- [ ] **Setup**—Open the Edit List dialog box shown earlier in Figure 7.9. It makes it easy to add buddies to your list while chatting, or whatever else, online.
- [ ] **Buddy Chat**—Invite your buddy to come talk with you in a private room—Buddy Chat will even create the private room for you, if you want.

COFFEE BREAK

You can add friends to your Buddy List even if they aren't AOL members—as long as they have an Internet address, you can enter *that*.

That's all *you* have to do to add your friends. However, your Internet friends have to download and install some software on their computers. Use the keyword INTERNET MESSENGER to send a message to your friends to download and install the software. After they do, they'll pop up on your Buddy List when they log on to the Internet, and you'll be able to IM them as if they were in a chat room with you.

Buddy Lists are an easy way to know where your online friends are at all times.

AOL Live!

AOL Live! is the area online where you can learn about, and enter, any of the many celebrity chats held online. You can meet famous actors, politicians, musicians, and even the occasional goof who writes computer books.

7

To get to AOL Live! use the keyword LIVE, to open the window shown in Figure 7.10. It highlights all the guests online today (click Today's Live Events) and future events (click Coming Attractions). It's worth a visit to pop in and click around, you never know *who's* going to be making a guest shot online.

Figure 7.10.

AOL Live! keeps you up-to-date with coming attractions.

TIME SAVER

To quickly get to all of AOL's event rooms, use the keyword INTERMISSION. Click the Auditorium Entrances button, and a list of all the special event rooms online appears. Double-click a name in the list to enter the room.

Summary

In this hour, you learned the basics of online chat, including some of the nifty features such as private rooms and Instant Messages.

Workshop

Use the following workshop to help solidify the skills you learned in this hour.

Q&A

Q **An Instant Message popped up on my screen from the billing department at America Online. It said there's problem with my account and asked me for my account information. What should I do?**

A Ignore it. America Online will *never* ask you for your password. AOL doesn't communicate with members through Instant Messages. Never give your password to anyone.

Q What's the difference between a private room and Instant Messages?

A Instant Messages are great for quick conversations or little asides during a chat session. If you're going to have a long group or one-on-one session, however, use a private room.

Quiz

Use the following quiz to bone up on your chatting knowledge.

Questions

1. If you want to know more about someone who is in a chat room, you should
    a. Double-click her name in the list of people in the room, then click Get Info.
    b. Drag her name from the list and drop it on your desktop.
    c. There isn't any way to find out more.
2. If someone becomes abusive in a chat room, you should
    a. Tell him to shut up.
    b. Click the Notify AOL button and report it.
    c. Never go to that chat room again.
3. The best way to keep track of which of your friends are online is to
    a. Look them up in the Member Directory.
    b. Call them on the phone and ask them if they're online.
    c. Use a Buddy List.

Answers

1. **a.**
2. **b.**
3. **c.**

Activities

Chat, for Pete's sake. Find a chat room that interests you and get talking. Then try using some of the features covered in this hour:

- ☐ Send an Instant Message.
- ☐ Go to a private room.
- ☐ Stylize some text.

7

Hour 8

Channels, Channels, and More Channels

The Channels are the heart and soul of America Online. Everything else is either included within or revolves around these 19 organizing topics, or categories. In fact, almost everything you've seen so far is part of a Channel—even though it might not *look* that way. For instance, when you use a keyword to jump to any forum online, you are actually diving right into a Channel. You've just bypassed the main Channel screen.

You've already learned some of the basics of Channel surfing, but this hour takes a more in-depth look at how the Channels work, and what you'll find in them.

This hour covers

- ☐ The main Channels screen
- ☐ How to use AOL Find to search all of AOL for what you want
- ☐ How to use Search & Explore to search a Channel
- ☐ Navigation tips

The Main Channels Screen

America Online is organized around its Channels, that's why the Channels screen is one of the first things to appear when you sign on. It's second only to the Welcome screen, and only because the Welcome screen shows you what's hot and happening online right when you sign on.

To get to the Channels screen, click the big, fat Channels button on the Welcome screen. The Channels screen will move front and center on your monitor (see Figure 8.1).

Figure 8.1.

The Channels screen—just click-and-go from here.

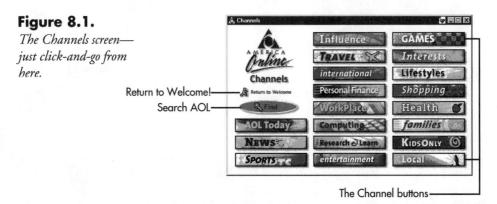

The Channels screen shows the 19 Channel buttons, the Return to Welcome button, and the Find button. You'll take a brief look at some of these Channels later in this hour, in the section "Checking Out the Channels."

Navigating the Channels

Each Channel has its own subject, or topic (News, Sports, and so on), but they all work pretty much the same way. When you click the button for any Channel, you open its main screen. All the Channel main screens include a set of buttons that take you to featured areas in the Channel, as well as buttons for the Channel's various departments (see Figure 8.2).

JUST A MINUTE

The first time you enter a Channel, you open a main Channel window like the one shown in Figure 8.2. This window is like New York City—*it never closes.* Well, at least not until you sign off AOL. If you click the close box on it, the window minimizes and tucks itself in the corner of the AOL screen. To restore it to normal size, click the minimized window—a menu pops up. Click Restore. If you're using Windows 95, you can also click the restore button right on the minimized window.

8

Figure 8.2.

The Lifestyles Channel—
it's all about how
you live.

Featured items

Easy access
to the other
Channels

You are here!

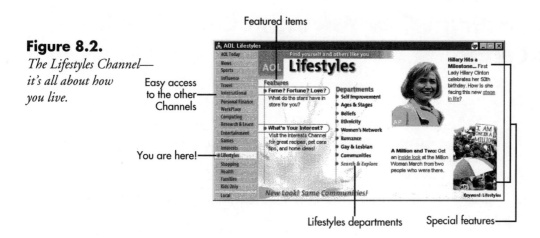

Lifestyles departments   Special features

Almost *everything* on a Channel's main screen is a link or button that you can click to take you to an area in the Channel. How do you know when you can click something online? Your arrow cursor turns into a pointing hand—it's one of the few times when it *is* polite to point, just ask Miss Manners.

To explore the contents of any Channel, find an item that interests you and click it. The related area will open in a new window. You can continue to explore whatever strikes your fancy—you'll probably open a fleet of windows in the process.

TIME SAVER

AOL's Window menu keeps track of all the windows you've got open. To return to a window you've lost track of, click the Windows menu, then select the window to which you want to return. They're all listed by name at the bottom of the menu.

If you've got a *lot* of windows open, you may need to select More Windows from the menu. It opens a list box of all the windows you've got open. Then just double-click the window you want. You can also use the back and forward pointing arrows on the toolbar to move back and forward through recently visited areas.

When you're done exploring *that* Channel, you can close all the intermediate windows you've opened until you're back at the Channel's main window. After you get there, you can click another Channel button on the left side of the window and explore other areas online. (You did read that *Just a Minute* back there, didn't you?)

Finding What You Want Online with Find Central

Sometimes browsing your way through AOL just won't cut it. There's something you absolutely, positively have to see, do, or learn, and you have to see, do, or learn it *now*.

You can sidestep all the random browsing and use the Channels screen's Find button to zero in on what you need to find. It gives you access to powerful search tools that let you browse through lists of the contents of every Channel, the power to search every Channel for a particular word or phrase, and a lot more.

Click the Find button on the main Channels screen to open the Find Central window shown in Figure 8.3.

Figure 8.3.
Find Central gives you six ways to search AOL.

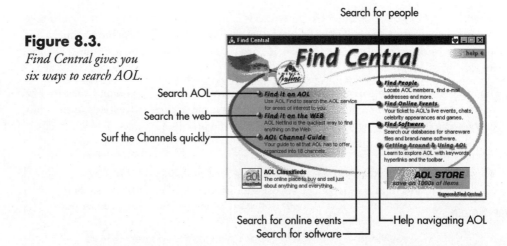

Search for people

Search AOL

Search the web

Surf the Channels quickly

Search for online events

Search for software

Help navigating AOL

To help you navigate the Channels, we'll look at two of the search options on Find Central now—Find it On AOL and the AOL Channel Guide. The other items will be covered in their appropriate hours throughout the book. (Find Software, for instance, was covered in Hour 5, "Downloading Files and Searching Databases.")

The AOL Channel Guide

If you're not in too much of a hurry to find what you want, you can browse a condensed version of the Channels, called the AOL Channel Guide. It lets you scroll through a complete listing of each Channel's contents (see Figure 8.4).

Figure 8.4.
The AOL Channel Guide.

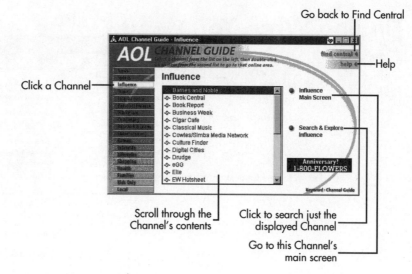

Go back to Find Central

Click a Channel

Help

Scroll through the
Channel's contents

Click to search just the
displayed Channel

Go to this Channel's
main screen

TIME SAVER

If all you really want to find is what cool stuff is happening online today, don't *search* anything—click the AOL Today button on the Channels display (or the toolbar's Channels menu), and you'll find out about *everything* going on, online.

To get to the Channel Guide, click the AOL Channel Guide button on the Find Central screen. The Channel Guide window will open. Click a Channel button on the left side of the window, and the list box at the center will display a complete list of each forum and area in that Channel. Scroll through the list until you find an entry of interest, then double-click on the entry to go to that area.

At the right side of the Channel Guide, there are two buttons. The top button will take you to the main screen for the currently displayed Channel (without having to go back to the Channels screen).

The second button gives you the option to Search & Explore the displayed Channel. This gives a searching tool similar to AOL Find (coming up next), but limited to *only the displayed Channel.* That way, if you know what you want is somewhere in the Influence Channel, you can save time by limiting the search to that Channel. You can see the Search & Explore window for the Influence Channel in Figure 8.5.

Help

Figure 8.5.

*Searching and
exploring the
Influence
Channel.*

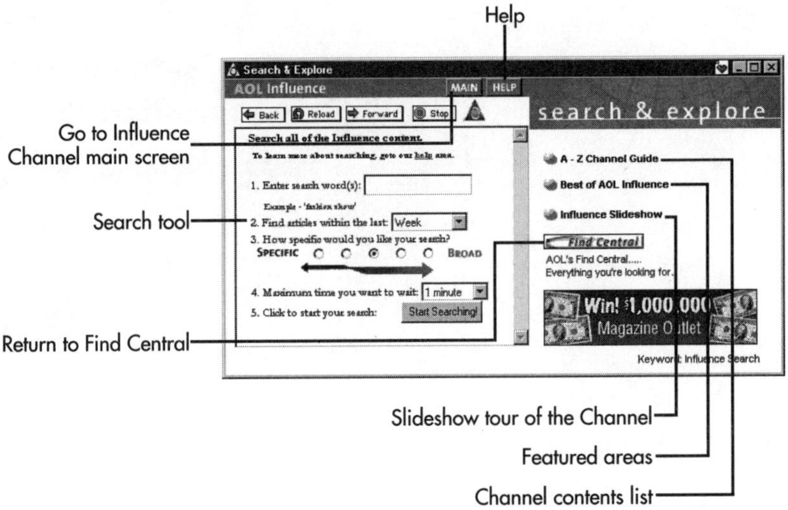

Go to Influence
Channel main screen

Search tool

Return to Find Central

Slideshow tour of the Channel
Featured areas
Channel contents list

Search & Explore gives you a number of ways to find what you want in the selected Channel. At the right of the window, you can open an A–Z list of the Channel's contents (like the Channel Guide shown earlier in Figure 8.4); you can get a list of featured areas; and you can even see a little slideshow tour of the Channel.

TIME SAVER

> If you need to Search & Explore a Channel, you don't have to go to Find Central, then to the Channel Guide, then to the Guide for that Channel... that's a lot of work. You'll find a Search & Explore button on each Channel's main screen—just select the Channel you want from the Channel menu on the toolbar, then click Search & Explore when the Channel's main screen opens.

To the left is the searching tool. Searching a Channel is a simple, five-step process—what the heck, it's so easy, let's search for something.

Search & Explore Mission

If you aren't already at the Search & Explore window for the Influence Channel, do this first:

1. Click Find on the AOL Channels display to Open Find Central.

2. On AOL Find Central, click the AOL Channel Guide to open the Channel Guide. Click Influence on the left side of the Channel Guide.

3. Click Search & Explore Influence on the right side of the Channel Guide.

8

When the Search & Explore screen opens, you're ready to search:

1. In the text box on line one of the search page, enter a word or phrase that interests you—it doesn't matter what, because this is an experiment. If you can't think of one, try *cigar*.

2. On line two, select a time frame in which to search. Just select one from the drop-down menu—week, month, or all dates.

3. If you care to, on line three select a level of specificity: from very specific to very broad—or just leave the default, middle-of-the-road selection.

4. Line four enables you to set how much time you want to wait—the more time you allow, the more thorough the search. Select a time from the drop-down menu based on your own level of impatience.

 5. Click the Start Searching button.

After the set amount of time, AOL will return a list of items from the Influence Channel that matches your search word or phrase (like the one shown in Figure 8.6). Explore at will—just click an underlined item to visit the related area.

Figure 8.6.
The results of my search, using "Cigar" as the search word.

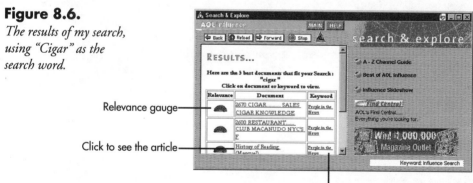

Relevance gauge

Click to see the article

Click to go to the area that contains the article

Using AOL Find

To search through everything on AOL, click Find it on AOL on the Find Central screen. That opens the AOL Find window shown in Figure 8.7. It's similar to the Search & Explore page you just used.

At the top of the AOL Find window is a text box where you enter a word or phrase that is descriptive of what you want to find. This can be a name, a topic, a phrase, and so on. Below that, select whether to make the search Specific or Broad—just click the one you want. When you've entered a word or phrase, and selected Specific or Broad, click the Find button.

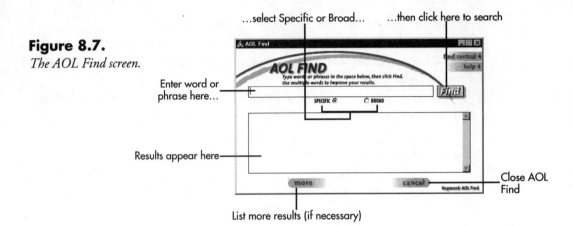

Figure 8.7.
The AOL Find screen.

...select Specific or Broad...   ...then click here to search

Enter word or phrase here...

Results appear here

Close AOL Find

List more results (if necessary)

AOL will think about it for a moment or two. The results of your search will be displayed in the large text box at the bottom of the window. Double-click an entry to visit the related area.

If you get a *lot* of matches—more than 25 or so—you may need to click the More button at the bottom of the window to scroll through the entire list. If you don't get *any* matches, you might want to try a more, or less, specific search or a different search word or phrase. Click the Help button for tips on phrasing your search request.

Summary

In this hour, you've learned how to navigate the Channels and search for what you want to find online.

Workshop

Use the following workshop to solidify the skills you've learned in this hour.

Q&A

Q I'm tired of all that clicking—do I really have to go through Find Central every time I want to Search & Explore a Channel?

A Not at all. There's a Search & Explore button on every Channel's main screen. If you'd prefer, just go to the Channel you want to search, then click its Search & Explore button.

Q **Are some forums/services available in more than one area?**

A Definitely. A lot of forums are listed as part of different Channels—sort of like a cross reference, or cross index.

Quiz

Use the following quiz to check your knowledge of Channels.

Questions

1. Using AOL Find is a way to

    a. Locate your car keys

    b. Search all 19 Channels for a particular topic

    c. Search one Channel for a particular topic

2. True or False: You close a Channel's main screen the same way you close any other window online.

    a. True

    b. False

3. With the Channel Guide, you can

    a. Find out what's on television tonight

    b. Quickly browse a Channel's contents

    c. Learn about psychics who channel spirit guides to learn about past lives

    d. All of the above

Answers

1. **b.**

2. **b.**

3. **b** *or* **d.** It's a trick question—if you actually *use* the Channel Guide, you'll probably be able to do all these things.

Activity

Use your newly learned navigation and searching skills to see if AOL has an area or information about:

☐ Your favorite hobby

☐ Your ethnic background

☐ Your favorite historical figure

☐ Your favorite *anything*

Part III

Getting Started on the Internet

Hour

Hour 9

Using AOL to Get to the Internet

"Check us out on the web at www.blah-blah-blah.com." You hear this at the end of just about every television commercial; you see it in newspaper ads, on business cards, on company brochures and letterheads, and on billboards. You even hear it from friends.

The World Wide Web has been a hot topic in the business world for the past couple years.

The Internet, however, is a lot more than just the World Wide Web. When it all started, the creators never dreamed that it might become an everyday part of life. In fact, the Internet started in the 1960s as a tool of the military, it graduated to being used by colleges and universities, and only after that did it become a tool for commercial and personal use.

This hour gets you started as an Internet user, specifically as an Internet user by way of AOL. This hour covers the following topics:

- [ ] What the Internet is
- [ ] Some Internet basics

☐ The difference between AOL and the Internet

☐ How AOL's Internet connection works

☐ How to get on the Internet via AOL

☐ The Internet's subdivisions

What Is the Internet?

That's a tough one. As many different definitions exist for the Internet as there are members of America Online—over eight million.

To understand what the Internet *is*, you have to understand what it *is not*. The following statements are all true concerning the Internet:

☐ The Internet is not owned or controlled by any company or individual. The Internet is not "owned" at all.

☐ No single person or company is making a ton of money off the Internet craze.

☐ The Internet is not a finite resource that will soon run out of capacity—although the phone lines (and numbers) people use to access the Net are getting scarce.

☐ The Internet doesn't exist in any one computer.

That's what the Internet *is not*. The following sections tell you what the Internet *is*.

An Internet Connection

To understand what the Internet is, and how it works, let's take a look at a single connection—the one you make when your computer gets on the Internet.

Your computer dials an access number (by way of your modem) that connects your computer to an Internet service provider, or ISP.

 Internet service provider (ISP)—A business that offers regular people an inexpensive way to connect to the Internet. You dial in to the ISP's computers and use them to access the Internet.

When you connect to the ISP, you're connecting to the ISP's computer, called a *server*. That server is hooked into the Internet by way of high-speed digital lines that are more stable than regular modem connections. When I say, "That server is hooked into the Internet…," what I really mean is that the server is connected by high-speed lines to another server, which is connected to another server, and so on.

The Internet is all those individual servers, scattered all over the world. It's an *inter*national *net*work of computers, all linked together so you can move from the contents of one server to another with a minimum of fuss and delay.

9

AOL Makes It Simple

AOL has given its members access to the Internet for a couple of years now. It behaves like the ISP described previously: You connect to their servers, and from there you can get out into the larger world of the Internet. In fact, when you use AOL to connect to the World Wide Web, or send email to a friend's Internet account, AOL *is* your ISP.

Why not just get your own connection to the Internet and bypass the middleman? The cost of getting a direct connection to the Internet is simply too high for most folks—a dedicated server and high-speed digital phone lines aren't cheap.

9

Understanding Internet Addresses

Just about every hour from here on contains some Internet addresses. To understand them, you need to break them down.

JUST A MINUTE

> Just like Internet email addresses (discussed in Hour 4, "Using Email"), it is important that you carefully type your Internet addresses. The smallest mistake (a blank space or a misplaced slash) and you'll either get the wrong web page, or no web page at all—just an error message.

You can start with that phony address from the beginning of this hour: `www.blah-blah-blah.com`. To understand it, take a look at it backwards.

The Last Part

The last part of the address (.com in this case) is called the domain, or top-level domain. The top-level domain is the large-scale category of the address; it defines either the country in which the site is located or the type of site it is.

In the United States, domains are divided by types:

- [ ] **com**—Business or commercial sites
- [ ] **edu**—Educational institutions
- [ ] **gov**—Governmental sites
- [ ] **mil**—Military institutions
- [ ] **net**—Network resources
- [ ] **org**—Other organizations, such as nonprofit ones

Elsewhere in the world, top-level domains are organized by country. For example, if an address ends in `.uk`, it is a site located in the United Kingdom. (Occasionally, you'll find a site here in the United States whose address ends with `.us`—it's unusual, but it happens.)

The Middle Part

In our example, the middle part of the address is `blah-blah-blah`. It identifies the specific computer at our fake company, on which the blah-blah-blah site is located. That's called *the domain name* (not to be confused with the *top-level domain* in the last section).

Because there are so many sites on the Internet, Internet addresses are like snowflakes: no two are exactly alike. Domain names are registered by an organization called InterNIC. They dole out the domain names to the Internet service providers, who in turn apply them to the computers on their networks.

JUST A MINUTE

> Internet addresses are *really* called Internet Protocol (or IP) addresses, but in daily use we drop the "protocol." The names are actually strings of numbers separated by periods, such as `125.95.198.2`. The numbers are much easier for the computers to deal with. However, they're translated into English, so just plain folks can understand (and remember) them.

The First Part

The first part of the address defines what type of site it is. For example, if the address starts with www, then it's a site on the World Wide Web. You'll find out more about the different types of sites in the coming hours.

It's also important to note that not all sites break down so neatly into an address. Many Internet addresses are much longer, with more complicated internal divisions, to identify particular units of a much larger organization.

The Difference Between AOL and the Internet

A lot of similarities exist between AOL and the Internet—they both offer email, chat, downloads, message boards, forums, and so on. The primary difference, however, is easy to define.

America Online is an online service unto itself. It's a company, with a board of directors and stockholders, and all that good stuff. It offers its own set of services (such as the ones mentioned in the preceding paragraph) that are available only to its subscribers.

The Internet is much, much bigger than AOL, and a lot more people use it—hundreds of millions, if not billions. But you won't find those people in an AOL chat room unless they also have their own AOL account.

9

So you, as an America Online member, have the best of both worlds. You have easy access to America Online's services, and through America Online, you have access to the Internet as well.

Using AOL to Get to the Internet

Previously, users had to go through an elaborate sequence to get from America Online to the Internet. America Online and the Internet were completely separate entities and they were treated as such. You were even charged an extra hourly fee for time spent on the Internet, as opposed to the time spent within AOL's cozy boundaries.

Times have changed and for the better. Not only are you no longer charged a separate fee for Internet access through AOL, but the line between the two has become so blurred, it's almost invisible.

Getting on the Internet from AOL is easier than ever. You might not even know you've left AOL and gone onto the Internet.

In the early days of America Online, Internet access was achieved through a separate browser window, so you were either on AOL or the Internet. When you got on the Internet, you kissed AOL's features good-bye. Even worse, AOL's browser was clunky, cumbersome, and incompatible with many sites. In short, it stunk.

Now AOL comes with Microsoft's high-tech browser, the Internet Explorer, built in—eliminating all the old problems. You can even be on the Internet while still using all of AOL's features.

There are basically two ways to get on the Internet from AOL—either go to the Internet Connection and set off on a personal Internet quest, or click one of the many links online that take you to an Internet site—typically a web page.

Links Online

A link is a bit of colored, high-lighted text which, when you click it, takes you to a site on the Internet.

Tons of Internet links are scattered all over America Online. In the Figure 9.1, the cursor is pointing at a link in the Pets forum (keyword PETS). When you point at a link, its actual address pops up in a small text box. That's one way to tell that a link is going to take you to the Internet, instead of another area on AOL.

Figure 9.1.
Most areas online offer links to the Internet, just click and go.

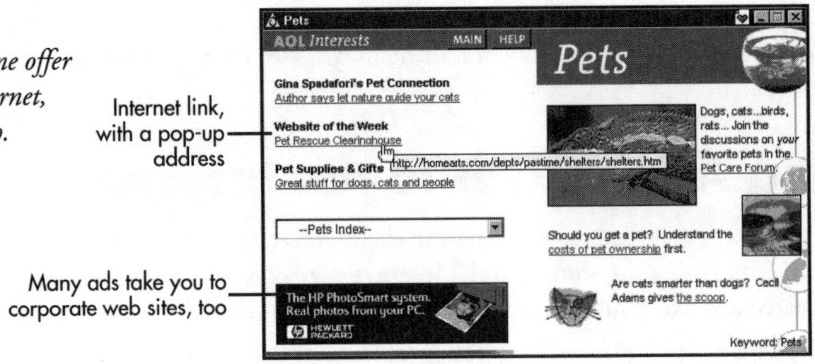

Internet link, with a pop-up address

Many ads take you to corporate web sites, too

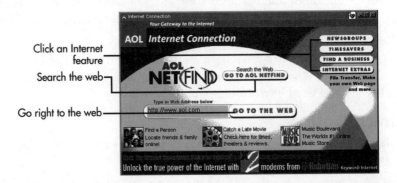

Links like these smoothly integrate AOL's contents with the Internet. They're an easy, painless way to explore your interests both in an AOL forum and on a web page.

Sometimes you just *know* that what you want (whatever it might be) is on the Net. You can cut to the chase and get right on the Internet by way of AOL's Internet Connection.

Internet Connection

Any time you just want to kick back and surf the Internet, head for the Internet Connection. To get there, click the Internet button on AOL's toolbar, and then click Internet Connection. The Internet Connection window opens right up (see Figure 9.2).

Figure 9.2.
The Internet Connection.

Click an Internet feature

Search the web

Go right to the web

Internet Connection can take you right to your favorite Internet features: newsgroups, web search, file transfers, and more just with the click of a button. If you know the address for the site you want to visit, you can simply type it in the Go to the Web text box at the center of the screen, and then click the Go to the Web button.

9

TIME SAVER

Actually, if you know the address for a site you want to visit, you don't have to go to the Internet Connection. Use the address like an AOL keyword: Click in the text box on the bottom of the AOL toolbar; carefully type the Internet address; and then click the Go button. You're on your way.

9

What follows is a brief introduction to each of the things you can do on the Net. They're covered in detail in the subsequent hours of this section of the book.

The World Wide Web

The World Wide Web is the hottest area of the Internet. Most of the Internet addresses you'll hear about on TV and in magazines are for web sites. The web is hot because its easy point-and-click navigation makes it simple for almost *anyone* to get around.

Plus, it's just cool—with excellent graphics, sound, animation, and the most bizarre mix of technology and pop culture you'll probably ever see. The web is covered in Hour 12, "The World Wide Web."

Newsgroups

Newsgroups are similar to AOL's message boards, but they're available to anyone on the Internet, not just AOL members. Newsgroups are devoted to just about any subject you can think of—and then a couple of thousand more, besides.

With newsgroups, you can post messages, respond to the postings of others, or just browse your way through any of thousands of topics that might interest you.

Newsgroups are covered in detail in Hour 10, "Newsgroups and Mailing Lists."

FTP

FTP stands for File Transfer Protocol, which is a fancy, formal way of saying *uploading and downloading files*. If you're amazed by the number of files you can find on AOL, just wait until you get a load of what's available on the Internet. FTP is covered in Hour 11, "FTP, Gopher, and All That Jazz."

Gopher

Gopher is a tool to help you search for, find, and read documents from all over the world. Although it was originally an indispensable part of the Internet, it's been overshadowed by the many search pages available on the web—including AOL's own NetFind page.

Gopher is covered in Hour 11, and web search pages are covered in Hour 12.

Summary

In this hour, you learned the basics of Internet access through AOL. You also learned some of the basic terms of the Internet. There's more to learn, but you have enough to get started. You'll build on what you've learned here in subsequent hours.

Workshop

Use the following workshop to solidify the skills you have learned in this hour.

Q&A

Q A friend of mine told me that he doesn't need to pay for America Online because he can just go to AOL's site on the web. Is this true?

A No. America Online does maintain a site on the World Wide Web (www.aol.com) that can be accessed by anyone on the Internet. However, that's just a site *about* AOL, it doesn't have AOL's content—no chat rooms, no file libraries, no forums.

Q How important is it for me to know the anatomy of an address on the Internet?

A It's not crucial. The anatomy of an address explains more about how the Internet works—otherwise, it's just an exercise in technical typing. It's more important to know *how* to get around, and the next three hours explain that.

Quiz

Take the following quiz to test your knowledge of AOL's Internet offerings.

Questions

1. True or False: The Internet is owned by one really rich guy in the state of Washington.
   a. True
   b. False

2. Which of the following is a true statement?
   a. To get full Internet access, you need an Internet service provider, not just America Online.
   b. You don't need an Internet service provider because AOL gives you full Internet access.

3. Using the Internet with AOL is easier now than it was in the past because
   a. Internet access is fully integrated into America Online.
   b. You don't have to pay additional access charges.

9

    c. Both of the above.

    d. None of the above.

Answers

1. **b.**

2. **b.**

3. **c.**

Activity

Go into your favorite Channel, Forum, or area online, and look for links to Internet sites. Use them to check out the Internet. If you like the sites you find, go ahead and add them to your Favorite Places—you remember how, don't you? (Skip back to Hour 3, "Exploring America Online," if you don't.)

Hour 10

Newsgroups and Mailing Lists

This hour, and the two that follow, gives you a brief look at some of the different aspects of the Internet—some of its breadth, if not its depth.

This hour concentrates on newsgroups and mailing lists, two ways for you to interact with other Internet users. Newsgroups and mailing lists are similar in nature, yet markedly different in how they work. Each has definite benefits, and both have some drawbacks. After you have a look at them, you can decide if you find either (or both) appealing.

This hour covers the following:

- ☐ How to find newsgroups
- ☐ How to join newsgroups
- ☐ How to read newsgroups
- ☐ How to post messages to newsgroups
- ☐ How mailing lists work
- ☐ How to find mailing lists
- ☐ How to subscribe to mailing lists
- ☐ How to unsubscribe to mailing lists

Newsgroup Basics

Newsgroups are similar to the message boards you find on AOL. Newsgroups are Internet message boards, organized by topic, where people from all over the world post and read messages from other people from all over the world.

Newsgroups are available on just about any subject you can imagine—and then add a couple thousand more for the subjects you *can't* imagine.

Newsgroups are organized by category. Some of these broad categories include:

- ☐ **biz**—Business-related groups
- ☐ **alt**—Newsgroups on alternative subjects (and one of the busiest, most bizarre categories going)
- ☐ **comp**—Computers, computer science, and software
- ☐ **sci**—Science
- ☐ **misc**—Groups that don't fall under any other category
- ☐ **soc**—Social issues
- ☐ **news**—General news
- ☐ **rec**—Groups aimed toward hobbies and recreational activities

Somewhere out there, there has to be at least *one* newsgroup you'll find interesting.

Finding and Reading Newsgroups

America Online maintains a huge list of Usenet newsgroups right online, with all the tools you need to read and reply to postings, and post new messages of your own.

 Usenet—Shortened form of *User's Network*. Usenet is the largest (and some say best) newsgroup collection on the Internet.

To get started, click the Internet icon on the toolbar, then select Newsgroups from the drop-down menu. The main Newsgroups dialog box opens as shown in Figure 10.1.

JUST A MINUTE

> Notice the Parental Controls button in Figure 10.1. Because newsgroups are, for the most part, uncensored, and cover a variety of inappropriate topics for children, you may not want to let your youngsters have access to them. Parental Controls let you block your children from using the newsgroups. You can read all about them in Hour 21, "Keeping Parental Control."

Figure 10.1.

The Usenet newsgroups start here.

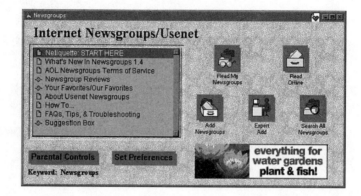

Next, click the Read My Newsgroups button to open the Read My Newsgroups dialog. Then select a newsgroup to read, your screen should be similar to the screen shown in Figure 10.2.

Figure 10.2.

AOL gives everyone a handful of newsgroups to start.

Marks all your groups as read

Lists all messages in group

Lists messages you haven't read in group

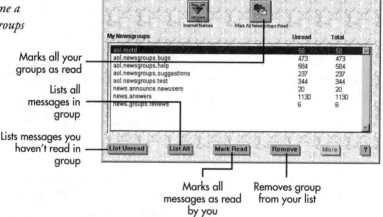

Marks all messages as read by you

Removes group from your list

The folks at AOL have already picked some newsgroups for you. Informational newsgroups are listed to help you figure out how newsgroups work. I recommend you keep them for awhile—they often have some valuable information. (You can delete them later, if you like: Click on a newsgroup in the list, then click Remove.)

At the right side of the newsgroup list in Figure 10.2, you'll notice two columns labeled Unread and Total. Those numbers show you the total number of messages in each newsgroup, and how many of them are Unread by you. Because you haven't opened any of them, the numbers in the two columns are the same.

Reading Messages

To read messages in a newsgroup, double-click the group of your choice. A list of subject lines for the messages appears (see Figure 10.3).

Figure 10.3.

A list of messages in a newsgroup.

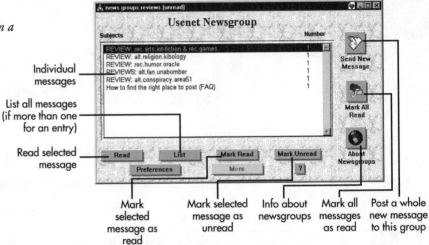

To read a message, just double-click the subject line and the message will open.

Newsgroups have a built-in way for you to keep from rereading the same messages over and over again. When you read a message, it's marked as read. The List Unread button only shows you the messages that you haven't read.

You can mark an uninteresting series of messages as read (even if you haven't read them), and they won't come back to haunt you. You can also mark an interesting message as *unread* so it will appear in your list the next time you click List Unread. You'll find Mark Read buttons on both message lists, and newsgroup lists, so you can list either a message or the entire current crop of messages in a group as read. It's a feature that cuts down on the clutter in your newsgroups.

The other buttons in the Read My Newsgroups dialog box shown in Figure 10.2 are:

☐ **List All**—Shows all messages in the newsgroup, even those you've read.

☐ **Mark Read**—Marks all the messages in a particular newsgroup as having been read. This is a way for you to start from scratch. If you do this, the next time you enter the newsgroup and click List Unread, the list will be only new messages.

☐ **Remove**—Takes a newsgroup out of the list of newsgroups that you like to read.

☐ **Mark All Newsgroups Read**—Marks every message in all your newsgroups as having been read.

10

Replying to Messages

When you find a message to which you'd like to respond, click the Reply to Group button on the message window. It opens a blank reply form, already addressed to the newsgroup and author of the original message.

Compose your reply in the Reply Window, and click Send. Off it goes.

If you want to reply to the author of the original, without posting a message to the newsgroup, click the E-mail to Author button. That opens a blank email form, already addressed to the author of the message. Compose your message and click Send like you would for any other email.

To create a completely new message in a newsgroup, click the Send New Message button on the group's message list (refer to Figure 10.3). A blank message form appears, addressed to the newsgroup. Type a subject for your message in the Subject text box, then type your message in the Message box. When you're done, click Send.

Finding Newsgroups

You don't have to be satisfied with *just* the newsgroups AOL has added to your newsgroups list. You can add any newsgroup you like, from the list of Usenet newsgroups online. Look back at Figure 10.1, and you'll see a button called Add Newsgroups. Click it, and you'll open the Add Newsgroups dialog box shown in Figure 10.4.

Figure 10.4.

Adding newsgroups to your list.

Categories ⎯⎯⎯⎯

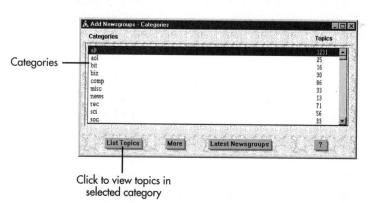

Click to view topics in
selected category

A list of categories appears that you can browse (alt, biz, and the others described in "Newsgroup Basics" earlier). Click a category that interests you, and then click the List Topics button to open the Topics window.

The Topics window alphabetically presents all the topics in the category you selected. Browse the list and find one that interests (or befuddles) you. Click the topic, and then click List Newsgroups.

A list of the newsgroups in that topic appears, like the one shown here in Figure 10.5. (If you care, the one shown in the figure is for alt.alien. I'm an *X-Files* junkie, what can I say?)

Figure 10.5.

Now you can add the newsgroups you like.

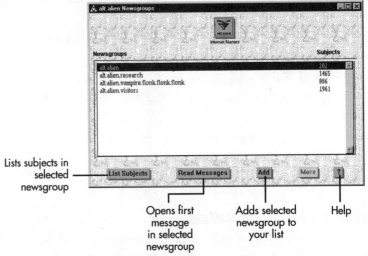

Lists subjects in selected newsgroup

Opens first message in selected newsgroup

Adds selected newsgroup to your list

Help

To see what a group is all about, click its name in the list and click List Subjects to browse the subjects of messages that have been posted, or click Read Messages to read a few. When you decide you *like* a newsgroup, and want to make it your own, close any intermediate windows you've opened until you're back at the newsgroup list shown in Figure 10.5. Click the newsgroup's name, and then click the Add button.

The selected newsgroup will be added to your list of newsgroups, and appear next time you click Read My Newsgroups—without all that burrowing through newsgroup windows to find it.

Netiquette and Newsgroups

Newsgroups have a code of conduct, one that anyone who posts messages should follow. You can learn all about it in the main Usenet Newsgroups window shown earlier in Figure 10.1. In the list box at the left of the screen, the first entry is Netiquette: START HERE. Double-click it to read about the ins and outs of correct behavior in newsgroups.

One of the most important things to remember is to keep your postings on topic: Don't veer off the newsgroup's topic. If you're posting in alt.alien.visitors, there had better be something about alien visitors in your posting.

10

It's also important to avoid over-criticizing other people who post in the group. If you disagree with someone's point, *argue the point*. Don't start calling someone names when you disagree with their opinion. That's called *flaming*, and it's rude as all get out.

On the flip side, if someone flames *you*, take a deep breath and get on with your life. Replying to a flame only fans it—and you may get burned.

Mailing List Basics

Mailing lists are similar in scope and content to what you'll find in the newsgroups—a huge variety of subjects thrashed about by an even larger number of people. The main difference between newsgroups and mailing lists is that mailing lists, as the name implies, are conducted via email.

To get on a mailing list, you must *subscribe* to it, like a magazine. Then the messages start appearing in your AOL mailbox. You read them and, if you care to, reply to them by way of email.

How Mailing Lists Work

After you find a mailing list to which you would like to subscribe (explained later in the "Finding Mailing Lists" section of this hour), you send email to the *listserver*. Often the listserver is a computer, sometimes it's a flesh-and-blood person. The listserver organizes, maintains, and sends the messages out to the members on the mailing list.

When your subscription request arrives, the listserver adds you to the mailing list. From that moment on, you receive any and all messages posted to the mailing list by other members. Any message you send to the list's email address is passed on to all the other members of the list as well.

The listserver computer acts as a reflector, bouncing all messages sent to it out to all the email addresses on its list. In a way, it's like sending a mass email message to a group in your Address Book. Only this is usually a much, much larger group.

The Problem with Mailing Lists

Mailing lists present one major problem—the number of messages you receive. If the mailing list has a lot of members, that can mean a lot of messages landing in your mailbox. This can clog your email account, and prevent you from getting email from say, your mom or a business associate.

I belong to *one,* relatively small mailing list. It sends me about 30–40 pieces of mail, three or four times a week—that's 90–160 messages per week. Don't say I didn't warn you.

10

I strongly recommend that you subscribe only to one or two mailing lists that *strongly* appeal to you. After you're on a list, you need to check your email regularly to keep things from building up.

TIME SAVER

> You can use Automatic AOL to send and receive your mailing list (and regular) email on a daily basis, and avoid that waxy yellow email buildup.
>
> You can also use Automatic AOL to take care of your incoming and outgoing newsgroup messages. This handy tool is explained in Hour 6, "Automatic AOL."

When all else fails, it's easy to *unsubscribe* from a mailing list, too (described later in this hour).

Finding Mailing Lists

America Online keeps a large list of mailing lists for you, so it isn't hard to find one or two to interest you. To begin, use the keyword MAILING LISTS to open the Mailing List Directory shown in Figure 10.6.

Figure 10.6.

AOL's Mailing List Directory.

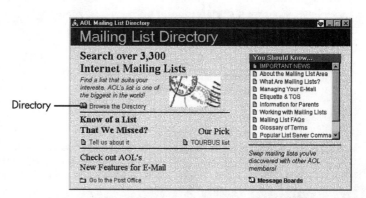

Click the Browse the Directory button, and you'll go to the Directory web page. There are two ways to find a mailing list from the directory web page:

- ☐ **Browse the Directory**—Scroll through the mailing list categories until you find one you like. Click the category name to open a page of mailing lists. Browse until you find a mailing list you might like.

10

☐ **Search**—If you sort of know what you're looking for, click Search at the top of the Directory web page. A standard search tool opens like the ones you've used elsewhere online. Enter a word or phrase to search for, and the software will return mailing lists that match your criteria.

When you've found a mailing list that interests you, click its name in the list. A complete description of that mailing list appears, including how to subscribe and unsubscribe to it. Figure 10.7 shows a typical mailing list description.

Figure 10.7.

Each mailing list description tells you how to subscribe and unsubscribe.

10

How to Subscribe...Sort Of

Most mailing lists work similarly, but the devil is in the details. All of them require that you send an email from the screen name to which you want your mail sent. Somewhere in that message (in the subject, or the body of the message) you include the word SUBSCRIBE. However, there are big differences.

Most subscription requests will be sent to different addresses. Some require that you put the name of the mailing list after SUBSCRIBE. There are other variations as well. The point is: Make sure you read the instructions for your particular mailing list before you subscribe.

Print a copy of the mailing list description (with its instructions) so you'll know how to *unsubscribe* should the need arise. You can also save a copy to your hard drive, if you prefer.

Unsubscribing to Mailing Lists

Unsubscribing is simple: It's usually the same as subscribing, using the word UNSUBSCRIBE in the message body or subject. Requests to be removed from a mailing list are sometimes sent to a different email address—another reason to keep a copy of the mailing list description and instructions.

Summary

In this hour, you have learned the basics of newsgroups and mailing lists.

Workshop

Use the following workshop to reinforce the skills you've learned in this hour.

Q&A

Q **If a subject I like has both a newsgroup and a mailing list, which would you recommend I join?**

A The newsgroup. That way, you can choose when you want to read messages and when you don't, and your email account won't be deluged with mail.

Q **A friend told me about a fun newsgroup, but I don't see it on AOL's list. What do I do?**

A In the main Newsgroup window, there is a button called Expert Add. This button is for people who know the name of a newsgroup they want to add to their list. Click Expert Add, then precisely enter the name of the group. If the newsgroup is one that's available through AOL (not all of them are, there's way too many), it will appear in your list.

Quiz

Take the following quiz to test your knowledge of newsgroups and mailing lists.

Questions

1. If you want to start fresh with all your newsgroups and not have to search through old messages, you should
    a. Click Mark All Newsgroups Read
    b. Click List Unread
    c. Click Remove

2. If you only want to display the messages in a newsgroup that you haven't read yet, you should
    a. Click Mark Read
    b. Click Remove
    c. Click List Unread

10

3. When you join a mailing list, you'll receive messages posted by
    a. Only the moderator of the mailing list
    b. All the members of the mailing list
    c. Only the members of the list with whom you agree

Answers
1. **a.**
2. **c.**
3. **b.**

Activities
1. Scout through the newsgroups list and find a few that you'd like to add to your list. There's no pressure; you still won't be forced to read the messages.
2. If you care to, go ahead and subscribe to *one* mailing list. Whatever you do, don't subscribe to ten of them, or you'll drown in a sea of email.

10

Hour 11

FTP, Gopher, and All That Jazz

If you are new to the online world you're probably thinking, "What the heck is *that* gibberish all about?" Well there's a lot more to the Internet than the World Wide Web (WWW). In fact, FTP and Gopher were around long before the World Wide Web came into being.

Before the Internet went WWW crazy, and everybody in the world got their own web site, the Internet was all about files—exchanging them, posting them on message boards, searching for them, reading them. Although the web now dominates the Internet, FTP and Gopher still serve their long-standing purposes.

In this hour, you'll learn

- ☐ What FTP is and how it works
- ☐ How to use FTP on America Online
- ☐ What Gopher is and how it works
- ☐ How to use Gopher on America Online

What Is FTP?

FTP stands for *File Transfer Protocol*, a fancy phrase for a common Internet activity. It's really nothing more than a mechanism through which you can upload and download files. Much like the uploading and downloading you can do on America Online, FTP enables you to get files from all over the Internet and share your files with others.

How FTP Works

To learn how FTP works, you first have to know the two sorts of FTP that are available to you—public and private. Private FTP sites are just that, private. Private sites are normally set up by companies with a remote workforce, for example, people who work from their homes via modem, or regional-manager types who spend a lot of time on the road.

Private sites are kept private by passwords and other security measures that keep people out who aren't affiliated with the company. Employees know how to get in, but competitors and hackers can't break in and get corporate secrets.

A lot of FTP sites are public and allow anonymous logins—anyone, anywhere can get into these sites and download files at will, without so much as a "mother may I?". Public sites are often used by software companies to distribute upgrades and fixes for software products, help files, and other relevant information.

The Basics of FTP

Just where is this FTP place? Well, there is no single FTP place. FTP sites exist all over the Internet.

After you locate an FTP site, finding files is relatively simple. The files stored at FTP sites are in directories. In the directories, you'll find category folders, then subcategory folders inside those, and so on. FTP files are sorted and stored the same way files are stored on your computer.

To use FTP on AOL, click the Internet icon on the toolbar. Then select FTP on the Internet drop-down menu. You'll go to AOL's FTP area shown in Figure 11.1.

To look for a particular file, or *kind* of file, click the Search for FTP Sites button to the left of the list box. You'll open a standard AOL search dialog box as shown in Figure 11.2. You use this search dialog box the same as the others you've used in earlier hours.

Enter a keyword or phrase to describe the sort of file you want, then click the Search button. The search results will appear in the text box at the bottom of the screen. Double-click an entry to go to the FTP site.

11

Figure 11.1.

FTP on AOL is as easy as ABC.

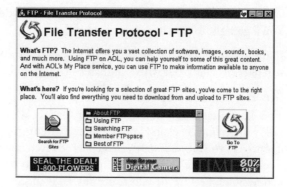

Figure 11.2.

Searching for FTP sites.

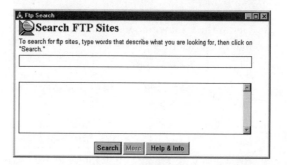

If you already know the address of the site you want, click the Go To FTP button on the main FTP window (refer to Figure 11.1). Clicking this button opens the FTP dialog box shown in Figure 11.3.

Figure 11.3.

Click the Other Site button if you know the address.

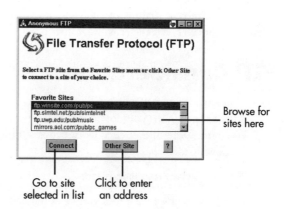

Click the Other Site button and carefully type in the address. Then click the Connect button. You'll go right to the site you entered.

In the following To Do, you're going to use the Other Site button to visit an FTP site. While you're there, check out what's available—you might find some cool stuff.

Going to an FTP Site

This To Do takes you to the WinZip FTP site. WinZip is the shareware file compression utility mentioned back in Hour 5, "Downloading Files and Searching Databases." You may not need it, you may not want it, you may not even care that such a thing exists. It is, however, a reliable FTP site that you can usually get into and explore (some are often busy and inaccessible). Feel free to substitute any FTP address you may know, or have found while exploring the FTP area.

1. Get to the FTP window shown previously in Figure 11.3 (click Go To FTP on the main FTP window).

2. Click the Other Site button.

3. In the address dialog box that opens, type ftp.winzip.com into the Site Address field.

4. Click Connect to open an FTP dialog box called Connected to FTP.winzip.com. It looks similar to one of AOL's file library lists.

5. Browse at will: Double-click folder icons to see their contents. Double-click "msg." entries to read the associated text file. Exe files are applications you may download, if you care to (the next step explains how).

6. To download a file, click the file's name, and then click the Download button. You'll be asked to specify where you want the file saved on your hard drive with a Save-type dialog box. Navigate to where you want the file saved, and then click Save. The transfer will commence.

FTP Considerations

You can download many different types of files. For example, WinZip (and any other software programs you download) will have the .exe extension, which indicates that it is a program. Other files such as word processor files, database files, spreadsheets, and so on can be downloaded also.

Keep these two things in mind:

☐ To use *document* files you've downloaded, you need to have an application capable of opening the file. A spreadsheet program is required to open a spreadsheet file, a graphics program to open a picture, and so on.

☐ When you download *software*, the program still needs to be installed on your
computer before you can use it. You either need to double-click the file's icon to
start the installation routine, or use Window's Run command.

CAUTION

Downloading anything from the Internet can be hazardous to your
computer's health. Internet file downloads are the primary way computer
viruses are spread. Practice safe computing: Get an antivirus utility
(download one, or buy one), and *use it* on any files you download.

It also helps if you save all your downloads to the same folder (your AOL
Downloads folder, for example). That way, you can set your antivirus
program to scan *that* folder and check all your downloaded files at once.

What Is Gopher?

Gopher is a graphics-based Internet browsing tool—the granddaddy of the web, you might
say. Gopher is used to navigate through Internet directories, locate files, and actually *view*
files online.

Created at the University of Minnesota, Gopher got its name for two reasons—for its
capability to "go-fer" information online, and for the school's mascot, the Golden Gopher.

Using Gopher on AOL

America Online makes using Gopher easy. You'll find Gopher in the Internet Connection.
To go there, use the keyword GOPHER. The Gopher dialog box appears as shown in Figure 11.4.

Figure 11.4.
*Your Gopher starting
place in AOL.*

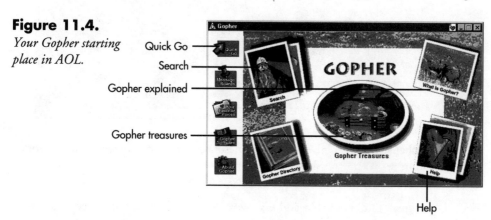

If you already know the address of the Gopher site you want, click the Quick Go button and type it in. If you're browsing, or don't know the exact name of the site you want, you can click Gopher Directory, and the Other Directories dialog box appears as shown in Figure 11.5.

Figure 11.5.
Gopher directories—double-click and go.

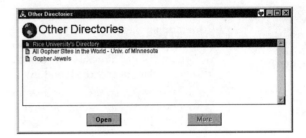

From here, you can get to any Gopher site in the world, just double-click an entry and see where it leads you.

Getting Started with Gopher

Because Gopher was created at the University of Minnesota, the best place to start with Gopher is right there, in Golden Gopher country. They maintain the Gopher site that's considered "The Mother of All Gophers."

The site can be found at gopher://gopher.micro.umn.edu (see Figure 11.6).

Figure 11.6.
The Mother of all Gopher sites.

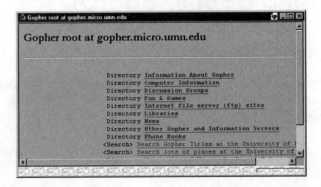

Another Gopher site at the University of Minnesota can lead you anywhere in the world. This is its address:

gopher://gopher.tc.umn.edu:70/11/Other%20Gopher%20and%20Information%20Servers.

Wait! Don't freak out about that address—you don't have to type it. There's an easier, Gopher way to get there. Back on the Gopher site in Figure 11.6, click the Other Gopher and Information Servers link. It takes you to the Gopher that gives you access, literally, to *All the Gopher Servers in the World.* It lists directories of Gopher sites from all around the globe. Be prepared, because if you connect to a Russian archive, you'll probably find yourself looking at pages in actual Russian. *Das vydanya!*

What's Up with the Icons?

The different directories and files you'll find on Gopher sites are sometimes identified by words or icons. The words are self-explanatory—<directory> means the item is a directory of other files or folders.

The icons, however, may be confusing at first. Three icons are commonly used:

- ☐ **A File Folder**—A folder means a directory, or subdirectory. It works like a folder on your hard drive—click it to get at the goodies inside.
- ☐ **File**—A file icon looks like a dog-eared page—one corner is folded over. These are usually text files. Click the icon, and the file displays on your screen. These may, however, open picture files as well.
- ☐ **Binoculars**—Binocular icons lead to a search utility that you can use to find the files you want.

Summary

In this hour, you learned the basics of using the Internet's FTP and Gopher tools through AOL.

Workshop

Use the following workshop to reinforce the skills you've learned in this hour.

Q&A

Q Can you give me an example of when I might need to use an FTP site?

A Sure. Your printer's not working right, and you call the manufacturer. The people there tell you to download their updated printer drivers from their FTP site. That kind of thing happens all the time to me, anyway.

Q What's an example of when I might need to go-fer something?

A Gopher sites are great for doing research because you'll find documents from libraries, university research departments, college archives, and more.

11

Quiz

Take the following quiz to test your knowledge of FTP and Gopher.

Questions

1. You can use FTP

    a. Only if you write a computer book

    b. To download files

    c. To create hypertext documents for the web

2. FTP sites are located

    a. In one big computer in the Midwest

    b. All on AOL

    c. All over the world

    d. None of the above

3. Gopher sites are

    a. Full of information and great for research

    b. Generally for entertainment only

    c. Places you can watch real gophers dig their holes

Answers

1. **b.**

2. **c.**

3. **a.** But, c is also correct if you want to be a wise guy about it.

Activity

Spend some time visiting FTP and Gopher sites to find out what's available to you.

Hour **12**

The World Wide Web

In the past two hours, you've learned about newsgroups, FTP, and Gopher. They're all vital, integral parts of the Internet, but I've saved the best for last: the World Wide Web (or WWW, or just the web).

Placing the WWW last is appropriate, because it's the most recent Internet innovation—and it's slowly but surely taking over the jobs of those older tools, particularly FTP and Gopher.

Although the web was conceived in the 1980s, it didn't really catch on until the early '90s—but after it did...the phrases "house on fire" and "bat out of hell" spring to mind. Seldom in the history of the world has any one development (*invention* somehow doesn't seem to fit, although it does apply) grown so rapidly.

In 1993, there were fewer than 100 servers that handled web documents. In 1998, there are *millions*. By the year 2000, the World Wide Web will probably have a place in the daily lives of most Americans.

In this hour, we'll boil this complex technology down to the basics—just enough to fill an hour of your time. This hour covers

- ☐ Web basics—sites, pages, links, and more
- ☐ Putting the web to use

☐ Navigating the web

☐ Searching and finding what you want

Learning to surf the web might seem daunting now, but it's really an easy, friendly environment. That's one of the main reasons why the web dominates the Internet. When most people say, the Internet, what they *really* mean is the World Wide Web.

Understanding the Basics

In the modern world, you constantly hear geeky-speak like: Internet address, web page, web site, home page, links, browser, and so on. Right now, it might sound like Greek to you, but you'll be able to *speak* geek with the rest by the end of the hour.

A *lot* of language is devoted to describing the web. Consider the following sections as one great big New Term box.

Addresses

You've already learned, in other hours, the anatomy of an Internet address and seen some examples. Just like a street address points to the location of a house, an Internet address points to a web page or site.

A web address is sometimes called a *URL*, or Uniform Resource Locator. URL is just a fancy-shmancy way of saying address.

Web Sites and Pages

One of the most often asked web-related questions is: *What's the difference between a web page and a web site?*

The answer is: Not a heck of a lot.

A *web page* is a single WWW document. A *web site* is a collection of related WWW documents, organized together as one package. When a company tells you to go to its web site, it means "go to our really cool set of web pages."

Figure 12.1 shows a typical web page (address: `http://www.thisweek-online.com`).

COFFEE BREAK

One of the common misconceptions about the Internet results from the use of the word *page*. Some folks believe that a web page is limited to 8 1/2×11 inches, like a sheet of paper. In truth, a web page can go on forever.

Some web pages *do* go on forever, making you scroll eternally for little tidbits of information. That's a *bad* thing, but don't get me started on bad web page designs...

12

Figure 12.1.

This is the first of many web pages on this web site.

Home Page

A *home page* is generally the first page of a web site. In addition to featured information, or graphics, you'll usually find an index that lets you move easily to the other pages on the site. Some sites treat their home page like a magazine cover: no real content is available, other than links to the index or site map.

CAUTION

> Home page is one of the few web terms with a double meaning. It also means the web page your web browser automatically goes to when you start it up. The page acts as your home base. This second meaning is more prevalent than "the first page of a set of related pages."

Links

Web pages are created using a set of formatting instructions called *Hypertext Markup Language (HTML)*. In addition to telling your computer where to place pictures, and what text to put in **boldface** or *italics*, it lets you turn text into *hypertext*.

Hypertext is simply a word or line of text that takes you to another page when you click on it. Back in Figure 12.1, all the words in the index at the left are *links* to other pages. If you click Sports, you'll go directly to the sports page.

A *link* is any hypertext that moves you to another page—it "links" one page to another. Most web pages have links in them. Links can be items in a list, such as those in Figure 12.1, or they can be words or phrases in an article, or other text. In the latter case, the links are colored and underlined to make them stand out more.

Links can also be pictures, icons, and buttons. Don't worry about spotting them. You can always spot a link because your cursor changes from an arrow to a pointing hand—like the one shown in Figure 12.2.

12

Figure 12.2.
Your arrow cursor changes to a hand when it touches a link.

Browser

A *browser* is the software you use to display and navigate web pages. Two of the most popular browsers in use today are Microsoft Internet Explorer and Netscape Navigator.

Microsoft's Internet Explorer 3.02 is built into America Online 4.0. When you are browsing the web on AOL, you're using Internet Explorer as your browser.

Putting the World Wide Web to Use

You'll find web pages covering every imaginable subject under the sun. People put up pages devoted to their pets, themselves, celebrities, hobbies, television shows, sports, science, you name it. If you don't believe me, try it: Use the AOL NetFind page (covered later in this hour) to search for the weirdest thing you can think of—dollars to donuts, you'll find a page devoted to it.

Within the past year or so, however, the fastest-growing genre of web site has been the corporate site. Businesses of all sizes are using the web as a form of interactive advertising, enabling consumers to see their products and message—a digital commercial, if you will—any time, day or night.

A perfect example of the corporate web site is the one shown in Figure 12.3, for Wilsons Leather.

Figure 12.3.
Retail outlets offer web sites like this one.

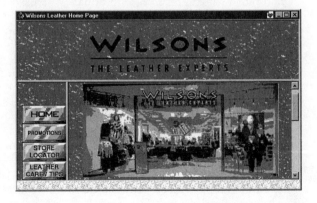

12

Wilsons is a retail chain that sells leather goods, you'll find them in most malls. Their web site includes a great deal of product information, pictures, and leather care tips—all of which are good for business. The site also offers a *store locator* that lets you, the web browser, find the Wilsons store that's closest to you—and that's *great* for business.

A lot of sites on the web let you actually buy the products advertised on the page. You fill out an order form, just as you would in a mail-order catalog. After you submit the form (which includes shipping and credit card information), your order is processed and delivered to your door.

CAUTION

> It's relatively rare, but there have been cases of people having their credit card number illegally intercepted online. The people intercepting the numbers then use them to fraudulently buy stuff (or to create fake credit cards with real account numbers). The Internet is becoming more secure, however, and that will make web commerce safer.
>
> Most Internet merchants offer "secure transactions," which means no one can get at your credit card information. You can easily tell when you're at a secure web page: The usual *http* in the address becomes *https*. The "S" is for "Secure."
>
> All the shopping you can do within the confines of America Online (not via the WWW) are guaranteed 100 percent secure. If you want to try online shopping, but are leery of shopping on the web, you may want to start with AOL's vendors in the Shopping Channel.

Although web commerce is becoming more commonplace, it's still in its infancy. When vendors come up with better security for online ordering, and people become more comfortable sending credit card information over the Internet, web commerce will grow tremendously.

12

Navigating the Web

Your web browser is the key to getting around on the WWW. Now that AOL has incorporated Internet Explorer into its software, you have access to a web browser with some *real* power.

Navigation Basics

The first part is simple: If you know the address of the site you want to go to, just type it in the text box on the toolbar. Click the Go button, and you're on your way (see Figure 12.4).

Figure 12.4.

AOL's navigation toolbar.

Type the URL here...   ...then click here

After you arrive at the page, you can wander freely by clicking links that spark your interest. After you've been through a few pages, you can use the navigation toolbar to move back and forth through the pages you've seen.

The navigation buttons shown on the toolbar in Figure 12.4 include the following:

☐ **Back**—The left pointing arrow takes you back to the page you just left. It's not just for people who can't make up their mind. For example, say you're at an index. You click a link in the index, but the linked page isn't helpful. To go back to the index, you can just click the Back (left pointing arrow) button.

☐ **Forward**—After you've gone back, you might want to go forward again. That's when you click the Forward button—that's the right pointing arrow. You can't click it unless you've previously used the Back button (otherwise, there's nowhere for you to go).

☐ **Stop**—If a page is taking a long time to load and you don't want to wait, click the Stop button—it's the circle with the X through it. Clicking the Stop button cancels whatever the browser is currently doing.

☐ **Reload**—Occasionally, a page won't load into your computer properly. If the graphics or text are jumbled, don't look right, or don't show up at all, click Reload. Reload is the spiral arrow button.

☐ **History List**—That little downward-pointing arrow (next to the Address box) opens a drop-down menu. The menu contains a list of the past 25 places you've visited, both on the web *and* AOL. To go back to a page (or area on AOL) you visited earlier in your session, click the down arrow, and then click the address.

TIME SAVER

Remember you can add web pages to your Favorite Places. Just drag the heart icon from the browser window, and drop it on the Favorite Places icon on the toolbar. That way, you can revisit your favorite pages whenever you log on. If you've forgotten about Favorite Places, refer to Hour 3, "Exploring America Online."

Searching for (and Finding) Sites

Searching has always been one of the more challenging aspects of any trip down the Information Superhighway. There are many, many ways to search the Internet, including several sites that are called *search pages*.

12

Search pages give you access to huge databases full of Internet addresses, all categorized neatly to make them easy to find. You plow through all the information in that database by way of a *search engine*—like the ones you've used to search for stuff on AOL.

AOL has its own search page, called AOL NetFind. Its motto: "Why search when you can *find*?" To use it, click the Internet icon on the toolbar, then select AOL NetFind. You'll go to the NetFind page shown in Figure 12.5.

Figure 12.5.
AOL's NetFind main page will point you in the right direction.

Enter a word or phrase here

Click here to search

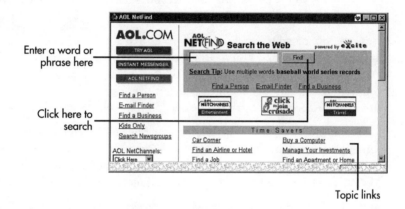

Topic links

AOL NetFind gives you two ways to search for links of interest to you: You can search, or you can browse. Browsing is more fun, if you have the time.

On the lower part of the NetFind page you'll see an index of Time Savers sites, arranged by category. Say you want to get some information on the proposed reorganization of the IRS. You could click the Your Government link, and go to the Government resources shown in Figure 12.6.

Figure 12.6.
Time Savers are links to commonly requested sites, grouped by category.

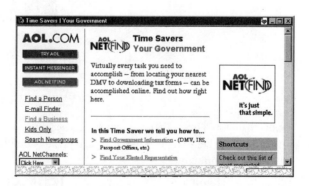

12

The page shown in Figure 12.6 contains government-related links broken down into different categories. These links take you to web pages that offer you more specific pages. You can keep browsing your way to the site you need, but it is time-consuming. *Fun*, but time-consuming.

If you don't have the time to spare—you need that information *now*—then go back to the main NetFind page. At the top of the NetFind home page, you'll find a search field. Like most of the searches you've performed on AOL, you enter a keyword or phrase about the thing you want to find, then click the Find button.

How you phrase your search, on the web as well as with one of AOL's searching tools, is important. The tips given for AOL searches (in Hour 5, "Downloading Files and Searching Databases," and other hours) also apply here. Too general a search word or phrase will net you hundreds (even *thousands*) of matches that aren't related to what you want to find, although too specific a search phrase may prevent you from finding *any* matches.

For example, if you want information on the Marriott hotels in Miami, enter just *hotels* and you might get millions of sites that include "hotel" somewhere on the page. Instead, enter "Marriott hotels," or even better "Marriott hotels and Miami" to locate the Marriotts in Miami. You'll get a much more specific (and more useful) list of matching sites.

AOL NetFind returns its matches with a page as shown in Figure 12.7. At the top, you'll usually find a box of Try These First links. These links are most likely what you want (at least, as far as NetFind could tell from your search word(s)).

Figure 12.7.
AOL NetFind's search results look like this.

Below that, you'll find other pages that matched your search word or phrase, and a percentage rating—the higher that percentage, the more likely that link is what you're looking for. Click an interesting link and go.

If you find a link that's really helpful, return to the Results page, and find that link again. Below it, you'll find a link called More Links Like This. Click it, and you'll go to a set of links to similar pages. Very handy.

12

TIME SAVER

> If you're looking for the site of a particular company or organization, try a *probable* address: Sandwich the name of the company or organization between www. and .com. If it doesn't work, you've lost nothing except a little time—but you'll be amazed at how often it *does* work.

Plug-in Mania

I *don't* mean those electric room deodorants. Plug-ins are little bits of software that expand the capabilities of your web browser. They give it, for example, the capability to run audio clips or movies, or some other fancy, funky, cool thing from the web. Internet Explorer is already capable of handling the web's latest crazes: Java and ActiveX—these tools can, literally, make a web page dance and sing.

Sometimes you'll run into a web page that says "You must have *this or that* plug-in to view this site." Which means, if you don't have *this or that* installed, you're going to miss out. Don't sweat it. More often than not, such sites also include links to pages where you can download the required plug-ins. Download the plug-in, and then follow the installation instructions (most are fairly painless).

If you want an idea of the number, and variety, of plug-ins available, visit this address: `http://multimedia.aol.com/external/plugins.htm`, or use the keyword `MMSHOWCASE`, and read more about them.

Summary

This hour covers the basics of the World Wide Web—how it works and how to get around on it.

Workshop

Use the following workshop to solidify the skills you've learned in this hour.

Q&A

Q Why do some people say "web page" when they really mean "web site"?

A The two aren't really interchangeable, but they're so close in meaning that the difference is negligible. Some "sites" are really only one "page." The technology is relatively new, and the bugs haven't been shaken out of the vocabulary yet.

12

Q What are some of the other search pages?

A Yahoo!, Excite, Infoseek, AltaVista, Lycos—the list goes on and on. To try one of these pages, stick its name between www. and .com.

Quiz

Take the following quiz to test your knowledge of the skills taught in this hour.

Questions

1. Which of the following is a true statement?
   a. A web page contains many web sites.
   b. A web site contains many web pages.
2. Hypertext is
   a. A word or line of text that takes you to another page
   b. A search engine
   c. An index of web pages
3. The best way to keep track of sites you like is
   a. To use the drop-down history list
   b. To mark them as Favorite Places
   c. To click the Back button

Answers

1. **b.**
2. **a.**
3. **b.** You *can* use the history list, but it changes as you visit sites. Favorite Places are saved on your hard drive, and permanently available.

Activity

Browse around on the web a little. Try a search using NetFind and follow some of the links. The only way to get comfortable with the web is to use it.

PART
IV

Personalizing and Customizing AOL

Hour

Hour 13

Creating Your Own America Online Web Page

Traffic on the Internet is at an all-time high. Current estimates are that about 4,000 web pages are added to the Internet on any single day. The doomsayers whine that it's only a matter of time before the whole Internet collapses, taking our precious phone system with it.

To that I say: *Hey, make your own personal web page on AOL!* That way, when the Internet self-destructs you can say, "I did my part!"

Seriously, no matter what the naysayers say, the Internet isn't about to crash and burn. Creating a personal web page on AOL can be fun, entertaining, and even *useful.* That's why this hour is all about making your own page for the World Wide Web. In this hour, you'll learn about:

☐ Features of AOL's Personal Publisher 3

☐ The cost of creating a home page

☐ Turning pictures into graphics

☐ Where to look for images

☐ Other helpful resources

So get ready to put your personal thumbprint on the World Wide Web.

The Basics of Personal Publisher 3

Personal Publisher 3 was added to AOL to take advantage of the newly integrated Internet Explorer, and its many capabilities. Unfortunately for previous America Online members, you can't magically change your old personal web page to the new format, you need to create a whole new page.

There are some structural changes, too. Under the old system, personal web pages were stored on a server with the address home.aol.com. The new pages are stored at members.aol.com. The server is the same, only the name has been changed—add your own *Dragnet* joke here.

Every screen name on AOL (which could be as many as 320 *million* names) is allocated 2MB of space on their web server with which to store their web pages.

CAUTION

> Later you'll learn about adding pictures and other graphics to your web page. Be forewarned that adding such images can take up a lot of hard drive space, and you might use up your free 2MB quickly if you get carried away.

Take a quick look at some of the features of the new Personal Publisher:

☐ You can add backgrounds of different colors.

☐ You can use images as links to other pages.

☐ Easier editing tools.

☐ Simple templates to help the design-impaired quickly create attractive pages.

☐ You can have more than one page, and you can link the pages together.

The best thing about Personal Publisher is that you don't have to know beans about HTML programming to create a page. (A little knowledge of HTML might help, but it's not *required*.)

Getting Started

To get started on your web page, you need to go to the Personal Publisher area. To get there, use the keyword PERSONAL PUBLISHER. Personal Publisher's main dialog box opens, as shown in Figure 13.1.

13

JUST A MINUTE

Hey! That's AOL 3.0 You're Using! Why yes. Yes it is. At the time of this writing, Personal Publisher wasn't compatible with AOL 4.0—*go figure*—but by the time you read this, it will be. There shouldn't be any major differences between the Personal Publisher you see here and the one you see with AOL 4.0.

Figure 13.1.
The Personal Publisher main dialog box.

JUST A MINUTE

I don't often recommend using an online tutorial—especially because this book is a tutorial in itself. In this case, however, I think the tutorial offered in the list box on the Personal Publisher screen can be valuable to you. Why not take a minute and go through it?

To start working on your web page, click the big Create a Page button in the middle of the dialog box. The Select Template dialog box appears as shown in Figure 13.2.

NEW TERM **Template**—A template is a predesigned form with fake text and graphics. You customize the template by replacing all the fake stuff with your own text and graphics—making it your own. You can also add other embellishments not included in the original design.

Figure 13.2.
You can create a page by starting with a template.

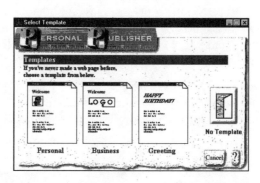

13

You can select one of three different page templates:

☐ **Personal**—Creates a page that provides personal information about you—like information you put in your Member Profile. You can add a picture of yourself, your pet anaconda, or whatever you like.

☐ **Business**—Creates a professional looking page appropriate for small- or home-based businesses. It's a great way to advertise your company's goods or services. Make sure to jazz up the page with your company logo.

☐ **Greeting**—Create a page that sends your greetings to the world. Just don't write one of those really sappy ones—I hate those.

☐ **No Template**—If you have some design experience and want to create a page without a template, click No Template. You can then create a page from scratch. This is a little challenging for newcomers, however.

After you decide which template you want, click it. You'll be walked through the creation process with easy, fill-in-the-blank forms as shown in Figure 13.3—it's the first step in customizing the Personal template.

Figure 13.3.

Creating a personal web page is easy with templates.

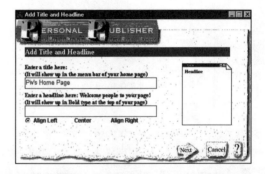

Turning Pictures into Graphics

Pictures are a natural addition to the graphics-based web page, but can be problematic for some people. Turning photographs and other art into graphics that a computer can use requires a scanner or digital camera—and most of us don't have one at home. (You may have access to one where you work, but always ask the boss if it's okay for you to use it, first. I wouldn't want you to get fired because of *me*.)

If you just plain don't have access to a scanner, you can use clip art and other digital photographs that you buy, or download from AOL. You should also check out Personal Publisher Graphics shown in Figure 13.4. To get there, use the keyword PPGRAPHICS.

13

Figure 13.4.
Personal Publisher Graphics is your online graphics resource.

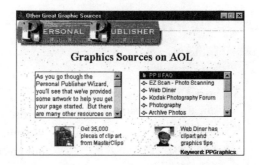

Personal Publisher Graphics offers all manner of tips, tricks, and advice on adding graphics to your web pages. You'll also find resources for downloading graphics from AOL, and even services that will scan your photographs for a small fee. Check it out.

Adding Other Art

Photographic images aren't the *only* way to spruce up a web page. You can add all manner of graphics—borders, ruled lines, cartoons, just about any digital graphic there is.

The web itself is a huge warehouse for *free* graphic files that anyone can use. Use the keyword NETFIND and do a search for clip art, icons, or whatever art you want.

CAUTION

> Before you add *any* art to your web page, make sure that it's really free for anyone to use. If anything you find is copyrighted, you can't use it— that's illegal.

A couple of AOL graphics-related areas you might want to check out are:

☐ **Quick Clips**—This area offers a collection of icons, bullets, lines, and graphics you can use on your home page.

☐ **AOL Graphics Libraries**—The file libraries on AOL are *loaded* with art you can use. The files have all been uploaded by AOL members, and they're free for you to use as you see fit.

Both of these areas appear in the list box on the main Personal Publisher dialog box (along with lots of other resources you can use). Just double-click an item in the list to visit the associated area.

13

Other Services

A couple of other places to go in America Online for more information or help with designing your web page include:

- ☐ **Advanced Tools**—Gives you lots of helpful information about web publishing and additional design resources. You'll find the Advanced Tools in the list box on the main Personal Publisher dialog box.

- ☐ **On The Net**—(keyword ON THE NET). On The Net, shown in Figure 13.5, offers all sorts of help to the up-and-coming webmaster, including: web publishing help, a multimedia showcase (for graphics, sounds, and other jazzy stuff), and access to advanced web publishing tools, such as AOLPress.

Figure 13.5.

On The Net has many tools to help you.

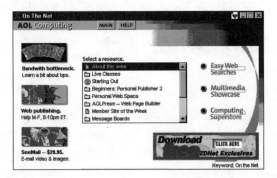

- ☐ **The Desktop & Web Publishing Forum**—Includes reference guides and web site evaluations—save this area for when you're getting really serious.

Summary

In this hour, you learned how to set up your own web page with AOL's Personal Publisher.

Workshop

Use the following workshop to refresh yourself on the skills you learned in this hour.

Q&A

Q Which version of HTML is supported by Personal Publisher?

A The browser supports HTML 3.2 tags, frames, and tables and some Netscape extensions.

Q I do have access to a scanner. How can I find out more about turning pictures into graphics?

A Try America Online's Digital Resource Center (keyword DIGITAL IMAGING) to get some helpful advice.

Quiz

Take the following quiz to test your knowledge of AOL's Personal Publisher.

Questions

1. How much free hard drive space do you get for your web page?

    a. About 2 inches worth

    b. 2MB

    c. 20MB

    d. 2GB (gigabytes)

2. True or False: You can create your own web page on AOL without knowing anything about HTML.

    a. True

    b. False

3. Which of the following is a true statement?

    a. You can easily convert your old AOL web page to the new Personal Publisher format.

    b. You can't convert your old web page to the new Personal Publisher format.

Answers

1. **b.**

2. **True.**

3. **b.** You have to make a new one—but it can look just like the old one, if you want.

Activity

Explore some of the web publishing resources available online. When you're comfortable with the idea, go ahead and use Personal Publisher to create your own web page masterpiece.

13

Hour **14**

Navigating Through America Online *Your* Way

The folks at America Online have spent a lot of time and money designing a service that is easy to use. Naturally, it's impossible for *anything* (including AOL) to meet all the needs of every person who uses it, so AOL has a pile of customizing features built-in.

You've already seen one of them briefly in Hour 3, "Exploring America Online," when you learned about using the toolbar's Favorite Places menu.

In this hour, you'll learn more ways to customize AOL, so you can tailor it to *your* particular needs. This hour covers

☐ More about Favorite Places

☐ How to add or change a screen name

☐ How to switch between screen names without signing off AOL

☐ How to change your password

☐ How to get started with My AOL

More ways to customize AOL exist than the ones you'll learn about here. There are tons of ways to tailor the way AOL behaves to suit you. Most of these other adjustments are made through your AOL Preferences. AOL Preferences are covered in Hour 15, "Setting Preferences."

Favorite Places

By now you've found a couple of places on AOL and the Internet that you like and want to visit again. You might have marked these spots as Favorite Places. Or, maybe you didn't. Well, in case you haven't, here's a little refresher course on adding and using Favorite Places.

Marking a Favorite Place

Adding something to your Favorite Places list couldn't be easier. When you find something (a web page, an AOL forum, anything) that you want to visit again, click and drag the little heart icon from the upper-right corner of the window, and drop it on the Favorite Places icon on the toolbar.

This works for *anything* that appears online with the little heart icon: Channels, chat rooms, forums, web pages—anything at all.

JUST A MINUTE

> You can also just click the heart icon. A small dialog box will appear and ask where you want this Favorite Place to go. You can add it to your Favorite Places, insert it in an email message, or send it in an Instant Message to a friend online. Just click the appropriate button.
>
> You can also click the Favorite Places icon on the toolbar, then select Add Top Window To Favorite Places.

Using a Favorite Place

To visit a Favorite Place, click the Favorite Places icon on the toolbar to see the drop-down menu. Click the name of the Favorite you want to visit, and you're on your way.

You may also select Favorite Places from that same menu to open a window (shown in the next section in Figure 14.1) that displays all your Favorites all the time. To visit a Favorite from the Favorite Places window, just double-click the name of the place you want to visit.

Organizing Favorite Places

When you click the Favorite Places icon on the toolbar icon, and then select Favorite Places, you'll open a window like the one shown in Figure 14.1 (assuming you've added items to your Favorite Places list). Not only can you use this window to go to your Favorites, you can use it to organize your Favorites, too.

14

Figure 14.1.
Your Favorite Places window can be customized.

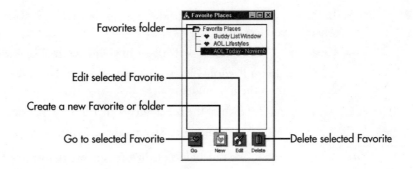

Favorites folder

Edit selected Favorite

Create a new Favorite or folder

Go to selected Favorite ——————— Delete selected Favorite

Going Back to a Favorite Place

You basically have two ways to get back to a Favorite Place after you've added it to your list:

- [ ] With the Favorite Places window open, double-click the name of the place you want to visit.
- [ ] Click the name of the place you want to visit, and then click the Go button.

Organizing Your Favorites

What happens when you've marked about 100 Favorite Places and have a list of Favorites as long as your arm? You get lost and confused, that's what. Kind of defeats the purpose, don't you think?

You can easily organize your list of Favorite Places. You can create organizing folders in which you can sort the various Favorites you've collected. For instance, you might want a folder for chat rooms you've added, another for web sites, and another for forums and other areas on AOL that you visit regularly.

You can simply drag and drop individual entries into the appropriate folder, keeping everything nice, tidy, and easier to find.

JUST A MINUTE

Not only does adding a folder organize your Favorite Places *window*, it also organizes your Favorite Places *menu* on the toolbar. Next time you use it, you'll find your favorites sorted into submenus with the same names as your organizing folders. *Very* cool.

Create an Organizing Folder in Your Favorite Places

To begin, open your Favorite Places window as described previously. Click the main Favorite Places folder to select it. You're ready to roll:

1. Click the New button to open a small Add New Folder/Favorite Place dialog box.
2. Click New Folder at the top of the dialog box.

14

3. In the text box, type a name for the new folder: Internet Sites, perhaps, or whatever you like.

4. Click OK. The new folder will appear in your Favorite Places window.

5. Click and drag a Favorite Places entry (one that fits the topic of the new folder), and drop it on the new folder.

6. Repeat step 5 for each of the other entries that fit into that category.

 7. Repeat steps 1–6 as necessary to organize your Favorite Places.

You *can* put folders inside the folders of the new folders you've created, but that, I think, overly complicates your Favorite Places. Keep it simple.

Figure 14.2 shows my list of Favorite Places after organization.

Figure 14.2.

*A nicely organized
Favorite Places window.*

You can use the New button to manually add Favorites to the list, but it's not as easy as just dragging and dropping the heart icon on the Favorite Places icon on your toolbar. As explained in Hour 3, it *is* convenient for manually adding web addresses to your list. Otherwise, it's just too complicated.

Editing Your Favorite Places

When you add Favorites to your Favorite Places list, they're named with the area's *full name*. That can make the names long and unwieldy. To change the name assigned to a Favorite Place, click its name in the Favorite Places window, then click the Edit button. A dialog box like the one shown in Figure 14.3 appears.

Figure 14.3.

*Editing the name of
a Favorite Place.*

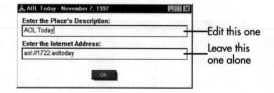

14

Edit the description entry in the Enter the Place's Description text box to say whatever you want, as long as you can remember where the entry will take you. *Don't* edit the Enter the Internet Address entry at the bottom. That's the address AOL uses to take you to the Favorite—if you edit it, you might never find it again...so be warned.

To delete an item from your Favorite Places list, click the entry you want to remove, and then click the Delete button. That sucker is history.

Adding and Changing Screen Names

The name you chose as your screen name when you first signed up with America Online is now and will forever be your Master Account screen name. You cannot change it, or delete it.

However, you can have up to four additional screen names on your AOL account. You can use the other screen names for members of your family, friends, or for yourself—one for work online, the other for play.

CAUTION

> You can only add, delete, or restore a screen name with your Master Account screen name—that is, the one you created when you first set up your AOL account. That way, none of the other folks with access to your computer can tinker with the available screen names.

To add a screen name, click the My AOL icon on the toolbar, and then select Screen Names from the My AOL menu. You can also use the keyword SCREEN NAME. Either way, the Create or Delete Screen Names dialog box appears as shown in Figure 14.4.

Figure 14.4.

The Create or Delete Screen Names dialog box: add, delete, or restore a screen name here.

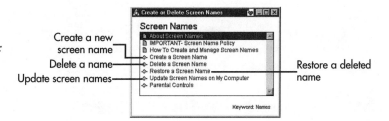

To add a new screen name to your account, double-click Create a Screen Name. The Create a Screen Name dialog box opens as shown in Figure 14.5. It should look familiar—it's just like the one you used to create your first screen name, way back in Hour 1, "Installing America Online and Signing Up."

14

Figure 14.5.

Creating a new screen name is a snap.

Type your new screen name in the Please Type the Screen Name You Want to Use text box, and then click Create a Screen Name. Chances are good that the one you chose is already in use—with more than 8 million members with up to five screen names each, the odds are against you.

AOL will alert you that the screen name you want is in use, and offer a variation. Usually it's the same screen name you entered with a string of numbers after it. If that's okay with you, click OK, otherwise try, try again.

After you've accepted a new screen name, AOL will ask you for a password for that screen name. You'll be asked to enter it twice, as you did when you entered your first screen name. Make sure it's different from the one for your primary screen name.

JUST A MINUTE

It's a great idea to let children in your house have their own screen names because you can set up Parental Controls at different levels for different screen names. Your 17-year-old can go places online that your 8-year-old can't—and it's all at your say so. Parental Controls are the topic of Hour 21, "Keeping Parental Control."

Congratulations. You've just given birth to a new online personality. You'll get a piece of email reminding you of the Terms of Service, and information about using the new screen name. Read it, it's a great little refresher.

Switching Screen Names

One of the coolest features of AOL 4.0 is the capability to switch between screen names without having to disconnect from the service and dial in again. Now that you have more than one screen name, why not try it?

14

Create an Organizing Folder in Your Favorite Places

To begin, open your Favorite Places window as described previously. Click the main Favorite Places folder to select it. You're ready to roll:

1. While signed on to AOL, click the Sign Off menu, and then select Switch Screen Names.

2. The Switch Screen Name dialog box opens with the list of your screen names, as shown in Figure 14.6. Click the screen name you want to use next, and then click Switch.

3. An alert appears that says, "You've been online for X minutes. Click OK to switch screen names." Click OK.

4. You'll be asked to type in the password for the screen name you're changing to. Carefully type in the password, and then click Switch.

Figure 14.6.

Switch screen names without having to sign off AOL—how convenient is that?

If this icon is yellow, this screen name has mail waiting for it

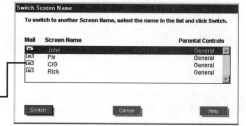

Changing Your Password

You should change the password for each of your screen names regularly. Once a month, or so—more often if you're paranoid, like me.

To change your password, sign on to AOL using the screen name with the password you want to change. Click the My AOL icon on the toolbar, and then select Passwords from the My AOL menu. The Change Your Password dialog box opens. Click the Change Password button. You'll be asked to enter three things in order: your current password, the new password, and the new password yet again (to make sure both entries match). Click OK, and your password is changed.

Don't forget to change the stored password for your Automatic AOL sessions (see Hour 6, "Automatic AOL," for details). Generally speaking, don't forget your new password.

14

Using My AOL

My AOL is your one stop customizing shop. It's an online, hold my hand while I do this, step-by-step tour of all your customizing features. It helps you do many of the things you learned in this hour, and many more.

To go to My AOL, click the My AOL button on the toolbar. Select Set Up AOL from the drop-down menu. You'll go to the Set Up AOL Now window shown in Figure 14.7.

Figure 14.7.

*My AOL provides
customizing help online.*

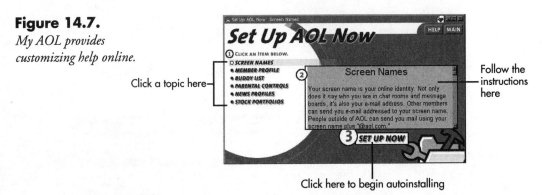

Click a topic here→

Follow the
instructions
here

Click here to begin autoinstalling

With My AOL you can set up your Member Profile, change passwords, create Buddy Lists, set the Parental Controls, and change some of your online preferences.

To use My AOL, click a topic on the left side of the window. Then read the informational text on the right side. My AOL is a great area that you should explore, especially if you're still a little squeamish about customizing AOL, even with all the assistance provided in this book.

Summary

In this hour, you've learned how to customize AOL to make it faster and easier for you to use.

Workshop

Use the following workshop to help you solidify the skills you've learned in this hour.

14

Q&A

Q Can I manually add an area from AOL to my list of Favorite Places?

A You can, but only if you know the exact AOL-type address for the area you want to add. For example, the address for the AOL Today Channel screen is `aol://1722:aoltoday`. It's much easier to drag and drop heart icons onto the Favorite Places icon on the toolbar. Really, it is.

Q If I use all five screen names for family members, why shouldn't I use the same password for all of them?

A If you do, you'll eliminate all the protection provided by Parental Controls. Your kids, armed with the proper password, will be able to use any account you've created and get at material online, or on the Internet, that you don't want them to see. Parental Controls is explained in detail in Hour 21.

Quiz

Take the following quiz to test your knowledge of the concepts taught in this hour.

Questions

1. True or False: You can't ever change your primary screen name, but you can change the password that goes with it.
    a. True
    b. False

2. Your Favorite Places list can include
    a. Places on America Online
    b. Internet sites
    c. Both

3. The complete list of keywords
    a. Must be memorized by all America Online members
    b. Is available online and can be printed
    c. Is stable and never changes

Answers

1. **a.**
2. **c.**
3. **b.**

14

Activities

Begin to customize America Online to suit the way you work (and play) online:

- ☐ Organize your Favorite Places list so it's easier to find the places you visit most.
- ☐ Go ahead and create additional screen names if you like.
- ☐ Visit My AOL, and see what other customizing options you have.

Hour 15

Setting Preferences

You've been working with this book, and AOL 4.0, for just a little over 14 hours. Somewhere in that time you may have said to yourself, "If only I could get AOL to work *this* way, it would be *perfect*." Well, that may not be just another idle daydream.

AOL, like almost any software on the market, offers you a set of customizing options. These options are called preferences and they let you tinker with how AOL looks and behaves.

In this hour, you'll learn how to set these AOL preferences:

- [ ] General
- [ ] Mail
- [ ] Chat
- [ ] Passwords
- [ ] Personal Filing Cabinet
- [ ] Buddy Lists
- [ ] World Wide Web

Who Knew I Had So Many Preferences?

AOL gives you a *lot* of customizing options. An awful lot, truth be told—more, at least, than can be demonstrated with a one-hour time limit. In this hour you'll learn about the preferences mentioned in the previous list, the preferences most readers will want to see and change.

Be aware that there *are* other preferences you can play with, including: Toolbar, Download, Graphics, Auto AOL, Spelling, Font, Language, and Marketing. Take some time to look at and tinker with them when this hour is up. Remember, you can't hurt anything by changing your preferences, so it's perfectly safe to play around with them and experiment.

All the preferences you'll see (and even those you *won't* see here) are usually a list of options that are turned on or off by clicking the check box in front of the specific option. When an option is checked, it's turned on. When it isn't checked, it's turned off.

Unless I mention otherwise, you can set these preferences offline.

General Preferences

General preferences affect AOL's general behavior, that is, things that aren't specifically related to email or your Buddy List. They affect what windows will open when you sign on to AOL, what size text will appear in, and whether AOL will make sounds for you while online—they're general as in wide-ranging, not as in minor or unimportant.

To view your General preferences, click the My AOL icon on the toolbar. From the My AOL drop-down menu, click Preferences. When the Preferences window opens, click the General button. The General Preferences dialog box opens, as shown in Figure 15.1.

Figure 15.1.

Your General preferences.

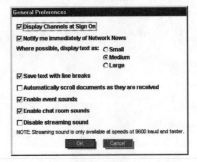

15

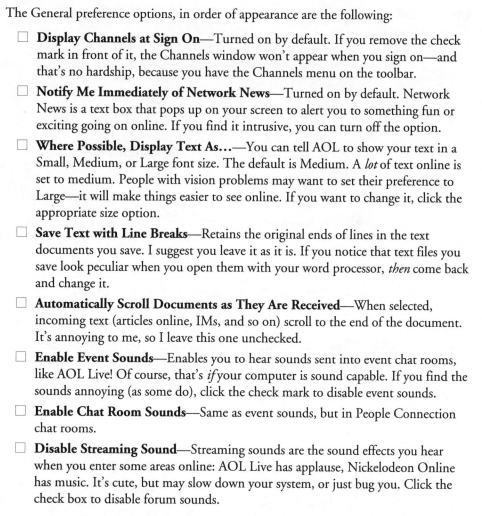

The General preference options, in order of appearance are the following:

- [ ] **Display Channels at Sign On**—Turned on by default. If you remove the check mark in front of it, the Channels window won't appear when you sign on—and that's no hardship, because you have the Channels menu on the toolbar.

- [ ] **Notify Me Immediately of Network News**—Turned on by default. Network News is a text box that pops up on your screen to alert you to something fun or exciting going on online. If you find it intrusive, you can turn off the option.

- [ ] **Where Possible, Display Text As...**—You can tell AOL to show your text in a Small, Medium, or Large font size. The default is Medium. A *lot* of text online is set to medium. People with vision problems may want to set their preference to Large—it will make things easier to see online. If you want to change it, click the appropriate size option.

- [ ] **Save Text with Line Breaks**—Retains the original ends of lines in the text documents you save. I suggest you leave it as it is. If you notice that text files you save look peculiar when you open them with your word processor, *then* come back and change it.

- [ ] **Automatically Scroll Documents as They Are Received**—When selected, incoming text (articles online, IMs, and so on) scroll to the end of the document. It's annoying to me, so I leave this one unchecked.

- [ ] **Enable Event Sounds**—Enables you to hear sounds sent into event chat rooms, like AOL Live! Of course, that's *if* your computer is sound capable. If you find the sounds annoying (as some do), click the check mark to disable event sounds.

- [ ] **Enable Chat Room Sounds**—Same as event sounds, but in People Connection chat rooms.

- [ ] **Disable Streaming Sound**—Streaming sounds are the sound effects you hear when you enter some areas online: AOL Live has applause, Nickelodeon Online has music. It's cute, but may slow down your system, or just bug you. Click the check box to disable forum sounds.

When you're finished tinkering with your General preferences, click OK, and you'll return to the main Preferences window.

Mail Preferences

You'll probably use email just about every day of your online life. Your Mail preferences enable you to customize how your email looks and behaves. To check out your Mail preferences, click the Mail icon on the Preferences window. The Mail Preferences dialog box appears, as shown in Figure 15.2.

Figure 15.2.

Your Mail preferences.

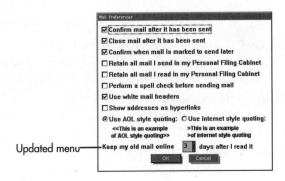

Updated menu

The Mail options are the following:

- [ ] **Confirm Mail After It Has Been Sent**—This option puts that little Your mail has been sent alert on the screen after you send mail. It's turned on by default. If you don't like it, click the check mark to disable it.

- [ ] **Close Mail After It Has Been Sent**—This option closes the email window after the message has been sent—it's a good way to know, at a glance, whether you've sent your mail or not. If you prefer that the message window stay open, click to remove the check mark.

- [ ] **Confirm When Mail Is Marked to Send Later**—This generates that Your mail has been saved for later delivery message when you click the Send Later button. If it annoys you, turn it off here.

- [ ] **Retain All Mail I Send in My Personal Filing Cabinet**—When checked, copies of *all* your outgoing email are stored in your PFC (covered in Hour 6, "Automatic AOL"). It's convenient if you frequently need to check and see what mail you've sent; however, it *does* eat up valuable hard drive space.

- [ ] **Retain All Mail I Read in My Personal Filing Cabinet**—Same as the last option, except it saves copies of *all* your incoming mail in your PFC. It's turned off by default. The same warnings about hard disk space apply here, too.

CAUTION

If you turn on either Retain All Mail... option described previously, go into your PFC once a week and delete unwanted items. Mail takes up a *lot* of hard drive space. It can also fragment your hard drive, which can slow down your computer. You'll need to occasionally use a defragmentation program (such as Windows 95's Disk Defragmenter).

- [ ] **Perform a Spell Check Before Sending Mail**—Automatically checks the spelling of your mail right after you click the Send button. It's a great option if you're a sloppy speller or bad typist.

15

☐ **Use White Mail Headers**—Keeps the address and delivery information in your email on a white background, in spite of what's been done to the color of the message text and background.

☐ **Show Addresses as Hyperlinks**—Turns email addresses into clickable links—when you click one, you automatically open a blank email form addressed to the screen name you clicked.

☐ **Keep My Old Mail Online *x* Days After I Read It**—This option helps you keep your mailbox cleaned up. You can elect to have mail deleted 1 to 7 days after reading.

The last options on the Mail Preferences dialog box concern how quoted text gets set off from the rest of the message. Examples of each type are given at the bottom of the dialog box, and you can judge for yourself which you want to use. Be aware, however, that 9 out of 10 computer geeks agree that Internet style quoting is required by etiquette standards. But who cares what they think? Click the one *you* like.

Chat Preferences

Your Chat preferences affect how chat and member names appear in the chat window. For these preferences, I suggest you experiment before deciding which to use—especially because how fast you read, and how easily you can pick out what you want on the chat window determines whether these options help or hinder you.

To view your Chat preferences, click the Chat button on the main Preferences window. The Chat Preferences dialog box will open, as shown in Figure 15.3.

Figure 15.3.

Your Chat preferences.

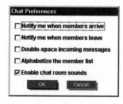

Chat preferences include the following:

☐ **Notify Me When Members Arrive**—This option sends a message like: `***Piv has entered the room***` into your chat room whenever someone new enters. It's off by default.

☐ **Notify Me When Members Leave**—Same as previous option, but the alert appears when someone *leaves* the room.

☐ **Double-Space Incoming Messages**—Puts a blank line between lines of chat—you may find it easier to read this way.

☐ **Alphabetize the Member List**—Sorts the list of people in the chat room alphabetically. With this option turned off, most recent additions to the room appear at
the top of the list, while folks who have been around for a while drift to the
bottom.

☐ **Enable Chat Room Sounds**—Enables your computer to play sounds sent into a
chat room by other chatters—your computer must be sound-capable, of course,
and you need to have a copy of the sound on *your* computer. (Appendix C, "Using
Smileys, Shorthands, and Sounds," explains how to send chat sounds yourself.)

Passwords Preferences

Passwords are the key to keeping your America Online account secure. The Password
preferences give you the option of *storing* your password so that you don't have to type one
in every time you sign on (or so you can use Automatic AOL to sign on while you're asleep
in your bed).

You *must* be signed on to AOL to change your Password preferences, and you can only store
the password for the screen name with which you are currently signed on.

To see your Password preferences (shown in Figure 15.4), click Passwords on the main
Preferences window.

Figure 15.4.

Storing your passwords.

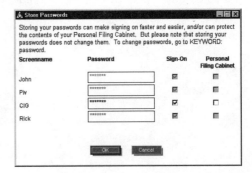

Type in the password for your screen name in the Password text box beside the name. The
password appears as asterisks, not the real letters, so type carefully.

Unless you're in a situation where you're the *only one* with access to your computer, I don't
recommend that you store your password—except (possibly) for use with Automatic AOL.
The added sense of security is well worth the extra second or two it takes to type in your
password.

15

15

Personal Filing Cabinet Preferences

The Personal Filing Cabinet is an extremely useful tool, but it can eat up a lot of your hard drive. You can use some of the Personal Filing Cabinet preferences to remind you to get in there and start deleting when the PFC gets too large.

To see your PFC preferences, click the Personal Filing Cabinet button on the main Preferences window. The Personal Filing Cabinet Preferences dialog box opens as shown in Figure 15.5.

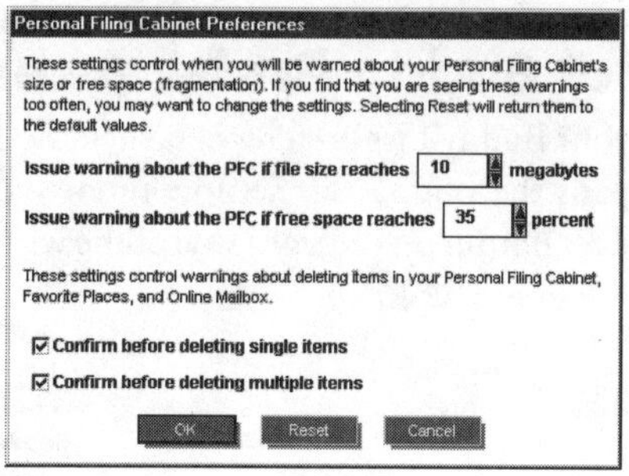

Figure 15.5.

Your Personal Filing Cabinet preferences.

The PFC options include the following:

- [ ] **Issue Warning About the PFC if File Size Reaches *x* Megabytes**—This lets you tell AOL when to warn you that your Filing Cabinet is stuffed to the gills, so you can go in and delete some items. The default setting is 10MB, which is a lot of space for email. You can change it to whatever you like. Double-click the number in the text box and type the new number.

- [ ] **Issue Warning About the PFC if Free Space Reaches *x* Percent**—This tells AOL to warn you that your Filing Cabinet is eating up free space you could be using elsewhere. It prompts the Compact PFC message mentioned earlier in Hour 6. If hard drive space is at a premium, you may want to set this number lower.

- [ ] **Confirm Before Deleting Single Items**—This option generates that Are you sure you want to delete that? message when you delete a letter or other single item from the PFC. Some users like the warning because it prevents accidental deletions, others don't. If it annoys you, turn it off here.

- [ ] **Confirm Before Deleting Multiple Items**—Works the same as the single items option, but with multiple items.

Buddy List Preferences

You learned about setting up Buddy Lists in Hour 7, "Chatting on America Online." Now you'll learn how to customize the performance of your Buddy List.

Your Buddy List preferences aren't found on the main Preferences window. They're found on the Buddy List Setup window—which means you have to be signed on to AOL to tinker with these settings. You actually have *two* sets of Buddy List preferences: one is a general set, about how your Buddy List performs; the others are Privacy preferences that set who can and can't add you to their Buddy Lists.

General Buddy Preferences

To see your Buddy List preferences, click the Setup button on the Buddies Online window. That opens the Buddy List setup window you used to create a list. Click the Buddy List Preferences button on the right side of the window to open the Buddy List Preferences dialog box (see Figure 15.6).

Figure 15.6.

Your Buddy List preferences.

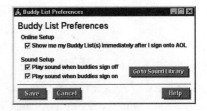

The general Buddy List preferences are the following:

- [ ] **Show Me My Buddy List(s) Immediately After I Sign On to AOL**—This automatically opens the Buddies Online window when you connect to AOL. If you turn off this option, you can open the list with the keyword BUDDYVIEW.

- [ ] **Play Sound When Buddies Sign Off**—When someone from your list signs off, this option plays a sound to alert you. It's helpful for those times when your Buddies Online window is hidden behind other windows.

- [ ] **Play Sound When Buddies Sign On**—Same as previous option, but the sound happens when one of your buddies sign on to AOL.

JUST A MINUTE

You can add some funky sounds to your Buddy List. Click the Go To Sound Library button on the Preferences window, and download some. Instructions are available online for installing and using your new sounds.

15

Privacy Preferences

To view your Privacy preferences, click the Privacy Preferences button on the bottom of the Buddy List Setup window. The Privacy Preferences dialog box appears as shown in Figure 15.7.

Figure 15.7.

Your Privacy preferences.

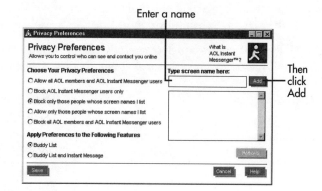

You may select one of the following Privacy preferences:

- [ ] **Allow All AOL Members and AOL Instant Messenger Users**—This allows anyone on AOL, or who uses AOL's Instant Messenger, to add you to their Buddy List. In short, no privacy at all.

- [ ] **Block AOL Instant Messenger Users Only**—This prevents folks on the Internet, using Instant Messenger, from adding you to their Buddy Lists.

- [ ] **Block Only Those People Whose Screen Names I List**—Enables you to block specific people from adding you to their Buddy Lists. Anyone not listed may add you to their Buddy List.

- [ ] **Allow Only Those People Whose Screen Names I List**—Enables you to block everyone, except the names you specify, from adding you to their Buddy Lists.

- [ ] **Block All AOL Members and AOL Instant Messenger Users**—Complete and total privacy—no one will be able to spot you with their Buddy List.

You may then apply this preference to either Buddy List users, or Buddy List and Instant Message users. Selecting the latter not only hides you from people's Buddy Lists, but renders you invisible to the Available? button on the Instant Message window.

To add a name to the list of blocked/allowed screen names, click to place the cursor in the Type Screen Name Here text box, and type the person's screen name or Internet address. Click Add. It will appear in the list box below the Add button.

World Wide Web Preferences

When AOL adopted Microsoft's Internet Explorer as its web browser, the AOL web preferences went from a handful, to a *big* handful—five tabbed pages worth. To cover them all would take an hour unto itself, so we're going to skip some of the more mundane and esoteric web preferences and cover only the ones that can affect your system's performance—the web can be painfully slow at times, no sense aggravating yourself further, right?

To get at your web preferences, click the Web button on the main Preferences window. The AOL Internet Properties dialog box appears as shown in Figure 15.8.

Figure 15.8.

The AOL Internet Properties dialog box.

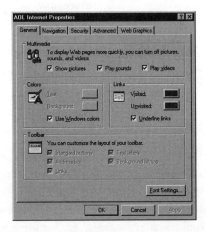

The General tab preferences affect the appearance of web pages as they pop onto your screen. In the Multimedia section of the General tab, you have the option of having the Explorer display pictures, play sounds, and play videos that are built-in to some web pages.

These options, although fun, can make pages load slowly. If you have an older computer, or a 14.4 (or slower) modem, you may want to disable one or more of these options. If you don't have a sound-capable computer, you may as well turn off the sound option—you can't hear the sounds anyway.

Another browser function that can affect your system's performance (and the amount of free hard drive space you have) is the cache of temporary Internet files that gets stored on your hard drive.

Like all browser software, the AOL browser stores a copy of each web page you visit on your computer's hard drive for future reference. This helps your computer display the page more quickly if you return to that page later.

You could have *hundreds* of these temporary files, eating up *megabytes* of space on your hard drive. Every now and then, you should get rid of them.

Dump Those Temporary Files

Those temporary files can be a pain in the...hard drive. Get rid of them:

1. Open your web preferences (the AOL Internet Properties dialog box) as shown in Figure 15.8.

2. Click the Advanced tab.

3. Click the Settings button (it's in the middle to the right of the display).

4. When the Settings window opens, click the Empty Folder button.

5. You'll be asked if you really want to delete those files. Click Yes.

When you're finished, check to see how much hard drive space you've freed up—if you use the web much, it could be a lot.

Summary

In this hour, you've learned how to set some of the more important preferences in your AOL software.

Workshop

Use this workshop to reaffirm some of the skills you've learned in this hour.

Q&A

Q I know that I can keep people from adding me to their Buddy Lists. Can I prevent someone from entering a chat room I'm in?

A Sorry, no. Keeping people from adding you to their Buddy Lists is about the only preference you can set that directly affects other members of the service. You can choose to ignore them by double-clicking their name and choosing the Ignore check box. That's *almost* as good as blocking them from your room.

Q America Online offers unlimited access. Why should I care if someone else at my office or home gets access to my account?

A True, someone else using your account won't affect your usage time bill. But it does give him or her access to your email, the ability to sign on with AOL's 10-cents-a-minute 800 number, and the ability to go shopping on your account. So, I'd keep those passwords a secret.

Quiz

Use this quiz to test your knowledge of preferences.

Questions

1. In the Chat Preferences dialog box, you can set up the software to announce

    a. When someone comes into or leaves a chat room.

    b. When you come into or leave a chat room.

    c. The score of your favorite team's game-in-progress.

2. If you don't clear the cache in your web preferences

    a. Your computer could explode.

    b. Your computer might respond slowly when you are surfing the Net.

    c. You could lose important documents.

3. If you store passwords

    a. Any America Online member can use your account remotely.

    b. You can log on to the service without typing your password all the time.

    c. You don't have to remember your password anymore.

Answers

1. **a.**

2. **b.**

3. **b.**

Activity

Go through the preferences discussed in this hour, if you haven't already, and set up things the way you like them. Then poke around in the preferences that weren't covered here, and experiment with what they do, too.

15

Hour 16

AOL Away from Home

If you are a homebody, someone who never goes out of town, never travels on business, and never takes a vacation, then go ahead and skip this hour. You can teach yourself America Online in *23* hours, I guess. Most of us, however, do go out of town for one reason or another from time to time. Part of the beauty of America Online is that you *can* take it with you. As an international service provider, AOL has local access numbers all over the world. After you've found one and dialed in, you'll find the same AOL you've come to know and love in the comfort of your own home.

Here's some of what you'll learn in this hour:

- ☐ General issues for travelers
- ☐ How business travelers can use America Online on the road
- ☐ How to get local access numbers away from home
- ☐ How to create a new location for AOL
- ☐ How to use your account on another person's computer

General Issues

If you're planning a trip, whether it's business or personal, it pays to be prepared. You don't want to get to your hotel room and be unable to use your America Online account because you've forgotten something simple, like a short length of phone line.

Let's take a look at a couple of things you'll want to do, have, or know before you hit the road.

Items You Won't Want to Forget

For a little bit of money, you can put together a kit of simple items you'll need when you travel. Some office supply stores have these items already put together in a kit for you. Here's what you might need:

- ☐ A travel case for your laptop computer and the rest of this stuff. If you forget your laptop, the rest of this list won't help much.

- ☐ An extra length of regular telephone cord. I take two—one that's very short (four inches) with a plug at each end and one that's about 10–15 feet long, also with a plug at each end.

- ☐ A modular coupler, the kind you can use to plug one line into another. I use it to create a telephone extension cord.

- ☐ A line splitter with an end that plugs into a wall jack, and the other end with two or three jacks for plugging in a phone and a modem.

- ☐ Your long-distance calling card or prepaid long-distance cards.

Other Travel Considerations

Beyond the hardware mentioned in the preceding section, you'll need to think about *where* you'll be using your computer while on your trip. Here are some things to check out:

- ☐ Check the types of hotel rooms available to you. Many hotels now offer special rooms for business travelers that are equipped with either a special jack for modem users or a *data port* built into the telephone. You use it to connect your modem to the hotel's phone line. If these amenities are not available, you *might* be able to unplug the phone from the wall and plug in your modem. In some hotels, the phones are hard-wired into the walls—to keep you from stealing the phone, I guess. Best to ask when you're making your reservations.

- ☐ While you're asking about the phone jack, ask about the hotel's phone system, too. PBX phone systems send more power through the phone lines, power that can fry your modem and possibly damage your computer. You can either avoid hotels with PBX systems, or buy an adapter, which protects both your modem and computer when connected to PBX systems. They're available in most computer stores and mail-order catalogs.

16

☐ Create location entries for your destination *and* the AOL 800 numbers. If all else fails, you can connect to AOL with the 800 numbers (1-800-724-0023 or 1-888-245-0113). It costs a little extra. You'll learn how to create locations later in this hour.

☐ If you are traveling overseas, you *really* need to be prepared. Among the things you might need are a voltage transformer and phone jack converter. I've heard stories about people who took all the time to convert their hair dryers and other accessory appliances to European voltages, only to overlook their laptops and end up frying their hard drives. Ouch.

America Online for the Business Traveler

You're heading out on a trip to meet with the company's biggest client. You'll probably want access to your email to keep up with what's going on at the office, get last minute instructions from your boss, and maybe send a little "I miss you" note home to your special someone.

Connecting to AOL while traveling is not as difficult as it might sound. There are just a couple of simple things you need to do to get ready to hit the road.

Find a Local Access Number

Folks who rarely travel might find it easier to just click Setup on the Sign On screen, and change your regular access numbers to those of the city you're visiting—and then change them back when you come home, of course. You do that the same way you selected your original access numbers back in Hour 1, "Installing America Online and Signing Up."

TIME SAVER

> If you travel to the same cities regularly, you'll find it much more convenient to create a *location entry* for each of your regular destinations. The how-to of creating locations is explained in the next section, "How to Create Location Entries."

Keep in mind that this method changes your local access numbers. If you're going to try it this way, wait until you arrive at your destination to change your access numbers. If you don't, you'll be connecting to AOL with long-distance numbers, which can become expensive. Remember to change them back, when you get home again.

To begin, fire up your America Online software. When the Sign On screen appears, click the Setup button to open the Connection Setup window, shown in Figure 16.1.

Figure 16.1.

Change your access numbers under the Connection Locations tab of the Connection Setup window.

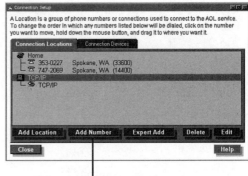

Click to add access numbers

Click on the first of your local access numbers (the ones with the little telephone icon preceding them in the list), then click the Delete button. Repeat until you're out of access numbers.

Next, click the Add Number button to open the AOL Setup dialog box, shown in Figure 16.2. It should look familiar—it's the same one you used in Hour 1 to select the numbers you just deleted.

Figure 16.2.

Enter the area code for your destination.

If necessary, select a country here
Enter an area code

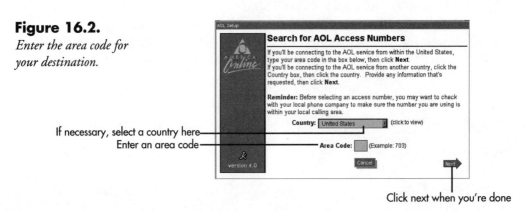

Click next when you're done

Enter the area code of the city you're visiting in the Area Code text box, then click the Next arrow. America Online gives you a list of numbers for that area code.

As I advised when you first signed up with AOL, you should select two or more access numbers. The first is for your primary access. The others are secondary access numbers in case the first is busy. Click a phone number from the list to select it. Then, click the Add arrow. Repeat for the secondary numbers.

After you've selected your access numbers, click the Sign On arrow, and you'll connect to AOL and get all the email you've missed while traveling.

How to Create Location Entries

If you travel a lot or travel to the same cities regularly, you'll want to create one or more location entries. Unlike changing the access numbers, location entries are saved on your hard drive and you can blithely switch between your home and travel locations with just a click of your mouse. It's *much* more convenient.

Create a Location Entry

1. Start your AOL software, and click the Setup button on the Sign On screen to open the Connection Setup screen shown earlier in Figure 16.1.

2. Click the Add Location button. The Add Location dialog box opens (see Figure 16.3). Enter a name for your new location in the Name text box. Then, click the Next arrow.

Figure 16.3.

The Add Location dialog box.

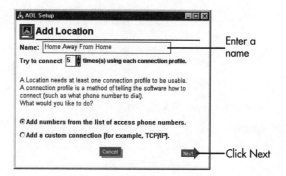

3. Next you'll get the Search for AOL Access Numbers screen shown previously in Figure 16.2. Enter the area code for your destination, and then click the Next arrow.

4. Select your access numbers, as you did in the preceding section. When you've chosen two or more numbers, click Done.

   You'll be returned to the Sign On screen, and your new location will appear in the Location menu. Make sure to re-select your Home location before you try to sign on to AOL (unless, of course, you're already at your destination—then you're ready to sign on).

When staying in hotels, or dialing in to AOL from an office building on the road, you may need to adjust your dialing settings. For example, most hotels require you dial an 8 or a 9 to get an outside line. You can tell your AOL software to do this automatically.

To change these dialing settings, click the Setup button on the Sign On screen. When the Connection Setup screen opens, select the Location entry for your destination by clicking its name. Next, click the Edit button. An Edit Location dialog box opens. It contains information similar to the Add Location dialog box shown previously in Figure 16.3, but looks a little different. Click the Edit button on the Edit Location dialog box to open the Edit Connection Profile shown in Figure 16.4.

Figure 16.4.

Your Connection Profile.

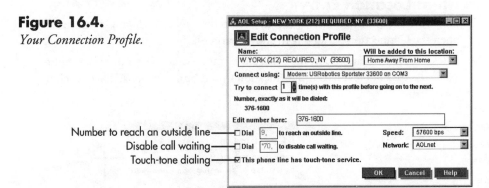

The three items you may need to change while traveling are shown in Figure 16.4.

NEW TERM   **Comma**   In punctuation, a comma (,) means take a little pause before continuing. It tells your modem to do the same thing: dial a 9, then wait a moment before dialing the rest of the number.

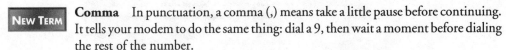

☐ Most hotels and office buildings usually require that you dial an 8 or a 9 to get an outside line. Click the Dial 9 to Reach an Outside Line check box. Verify that 9 is the correct number. If it isn't, select the 9, and enter the correct number followed by a comma (,).

☐ If the location you'll be calling from has call waiting service, click the Dial *70 to Disable Call Waiting check box. Incoming calls with call waiting can disrupt your connection to AOL.

☐ Most hotels and office buildings have touch-tone dialing. If you're staying with friends, they may have an old-fashioned rotary phone with an actual *dial.* If they do, click to remove the check mark labeled This Phone Line Has Touch-Tone Service.

After you have all your locations set up, complete with local access numbers for each, you'll want to make sure that you have the correct location selected each time you sign on to America Online.

16

CAUTION

Every time you sign on, check the Location listing to make sure you're using the right location. Otherwise, you might find yourself with a surprise long-distance bill because you're calling an access number in Texas when you are, in fact, in Minnesota.

It's easy to do. Just look at the Location box under the Screen Name and Password boxes on the Sign On screen. If it doesn't show the Location you want to use, click the arrow beside the Location, and select the correct one from the drop-down menu. You're ready to sign on.

16

Using Your Account from a Friend's House

If you don't have a laptop, you can still access your AOL account while traveling. You just have to rely on the kindness of strangers—or friends, relatives, or coworkers.

You can access your AOL account from any computer that has the AOL software installed.

Start America Online. Click the arrow next to the Select Screen Name field and select Guest from the drop-down menu. Your friend's Sign On screen will look like the one shown in Figure 16.5.

Figure 16.5.

Sign on as a guest from a friend's computer.

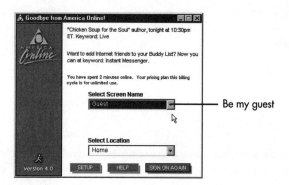

Be my guest

Click the Sign On button, and the computer dials in to America Online. Before you connect and hear that "Welcome," the Guest Sign-On window appears (see Figure 16.6).

Figure 16.6.

Enter your screen name and password to sign on as a guest.

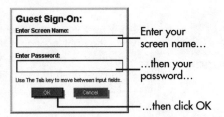

Type in your screen name, press the Tab key, and carefully type in your password. Click OK and you'll soon be cruising AOL as if you were at home sweet home. Just be forewarned: You won't have access to your Personal Filing Cabinet or Favorite Places—they're stored on the hard drive of your computer at home.

Summary

In this hour, you've learned a couple of different ways to access your AOL account while traveling—either with your laptop or with another America Online member's computer.

Workshop

Use the following workshop to help solidify the skills you've learned in this hour.

Q&A

Q **If I'm at my friend's house, why can't I just use their America Online account to access the service? It's the same deal, right?**

A True, it is the same America Online you've grown accustomed to. However, you would be using *their* account, which means you can't read your own email, for example. It's always better (and polite) to use your own account whenever possible.

Q **I signed on as a guest on my friend's computer, and everything works fine, except the screen looks a lot different to me. Why is that?**

A Chances are that they are using an older version of America Online's software than the one you're using. That's okay—the same forums and such are available. It just looks different. Perhaps their computer's hardware can't handle the advanced features of the newer software, or maybe they haven't taken the time to download it yet. Whatever you do, don't criticize them—they're being nice enough to let you use their computer.

16

Q When I use my friend's computer to sign on as a guest, Favorite Places and the Personal Filing Cabinet aren't available. Why?

A Your Favorite Places and Personal Filing Cabinet are stored on your hard drive, not on AOL's computers or your friend's computer. So those options are unavailable to you when you sign on as a guest.

Quiz

Use the following quiz to test your knowledge of using America Online on the road.

16

Questions

1. You should create location entries if

   a. You travel to the same location regularly

   b. You don't want the hassle of having to reset your access numbers when you return home

   c. Both of the above

   d. None of the above

2. Which of the following items would help you use America Online on a business trip?

   a. Two tin cans and a piece of string

   b. An extra length of telephone line

   c. The original AOL software CD

3. True or False: You should try to get a computer-friendly room when you're making hotel reservations.

   a. True

   b. False

Answers

1. **c.**

2. **b.**

3. **a.**

Activity

If you travel regularly, take a couple of minutes to set up location entries for each of your usual travel destinations. You'll have one less thing to do before your next trip.

PART V

Getting Information Online

Hour

Hour 17

Your Computer as a News Source

As a kid, I always thought that the way George Jetson read his newspaper was cool. He'd sit down in front of a computer screen and press a button, and the paper would pop up in front of his face.

Isn't it strange that *The Jetsons*, a cartoon created more than 30 years ago, was pretty accurate in the way it portrayed reading the paper in the future?

In this *information age*, people can get their news in a number of different ways—including some that look rather, *um*, Jetson-y. In this hour, you'll take a look at what America Online and the Internet have to offer to the information junkies of today's world. The topics discussed in this hour include the following:

- ☐ News sources on AOL
- ☐ How to search for news on AOL
- ☐ Finding your hometown news on the Local Channel
- ☐ How to save and print the articles you find
- ☐ AOL's online newspapers and magazines
- ☐ News sources on the Internet

News Sources on America Online

America Online offers an extremely comprehensive news source for its members—one good enough to make more than a few newspaper editors around the United States blush.

It all starts with the Top News Story button, which can be found on the AOL Welcome screen, shown in Figure 17.1. The text beside the button highlights a featured story. To read that story (plus the day's other top news), just click the button.

TIME SAVER

News From Anywhere Online   If you don't happen to be at the Welcome screen, you can get at the top news stories a couple of ways—select News from the Channels menu on the toolbar, click the News button on the left side of any Channel's Main Screen, or use the keyword NEWS.

Figure 17.1.

The Welcome screen gives you easy access to the news of the day.

Click here to see today's top news stories

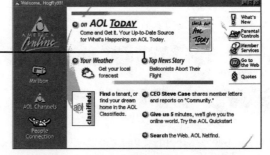

The impressive array of stories is provided by wire services such as Reuters (one of the world's leading news services), SportsTicker, Knight-Ridder/Tribune Business News, and PR Newswire. Occasionally, you'll find stories from other services, but Reuters provides the bulk of AOL's news.

When you click the News button, you're launched into America Online's News Channel—the News Channel's main screen is shown in Figure 17.2.

17

Figure 17.2.

Today's news works like a newspaper, but you don't get ink on your hands.

Top headlines here

Feature article

News departments

Featured news areas

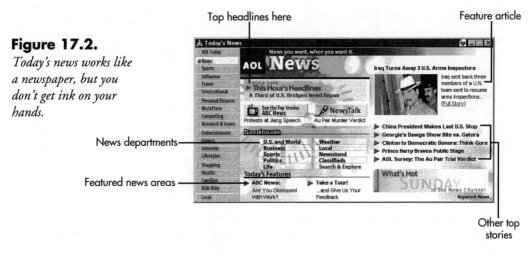

Other top stories

The News Channel works sort of like a newspaper. It's broken down into the typical assortment of departments, like sections of a paper. You'll find departments for U.S. and World news, Business, Sports, Politics, Life, Weather, Local news, and Classifieds. Don't be deceived by the newspaper metaphor—there's plenty of television-style reporting available on AOL, principally from *ABC News*.

To get a summary of the top news, click This Hour's Headlines (it's indicated in Figure 17.2), and you'll get a brief summary of the news.

The News Summary

The News Channel's headlines (shown in Figure 17.3) are very current; they're updated hourly, which means you can check out stories as they develop.

Click here to see more in-depth coverage of the top stories

Figure 17.3.

The hourly news summary keeps you up-to-date.

Click to visit a different news department

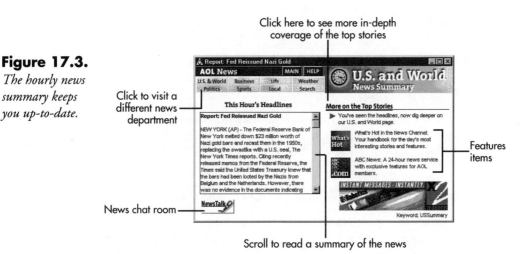

Features items

News chat room

Scroll to read a summary of the news

The screen is dominated by a text box labeled This Hour's Headlines. It contains what print journalists call *briefs*—short, two- or three-paragraph summaries of the top stories of the day. The top stories can be from any of the main news departments.

To get more detailed coverage of the top stories, you can click the More on the Top Stories link beside the summary text box. There you'll see full-length articles on the headline stories, plus photos and graphics all wrapped up in a neat little package.

If none of the top stories catch your eye, you can use the department buttons above the summary to go right to any of the news departments.

The News Departments

Each of the news departments contains a full complement of stories, photos, and features—enough information to fulfill the needs of the biggest info-addict. Figure 17.4 shows you the U.S. & World News department, which is laid out like all the News Channel's departments.

Figure 17.4.

U.S. & World News is typical of the News Channel's departments.

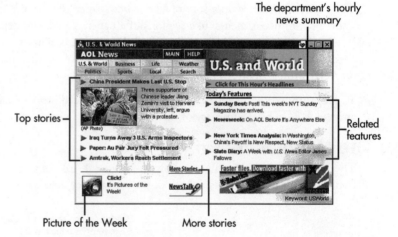

The day I visited U.S. & World, it featured four top news stories, plus another four news-related feature stories from sources as varied as *Newsweek* magazine and the *New York Times*. Each headline is a link to the full story; just click the link to read the related article.

The heading Click for This Hour's Headlines takes you to a summary of the top news stories for the current department. You also can see the news that didn't make the top news story cut by clicking the More Stories button below the headlines.

Searching for News on AOL

I'm sure it has happened to you: A friend tells you to check out an article in today's paper, then you spend 10 to 15 minutes trying to find the darned thing. Talk about frustrating!

17

Well, that won't happen online. You can make AOL look for the stories for you, while you enjoy that second cup of coffee.

If you look back at Figure 17.3, you'll notice that the department buttons (in the upper-left corner of the screen) include a Search button. Click the Search button, and you'll open the News Search window, as shown in Figure 17.5. It should be a familiar sight by now because you've used one just like it to search for other items online.

Figure 17.5.

You should already be familiar with the News Search screen.

Enter a word or
phrase here...

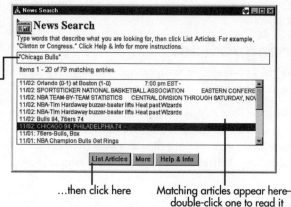

...then click here   Matching articles appear here—
                          double-click one to read it

All you need to do is enter a key word or phrase about the topic you want to find, then click the List Articles button. Remember, however, that Today's News is a *very* extensive news source. If you search for articles about Bill Clinton, you're going to get a list of articles a mile long.

Narrow your search as much as possible—that is, be as specific as you can. For example, if you want to search for stories about the Chicago Bulls, type in `"Chicago Bulls"`, as I have in Figure 17.5. Enclosing two or more words that *must* appear in a specific order in quotation marks will eliminate the majority of false matches. You won't get stories about the bull market on Wall Street or a huge list of stories that mention the great city of Chicago.

You also can use the modifiers *and, or,* and *not* between words and phrases, to focus on exactly what you want. For example, if you only want articles about Michael Jordan and the Bulls, you could enter: `"Michael Jordan"` and `"Chicago Bulls"`. AOL will search for stories that contain both sets of words.

Alternately, if you want stories about Mike that aren't related to the Bulls, you could enter `"Michael Jordan"` not `"Chicago Bulls"`. AOL will return a list of stories about Mike that do not include a reference to the Bulls.

Saving and Printing Articles

Back in the days of AOL's hourly billing, it was essential to be able to save a new article to your hard drive, so you could read them offline and save money on your bill. Well, those days are long gone, but it's still convenient to be able to save or print a copy of an interesting article—either for future reference or to share with a friend who might be interested in the story.

You can do either or both—save an article, print an article, or save an article so you can print it later.

Saving Articles

When a news story is the foremost window on your screen—that is, in the active window—you can easily save it to your hard drive or floppy disk.

With the article open, click the File menu, then click Save. That opens a standard Save dialog that you can use to name and save the file on your hard drive or a floppy disk. Windows users should be sure to end the filename with the extension .txt—something like article.txt, or anything to help you remember the file's content. File extensions aren't an issue for Mac users.

JUST A MINUTE

> **Save More Than the News**   You can save any text article you find on AOL, any time you like. If, by some chance, you cannot save a story, the Save option on the File menu will be grayed out.

Once you save an article, you can open it later with any word processor or your AOL software. AOL articles are plain text, so even basic word processors (such as Windows 95's WordPad or the Mac's Simple Text) can handle them.

Printing Articles

Printing an article works like saving one. With the article in the foremost window, click the Print icon on the toolbar, and the file will be sent directly to your printer.

You can also print an article by clicking the File menu and selecting Print. This gives you a standard print dialog, with which you can change your printer settings, should you need to.

17

CAUTION

I strongly recommend saving an article, then printing it once you sign off AOL. At best, printing while online may slow your system down, wasting valuable online time. At worst, your computer may lock up and you'll lose your connection to AOL. It isn't really an issue of computer power or RAM, but rather about how your system handles print jobs; what other software you have running; and whether your printer, modem, AOL, and whatever else you have running want your computer's full attention at the same instant.

Newspapers and Magazines Online

17

Most people have stacks of magazines or newspapers that have been sitting untouched for, well, *way* too long.

I'd tell you that now is the time for you to haul that mess to the recycling center, but doing that task would probably put this chapter over its hour time limit.

Anyway, America Online offers a solution for periodical build-up—paperless magazines and newspapers that you can read online in the Newsstand.

The Newsstand

AOL's Newsstand, like its namesake, is an area that collects all the online publications into one location for easy browsing. The easiest way to get to it (without digging through a lot of intermediate windows) is to use the keyword NEWSSTAND. You'll be browsing through your favorite magazines and newspapers before you know it. You can see the Newsstand in Figure 17.6.

Figure 17.6.

The Newsstand has tons of publications—and no annoying subscription cards or perfume samples.

Featured areas

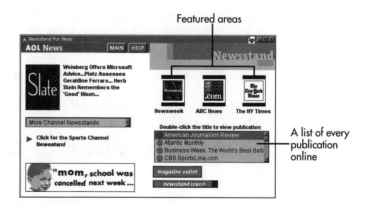

A list of every publication online

As with most areas online, the Newsstand has a selection of buttons that take you to featured areas online—just click a button and go. The large list box lets you scroll through every publication available on AOL. When you find one that interests you, double-click its name to visit its area online.

Don't get too attached to the Newsstand as shown here, though. It's a chameleon, changing its appearance on an almost daily basis. Different magazines, newspapers, and particular articles are featured regularly.

The online versions of these publications compare favorably with what you'll find on your corner newsstand, but they aren't always *exactly* the same as the copies you'd buy in a store. In some cases, you get a complete copy of a publication's most recent issue. In other cases, you get access to a periodical's back issues. Yet in other cases, you get a condensed, online version of the publication. However, in almost every case, you get the full text of the featured articles in the publication.

News Profiles

Back in Figure 17.6, at the upper left of the screen you'll see AOL.

AOL News Profiles is a very cool—and free—feature of the Newsstand. It's a *personal agent*, which means it searches for articles that meet the criteria you've selected in your News Profile. The articles that match your profile are automatically delivered to your online mailbox. Pair your News Profile with Automatic AOL (the name and subject of Hour 9, "Using AOL to Get to the Internet"), and you'll always have something interesting to read.

To set up your own News Profile, double-click the AOL News Profiles entry in the list box. An AOL News Profile window opens. Click Create a Profile, and follow the onscreen directions. You can complete your profile in only six easy steps.

Make sure to follow the instructions carefully. Also, remember to limit your news searches with very specific criteria—as described in the "News Sources on America Online" section earlier. If you don't limit your searches, you will be deluged with email that will clog your mailbox.

Should you find that your profile is returning news that doesn't really suit your interests, you can return to AOL News Profiles and use the Modify a Profile button to edit or completely change your existing profile.

Local News from Digital City

If you're looking for news from a specific city or area, Digital City is the place to go.

Click the Local button on the main Channels display, or select Local from the Channels menu on the toolbar. The Digital City screen, shown in Figure 17.7, will open.

17

Figure 17.7.

You can get Local News from the Local Channel and Digital City.

Or you can click the Local News button

You can zero in on your hometown by clicking the map

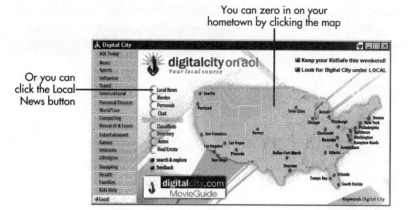

To home in on a particular city, click on a region of the map. Once you're in the region, click the city of your choice. You'll find all sorts of local resources, including news.

If local news is all you want, click the Local News button on the Digital City main screen (it's indicated in Figure 17.7), and you'll open a list of all the local news resources online, broken down by city name. Scroll through the list to find the city you want, then double-click its name.

News Sources on the Internet

There is no simple way to summarize all the news offerings you'll find on the Internet. There are, however, some good places to start. Just about any search engine—such as AOL NetFind, Yahoo!, Excite, and Lycos—will yield a huge number of news sites on the Net. If you don't remember what a search engine is, you may want to skip back to Hour 12, "The World Wide Web," to refresh your memory.

If you'd rather browse than search, you can find a great directory of Internet news sites at `http://www.ecola.com/news/`. This site takes you to the Ecola Newsstand, shown in Figure 17.8. While you're looking at Figure 17.8, get those *uncola, e coli,* and *Ebola* puns out of your system.

The Ecola Newsstand lets you search, by state, for newspapers that publish online editions. It's a great place to begin your quest for news on the Net.

17

Figure 17.8.

Search the Ecola Newsstand directory for news web sites.

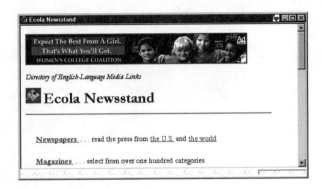

The Big Guys

Another way to find news on the Internet is to start with the big guys—those huge daily newspapers and weekly magazines that have their own web sites.

USA Today, the *New York Times,* the *Chicago Tribune, Time* magazine, and many others have outstanding online editions. Their web addresses can be found in their paper versions (if you have a copy), or you can exercise your web-searching skills with AOL NetFind. (Did I mention that web search tools are covered back in Hour 12?)

The Little Guys

You might be surprised to find, however, that a lot of smaller publications—and not just dailies—maintain online editions. Again, the Ecola News site maintains an up-to-date list of the sites of newspapers of all different sizes.

Check with your local paper to see whether it has a site. You'll find references to the site salted throughout the paper—probably on the editorial and classified sections, too.

Don't scoff at the idea of your local paper having a web site; at least check before you scoff. Some small papers, in some pretty small towns, have fairly elaborate web sites. Check out Figure 17.9, which shows the web site of the *Scranton Times* and *Tribune* in Scranton, Pennsylvania—a small-town newspaper, if ever there was one.

These local sites can be great resources for news, advertisements, classifieds, and more. Many have links to connect you with your local government, schools, and area businesses. I regularly use my local paper's site to check movie times.

If you've left your hometown and are feeling homesick, local newspaper sites keep you in touch with community events and other goings-on, so you won't feel so far from home.

17

Figure 17.9.

Many small, local newspapers have web sites. Really.

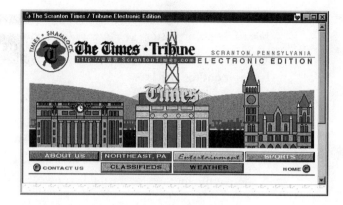

Summary

In this hour you explored many of the news sources available on both AOL and the Internet. Online news is a great way to keep up with current events, without getting buried under a pile of newspapers and magazines or spending hours staring at the TV.

Workshop

Use the following workshop to solidify the skills you've learned in this hour.

Q&A

Q Are there any places to chat about the news?

A Of course there are. Go into People Connection, and you'll find a number of chat rooms that are centered on news topics, especially politics and sports. You also can click the News Talk button, found on many of the News Channel's screens.

Q I've seen some news sites on the Internet that had some incorrect information. What gives?

A Not all sites that claim to contain news have "news" in the unbiased, verify-your-facts, journalistic sense of the word. Many organizations use the Internet to further their own cause with biased, *faux*-news presented in an authoritative news reporting style. As a general rule of thumb, when you're dealing with an unknown source on the Internet, take everything you read with a large grain of salt.

Quiz

Take the following quiz to test your knowledge of news sources on America Online and the Internet.

Questions

1. While reading a news story on America Online, you can do which of the following?

   a. Save the article to your hard drive.

   b. Print out the article.

   c. Both of the above.

   d. Neither of the above.

2. If you can't find a specific publication on AOL, you should

   a. Give up. The publication doesn't exist online.

   b. Search the Internet for the publication.

   c. Cancel your subscription to the publication.

3. You should be specific when you enter search criteria because if you're not

   a. You'll get way too many matches.

   b. You won't get any matches.

   c. America Online will get mad at you.

Answers

1. **c.**

2. **b.**

3. **a.**

Activity

Go get yourself some news!

Spend some time working your way through AOL's News Channel, then shoot off to the Internet. You'll be amazed at how many media outlets have web sites.

If you aren't sure where to start, try finding your local newspapers, either in Digital City or on the Internet.

17

Hour 18

Entertainment Online

If you want to get technical about it—most of this book is about your entertainment options online. More than half the time people spend on AOL is spent looking for entertainment. Chat, the Sports Channel, online shopping—it's all entertainment in one form or another.

This hour is about entertainment in the strictest sense—that is, the Entertainment Channel, with all the glitz, glamour, and gossip with which it's associated.

Whether you think of it as Hollywood, or Holly*weird*, the entertainment industry is always full of surprises. So is America Online. Its entertainment offerings are all over the map, from music to movies to television and more.

This hour covers the following:

- ☐ Hollywood Online
- ☐ *Entertainment Weekly*
- ☐ ABC Online
- ☐ Critic's Choice
- ☐ Columnists and Features
- ☐ Music and other entertainment features online
- ☐ Entertainment on the Internet

Hollywood Online

Are you a movie fan? Do you spend a lot of your free time in dark theaters, with surround-sound speakers pounding in your ears, and your fingers all greasy from buttery flavored popcorn?

Yeah, me too.

Not surprisingly, America Online has top-notch offerings for movie fans, including Hollywood Online. To get to Hollywood Online, you start with the Entertainment Channel, shown in Figure 18.1. To get to the Entertainment Channel, click the Entertainment button on the Channels screen, or select Entertainment from the Channels menu on the toolbar.

TIME SAVER

If you want to cut right to the chase, as they say in Hollywood, you can get to Hollywood Online by using the keyword HOLLYWOOD.

Figure 18.1.

The Entertainment Channel is entertainment central.

Click movies

After the Entertainment Channel's main screen is open, click the Movies button to go to the Movies area. From there, you get to Hollywood Online by selecting its name from the drop-down menu of movie-related areas. Hollywood Online, shown in Figure 18.2, will open its digital doors to you.

The movie marquee is actually two links to the main Hollywood Online areas: Coming Soon and Feature Presentations. One of my personal favorites is the Coming Soon area. Click on the left side of the marquee and you'll open the Coming Soon area shown in Figure 18.3.

Coming Soon offers movie fans a lot: You can read movie notes, see still photos from new releases, play games, download movie trailers, and much, much more.

18

Figure 18.2.
Welcome to Hollywood Online.

Movie previews

Current features and news

Forum options
(Chat, message
boards, and so on)

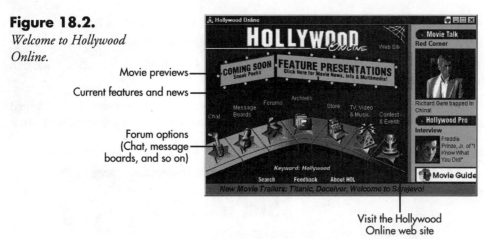

Visit the Hollywood
Online web site

Figure 18.3.
Coming Soon gives you the scoop on movies that are "Coming soon to a theater near you."

Movie &
Video
guides—
double-click
to view

Click a feature button

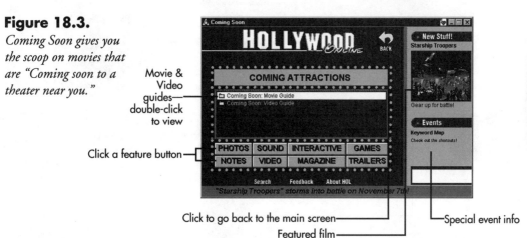

Click to go back to the main screen

Featured film

Special event info

18

Back on the main Hollywood Online screen are links to forums and chat rooms—some of America Online's liveliest. Often, you'll see announcements about the next celebrity to appear in its live chat room. Special events like these are always fun; be sure to mark your calendar.

Entertainment Weekly

Entertainment Weekly magazine sometimes gets lumped in with some of the other pop-culture or celebrity magazines that offer, well, a less journalistic approach to their profession. All right, all right, I mean trashy gossip magazines.

Entertainment Weekly is much more than gossip. It's all about movies, behind the scenes information, box office reports, trends, and, okay, a little gossip, too.

An online version of *Entertainment Weekly* is available with all the features, stories, and reviews that make the printed magazine so popular.

You'll find *Entertainment Weekly* in the same Movies drop-down menu as Hollywood Online, or you can use the keyword EW. When the *Entertainment Weekly* window opens, it will look like the one shown in Figure 18.4.

Figure 18.4.

Entertainment Weekly Online.

COFFEE BREAK

Entertainment Weekly on AOL is little more than a list box of features. That's because it's one of the areas online that blurs the distinction between AOL and the Internet. While there's an *Entertainment Weekly* window on AOL, and you can use a keyword to get to it, all the *Entertainment Weekly* content is on web pages on the Internet. Pretty cool, huh?

One of the best features of *Entertainment Weekly* on America Online is the weekly Parents' Guide, the item that's selected in Figure 18.4. The Parents' Guide offers helpful tips on which movies are appropriate, and more important, which aren't appropriate for your child to watch.

EW Interactive has some great things to offer: a full version of the magazine's current issue; a searching tool to let you find articles from past issues; a multimedia library; and more.

ABC Online

Television fans will want to check out ABC Online, also found in the Entertainment Channel. To get there fast, use the keyword ABC.

18

The main ABC Online screen (shown in Figure 18.5) gives you access to just about everything on ABC, including the soaps, news, sports, kids programming, and Oprah Winfrey. ABC Online also offers the usual assortment of forum features: chat, file libraries, message boards, games, and even a chance to shop.

Figure 18.5.

From soaps to Good Morning America, *ABC Online has it.*

Soapline Daily is a particularly popular area, especially for those who for one reason or another are forced to miss a day or two of their favorite daytime dramas. This area helps you catch up with who's doing what to whom, and all the other assorted, sordid happenings of daily life in these shows. Click the ABC Soaps button on the bottom of the main screen to get up to date with your favorite stories.

Folks not into the soaps can try the links to ABC News, ABC Sports, ABC Kidz, Oprah, and the ABC TV prime-time lineup of shows.

Critic's Choice

If you can't get enough of Siskel and Ebert, I have some advice for you: Check out Critics Inc. You can get there quickly using the keyword CRITICS. When the Critics Inc. window opens, you'll be able to wallow in reviews and opinions about movies, television, books, music, and more (see Figure 18.6).

JUST A MINUTE

You may notice that Critics' Choice isn't as pretty as some of the other areas online. Whenever there's a major overhaul to the AOL software (like the 4.0 upgrade), some cosmetic changes are usually made to all the areas online. It's like slapping on a fresh coat of paint. Look for Critics' Choice—and lots of other areas online—to get total makeovers in the coming months.

Figure 18.6.

Critics' Choice covers more than just movies.

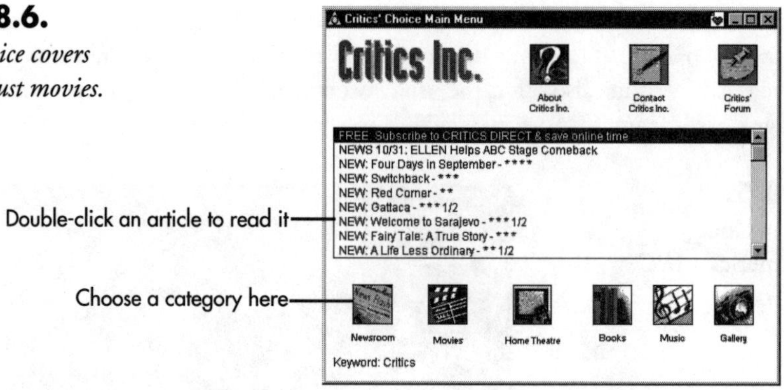

Double-click an article to read it —

Choose a category here —

First of all, Critics' Choice has a great chat room, where all you amateur critics have a chance to air your views alongside those of other Siskel and Ebert wannabes. To visit the chat room, click the Critics' Forum button to open the forum window. Then, click the Chat button.

Critics' Choice also has a great index full of reviews, but to really get down to business, you'll want to zip right to one of the main topic areas, to narrow your search and satisfy your craving for criticism quickly. The topic choices are Newsroom (for news), Movies, Home Theater (video rentals), Books, Music, and even a Gallery of files you can download.

Reviews from some of the top reviewers in the country are found here, reviews you could find only if you subscribed to every newspaper and magazine in the United States.

Cartoons

Are you a fan of the funnies?

Well, about 90 percent of the world is a *Dilbert* fan. The author, Scott Adams, is an America Online member and proud of it—his AOL email address is listed with the cartoon every day.

You can find *Dilbert,* and other comic strips, in AOL's Cartoons area. To get there, use the keyword FUNNIES. You'll land at the Funny Pages screen shown in Figure 18.7.

TIME SAVER

Want an instant chuckle? Click the AOL logo on the Welcome screen and you'll go to Daily Delights. It features a *Dilbert* cartoon in postcard form, which you can send to a friend, plus links to your daily horoscope and other areas.

18

Figure 18.7.

See you in the Funny Pages.

Cartoon Network

Dilbert

DC Comics   Web sites

Besides *Dilbert*, there are other cartoons you can read every day (including editorial cartoons by Mike Keefe), and check out the latest from the Cartoon Network (*Dexter's Laboratory* is a hoot).

Music, Music, Music

If you haven't noticed, the online world is a digital smorgasbord. Because the music industry is largely digital these days, the two are a perfect fit. The Music area in the Entertainment Channel demonstrates this admirably.

To go to the Music area, click the Music button on the Entertainment main screen, or use the keyword MUSIC. You can see the Music screen in Figure 18.8.

18

Figure 18.8.

Your link to the music industry.

New music releases

Drop-down menu of Music areas

Featured   Music
musical group genres

For the younger side of the demographic scale, you can visit MTV Online and *Rolling Stone*. For the—*uh*—*other* end of the demographic spectrum, you'll also find VH-1 online.

Music is such a personal taste kind of thing, that I'll leave you to explore on your own. Click the button for your favorite genre of music (Alt/Rock, Pop, R&B, Country, Classical, or Jazz) and soak up some sounds. If you'd care to swap stories and opinions with other music fans, check out the Music Message Center.

Music Message Center

The Music Message Center is a message board of epic proportions. It enables folks with varying degrees of musical knowledge and tastes to share their opinions with the rest of the listening public.

To get the Message Center, click the Word of Mouth button on any genre screen, and then click the Message Center button. The Message Center works like all message boards online and like the newsgroups discussed in Hour 10, "Newsgroups and Mailing Lists."

If you want to have some real fun, enter the Alt/Rock area and post a message along the lines of, "The Beatles were overrated," and wait to see the response. It can be quite, *er*, educational? Irrational? Inflammatory?

On second thought, don't do that. You don't want to start a flame war, or anything…

A favorite part of the Music Message Center is the Member Reviews board, where you can find out what other music fans think of the latest releases.

Watch Out for Streaming Audio and Video

One of the coolest features of AOL 4.0 is streaming audio and video. What is it? In some forums, you'll hear *background music* while you're looking at a screen. In another area, you'll be able to look at slideshows and video clips from your favorite TV shows and movies.

Want to check it out? The Nickelodeon Forum (keyword NICK) has streaming audio. You can use the keyword SLIDESHOW to get a peek at streaming video—including one of David Letterman's Top 10 Lists.

Streaming? It's *steaming*, as in hot.

Entertainment on the Internet

Millions, possibly billions, of web sites exist that are related in one way or another to entertainment. If you're up for the challenge of exploring on your own, you might want to

18

skip right to AOL NetFind (as discussed in Hour 12, "The World Wide Web") and search for your favorite entertainment topics. Otherwise, you might want to check out some of these links to the Internet that you'll find right on AOL.

If it's music you're after, you can select MuchMusic from the drop-down menu on the Music main screen. You'll go to the MuchMusic forum, and from there you can click the link to muchmusic.com. MuchMusic's web site is a mass of music information—you can take a peek at it in Figure 18.9.

Figure 18.9.

muchmusic.com *is your link to music on the web.*

If it's movies you like, I have two suggestions. First, you can skip back to Hollywood Online, and click its Web button on the main screen (refer to Figure 18.2).

Second, you can find out what's playing at your local Cineplex with MovieLink at http:// www.movielink.com. MovieLink lets you search for the movie listings in your area either by city or ZIP code.

Before you head to the theater, you might want to check out a review. Dozens of sites offer reviews. Many newspapers offer reviews within their larger web sites. To find them all, point your browser to the Yahoo! directory at http://www.yahoo.com. Click the Entertainment link, then the Movies and Films link, and finally, the Reviews link.

For the more browser-savvy among you, you can simply use this address as an AOL keyword, and sidestep all that clicking and linking: http://www.yahoo.com/Entertainment/ Movies_and_Films/Reviews/.

Summary

In this hour, you learned about many of the offerings of AOL's Entertainment Channel, and entertainment-related sites on the Internet.

Workshop

Use the following workshop to solidify your knowledge of entertainment on America Online and the Internet.

Q&A

Q What if I don't want to find out about the entertainment industry, but want to find something to keep me entertained while on America Online?

A A fair question. Check out the Games Channel, where you'll find lots of fun games to play online and others that can be downloaded and played on your own time.

Q What about Dave? I'm a big fan of David Letterman. Did America Online forget about me?

A Not a chance. If Stupid Human Tricks is your bag, check out the Late Show Online at the keyword LATE SHOW.

Quiz

Take the following quiz to find out if you know how to entertain yourself on AOL.

Questions

1. To find out about the entertainment industry, you should check which of the following?
    a. The News Channel
    b. The Entertainment Channel
    c. Both of the above

2. On ABC Online, you can do which of the following?
    a. Keep up with your soaps.
    b. Read about new shows coming in the fall.
    c. Read about ABC personalities.
    d. All of the above.

3. You can find information on Janet Jackson in which of these areas online?
    a. ABC Online
    b. MuchMusic
    c. Learning and Culture

18

Answers

1. **c.** The News Channel (covered in Hour 17, "Your Computer as a News Source") features Entertainment news, too.

2. **d.**

3. **b.**

Activities

1. Spend some time bopping around the Entertainment Channel and then see how many different links you can find to the Internet.

2. As a test, use the Entertainment Channel, and its web links, to see how much information you can find out about a movie that hasn't been released yet.

18

V

Hour **19**

Personal Finance

Every day millions of people put money away for this or that. Maybe they want to save for college expenses (a phrase that sends chills down the spines of most parents). Maybe they want to save for their retirement. Maybe they want to just plain *save*.

Regardless of the motivation, they sock money away in IRAs, stock portfolios, mutual funds, and the bond market. In short, they invest.

Every day the world markets rise and fall, and those whose futures are closely linked to these peaks and valleys struggle, trying to keep up with all the changes. Just how can you keep up with it?

AOL's Personal Finance Channel helps you not only keep up with your investments, but gives you the tools you need to make your investments work harder for you. In this hour, you'll learn how to use the Personal Finance Channel to

- ☐ Track your personal stock portfolio
- ☐ Research companies as potential investments
- ☐ Use the PC Financial Network
- ☐ Grow your business
- ☐ Locate entrepreneurs and investors on the Internet

Your Stock Portfolio

A stock portfolio is, basically, all the stock market investments you've made lumped together. To know if your stocks are performing well, you need to track them. In terms of tracking stocks, AOL's Portfolios area is an investor's best friend. Even better, you don't have to be a *real* investor to try it out—you can pretend, without risk, to see how you do as a Wall Street tycoon.

To begin, you need to get yourself to the Personal Finance Channel. You can click the Personal Finance button on the main Channels screen, use the Personal Finance button on the left side of any Channel's Main Screen, or select Personal Finance from the Channels menu on the AOL toolbar. You can even use the keyword PERSONAL FINANCE.

Click the Portfolios button to open the Portfolios window, as shown in Figure 19.1. You'll already have a portfolio in the list box, but it will be empty.

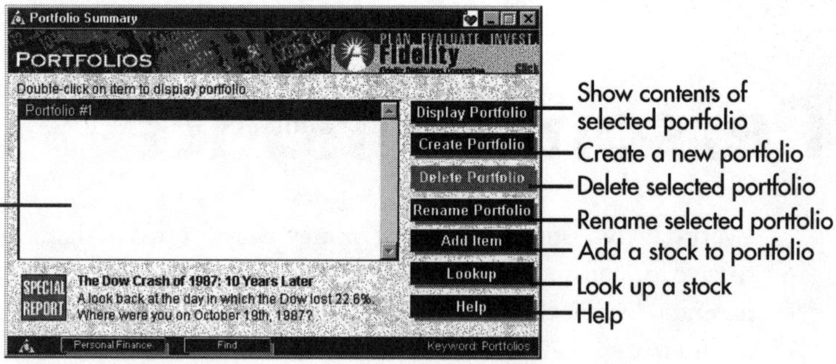

Figure 19.1.

Build a stock portfolio here—either real or imaginary.

Portfolios appear here

Show contents of selected portfolio
Create a new portfolio
Delete selected portfolio
Rename selected portfolio
Add a stock to portfolio
Look up a stock
Help

JUST A MINUTE

Remember, when you're building your portfolio, you *aren't actually buying anything*. You can add stocks you don't own to your portfolio, or even build a completely fictitious portfolio of real stocks. If you plan to invest without the help of a qualified financial planner, you should build a practice portfolio before you put your hard-earned money on the line. It will give you a chance to see how the market works, and how good you are at selecting performance stocks.

19

Starting a Portfolio

Nothing exciting will happen in your portfolio—actually, nothing *at all* will happen—until you put some stocks in there. Here's how to do it.

You've already got a generic portfolio called Portfolio #1. You can work with just that one, or you can get fancy. If you're a big-time investor, you might want to divide your stocks up by category and create a portfolio for each one. You can create up to 20 portfolios, with as many as 100 stocks in each one.

To create a portfolio, click the Create Portfolio button. You'll be asked to give the portfolio a name, and then you're ready to start adding stocks. You can call your portfolio(s) whatever you want.

Building a Portfolio

With one or more portfolios on hand, you're ready to begin adding stocks. You add stocks by using their market symbols—you know, that abbreviated gibberish that's always scrolling across the bottom of the screen on CNN and CNBC. They're also the symbols that appear in the financial section of your newspaper.

Most folks don't know stock market symbols off the top of their heads, and that's okay. The easiest way to add a stock to your portfolio neatly sidesteps the symbol issue. Because it's the easy method, why don't you play along?

Adding Stocks to Your Portfolio

It's easy to add an area to your Favorite Places. Simply find an area you like, then follow these easy steps:

1. In the Portfolios window, click the Lookup button to open a little Search Symbols dialog box.

2. Enter the first few characters of a company's name in the text box.

3. Click the Search By Company button. You'll open a list of companies whose names begin with the letters you've entered.

4. Scroll through the list until you find the company you want (you may need to click the More button to see all the company names in the list). Click on the name to select it.

5. Click Get Quote. You'll get a detailed quote on the stock you selected, like the one shown in Figure 19.2.

6. If the stock is one that you want to add to your portfolio, make a note of its Last Price (the fourth line of the quote), then click the Add to Portfolio button at the bottom of the quote.

19

Figure 19.2.
Adding a stock to your portfolio—the lazy way.

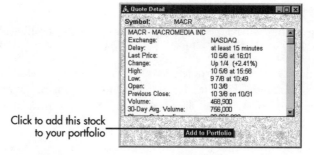

Click to add this stock
to your portfolio

7. AOL will ask to which portfolio you want the stock added. Click the name of the appropriate (or only) portfolio, and click the OK button.

8. Next you'll see an Enter Item dialog box with two text boxes. In the top box, enter the number of shares you want to add to your portfolio. Below that, enter the amount you paid for the stock. If you're just pretending, enter the Last Price from the Quote screen. Click OK.

 You can repeat the process for as many stocks as you'd care to add to your portfolio, up to 100 stocks.

Displaying a Portfolio

After you've built your portfolio, you can check its current value and your profit or loss, anytime you're online.

To check a portfolio, click the name of the portfolio in the Portfolios window, then click the Display Portfolio button. The portfolio will open in a window like the one shown in Figure 19.3.

Individual stocks   Total value, plus profit or loss on investment

Figure 19.3.
Your stock portfolio tracks the progress of investments. Hey, I did pretty well...

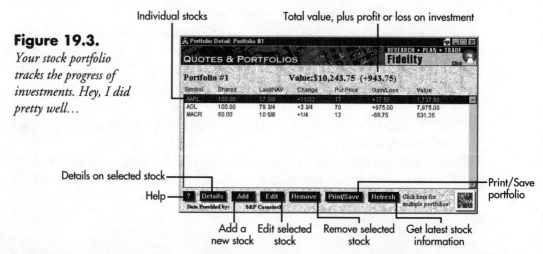

Details on selected stock
Help
Add a new stock
Edit selected stock
Remove selected stock
Get latest stock information
Print/Save portfolio

Conducting Company Research

Before you actually buy stock, it's a good idea to look into the company a little bit. Unless it's a company you know well, you'd be well advised to *look* into it before you *buy* into it.

Even if you're only pretending, it's still a good idea to research a company before you buy their stock. It will prepare you for those hard choices when you actually decide to take the plunge (sorry, probably shouldn't use the word *plunge* in reference to the market).

To research a company's track record on the market, add it to your portfolio, as you did in the To Do exercise previously. Then follow these steps:

1. Display your portfolio.
2. Click the company name, and click the Details button on the bottom of the Portfolio window (the Details button was shown earlier in Figure 19.3).

   The Details button gives you a window much like the stock quote you saw back in Figure 19.2, except for one difference—along the bottom of the quote, there are three buttons. Each button gives you valuable information about the company and its stock:

   ☐ **Market News**—Gives you the latest news about the stock market. Although it may not feature the company you're looking at, it *will* give you a feel for trends in the market as a whole.

   ☐ **Historical**—Gives you the performance of the stock over a longer period of time. For stocks, you'll see highs, lows, and opening and closing prices. For mutual funds, you'll see a line graph.

   ☐ **News By Ticker**—Offers news stories, such as Market News, but you'll only see stories about the company you're researching, so it's right-to-the-point information. This information is recent, only going back a few weeks.

If you take your time and do your homework, you'll be a much wiser (and happier) investor.

DLJ Direct

If you're ready to invest some real dollars, you might want to start with DLJ Direct (you may have heard of it under its previous name, *The PC Financial Network*).

DLJ (for Donaldson, Lufkin, and Jennette) Direct gives you the chance to invest your money in real time, through your computer and AOL, all in the comfort of your own home. To get to DLJ Direct, use the keyword DLJdirect. You'll arrive at the screen shown in Figure 19.4.

19

Figure 19.4.

Buy, sell, and trade with DLJ Direct.

The Demo Account option is a great way to get some practice before you really invest. It works much the same as the phony portfolio you created earlier.

DLJ Direct is a company offering real financial services, so (beyond the Demo Account) real money is involved when you open an account with them. After you open your account, you can buy, sell, or trade at any time, and the whole thing takes place electronically.

AOL doesn't add any extra fees when you use this service, but you will have to pay commissions to DLJ Direct for your transactions.

CAUTION

Remember, this is real money you'll be dealing with here. Anything you do within this area is at your own risk. Make sure you are making informed decisions before you conduct your financial business. You should also know that AOL does *not* guarantee that the information presented online is accurate. It's *Enter at your own risk* all the way.

Your Business

Your Business is a resource for small businesses. Actually, it doesn't matter if your business concern is large or small. The Your Business area is *really* helpful. It's geared toward entrepreneurs, folks who want to be entrepreneurs, or even those who hope to be one when they grow up (like I do).

Your Business is the place to get all the information you need to get yourself started or to get some helpful advice to keep your business moving forward. You can see Your Business in Figure 19.5. You can get there by using the keyword YOUR BUSINESS.

JUST A MINUTE

Okay, okay, okay. So Your Business is part of the Work Place Channel. So shoot me. It still has to do with your Personal Finance, especially if you're an entrepreneur.

Figure 19.5.

Your Business has services for the entrepreneur.

Among the services available in Your Business, you'll find lists of regional city, state, and government resources to help you along the way (click Regional Resources on the Your Business window). You can also get advice on Getting Started, Sales & Marketing, Doing Business Online, and more. Click the button for the topic you want on the right side of the Your Business window.

The Business Strategies Forum message boards are helpful, too (click Chat & Messages on the main screen). Business people use the message boards to share their ideas, concerns, and solutions with other entrepreneurs online. Specific boards are dedicated to marketing, home businesses, government, consultants, and more.

Personal Finance on the Internet

The Internet, as limitless as it is, offers thousands of finance-related sites.

As always, you can start with a search of your topic of choice, using one of the major search engines. Be warned that your search may result in a list of sites way too long for any one to explore.

A better option might be to use AOL NetFind Investment Time Savers and the Wall Street Journal Interactive Edition discussed in the following sections.

AOL NetFind Investment Time Savers

AOL NetFind Investment Time Savers is an index page on AOL's NetFind. It puts together a sort of clearinghouse of investment-related sites on the Internet (see Figure 19.6). Although it covers much more than investment, a number of personal finance and business-related indexes are available.

Figure 19.6.

NetFind Investment Time Savers has tips for investors.

To get to the NetFind Investment area, click the Internet menu on AOL's toolbar, then select AOL NetFind. On the main NetFind page, click the Investment (or Business, or whichever) Time Savers link. The URL savvy can go directly to the page shown in Figure 19.6 by using this address as a keyword: `http://www.aol.com/netfind/timesavers/money.html`.

For more on using AOL NetFind, skip back to Hour 12, "The World Wide Web."

The *Wall Street Journal,* Interactive Edition

The *Wall Street Journal* has been *the* newspaper for business people and investors for years and years. Now, WSJ's Interactive Edition works that old Wall Street magic in cyberspace.

To go there, use this address as an AOL keyword: `http://update.wsj.com`.

Good advice doesn't come cheap, and any investor will tell you that sometimes you have to spend a little money to make money. To that end, I must inform you that after you read WSJ's basic information page, the rest of the site can be read by subscription only.

Typically, you get a free trial period when you agree to sign up, and you may cancel without charge any time before the trial period is up.

The online edition is structured like the newspaper, but the Interactive Edition's stories, tables, graphics, and so on are all updated throughout the course of the business day. There is no "daily edition," the Interactive Edition is always hot off the press.

Straight from the Source

If you want market information, go to the marketplace. Use these addresses as keywords, and you'll zip right to these market sites:

19

☐ **The New York Stock Exchange**—http://www.nyse.com

☐ **The NASDAQ Stock Market**—http://www.nasdaq.com

Summary

In this hour, you learned where to go on both AOL and the Internet for some helpful resources and advice about managing your personal finances. What you choose to do with that knowledge is, of course, your business.

Workshop

Use the following workshop to reaffirm what you've learned in this hour.

Q&A

Q I found a site on the Internet that promises me the chance to make millions if I agree to invest. It says I can use a cash advance from my credit card to open my account. What should I do?

A RUN AWAY! The Internet, for all its practical uses, can be used by some to run scams against ordinary people. Just like you shouldn't give out your credit card number to strangers on the phone, don't give it on the Internet or AOL. You're just asking for trouble.

Q You mentioned AOL NetFind's Business Time Savers. Don't the other search engines have similar features?

A Yes, they do. If you prefer another search page, go ahead and use it. It will link you to many of the same sites.

19

Quiz

Take the following quiz to test your knowledge of Personal Finance on America Online and the Internet.

Questions

1. I can use a portfolio within America Online to
    a. Buy stocks
    b. Sell stocks
    c. Keep track of investments
2. Some good places to check for information on a company are
    a. Get Quote
    b. News by Ticker

    c. Both of the above

    d. None of the above

3. Business Strategies Forum Message Boards offer

    a. Information for investors

    b. Information for business owners/managers

    c. Information for stock brokers

Answers

1. **c.**

2. **c.**

3. **b.**

Activity

A large number of business- and finance-related areas on AOL were not covered here. Take some time to snoop around and explore other areas—you might find some that are useful to you.

19

Hour 20

Sports Online

As the online world began to attract the attention of the newly computer-literate masses, one of the first subjects to appear with really top-notch content was—you guessed it—sports.

Since then (that is a couple of years ago, which may as well be a century in technological years), sports coverage online has increased dramatically, along with the rest of the online world. In this hour, you'll get a basic idea of what's available on America Online and the Internet for sports fans—and do it in about the same time it takes Tiger Woods to make three birdies and an eagle at Augusta National.

We'll focus, of course, on sports areas on AOL, but don't overlook what the Internet has to offer sports fans—it's amazing, both in quantity and quality.

In this hour, you'll learn

- ☐ Sports Channel basics
- ☐ How to check the scores and statistics
- ☐ Where to find sports news stories
- ☐ How to join a Fantasy sports team online
- ☐ The top sports sites on the Internet

Sports Channel Basics

We sports nuts love a good sports channel. We were intrigued when ESPN debuted as the first all-sports television network. In a short period of time, we were more than intrigued—we were hooked.

Then came ESPN2, CNNSI, ESPN News, and the many regional and local sports channels across the country. Apparently, we just can't get enough sports coverage.

America Online has its own Sports Channel, and although it's different from its cable counterparts (more interactive, for example), it has a lot of similarities.

America Online's Sports Channel offers up-to-the-minute scores, stats, stories, live chat, and more. Let's start by taking a look at the Sports Channel's main window, shown in Figure 20.1. To get here, click the Sports button on the main Channels display (or any Channel's Main Screen). You can also select Sports from the Channels menu on the AOL toolbar.

Figure 20.1.

The main Sports Channel window is your starting point.

The Sports Channel Main Screen has the typical features of all Channel screens—featured stories, links to favorite areas, and buttons for the Channel's departments. The Sports Channel screen is dominated by buttons for the three most popular areas in the Channel—the Scoreboard, News Top Stories, and the Grandstand.

Beside those three links, you'll find a list of sports you can click to visit the related forum.

Just click the sport of your choice to get a specialized window completely devoted to that sport. If your favorite sport isn't listed here, it may be listed under More Sports (which opens an additional list), or may be grouped under the Fitness, Outdoor, or Extreme headings.

20

COFFEE BREAK

If you want even *more* coverage of a sport such as hockey (that's more popular in Canada), or even cricket (that's popular in the United Kingdom), you can go to keyword CANADA or UK, and visit *their* sports areas. How cool is that?

Most sports junkies need an immediate fix of scores and stats. You have a couple of options for getting them as you'll see in the following sections.

Scores and Statistics

As sports fans, we crave constant updates—*What's the score? What's the score? What's the score?*—until we're asked to leave the room, or to *please* turn off the radio in church.

Click a Sport

Need to know what's happening in the NBA? Go to the Sports Channel and click Pro Basketball on the main screen. You'll open the Pro Basketball forum, shown in Figure 20.2.

Figure 20.2.

Every sport's forum offers scores and statistics with just a click or two.

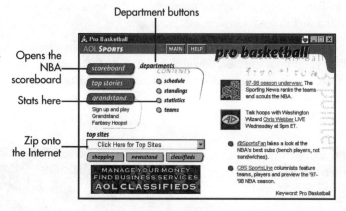

After you've opened the forum of your choice, it's easy to get a list of up-to-the-minute scores for that sport: Just click the Scoreboard button. For statistics, click Statistics in the Departments list.

The Big Scoreboard

Back on the Sports Channel Main Screen (refer to Figure 20.1), you can go right to the granddaddy of all scoreboards by clicking the Scoreboard button. It opens the window shown in Figure 20.3, and gives you access to scores for the NBA, NCAAFB, NBA, and NHL.

20

Click to open a scoreboard

Figure 20.3.

The Scoreboard gives you all the available scores and more.

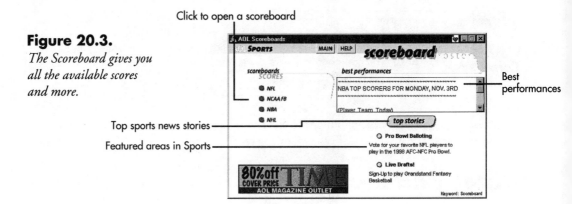

Best performances

Top sports news stories

Featured areas in Sports

From here, you have access to scores from every major sport, including collegiate scores.

STATS Sports

If you think that scores are just numbers, then you haven't visited STATS Sports online—or read your local newspaper lately. Besides the score of the big game, we sports fans crave tons of *statistics*. Do you know what Ken Griffey Jr.'s batting average is against left-handers on Tuesday nights in which the game-time temperature was 75 degrees or higher and there was a slight breeze blowing in?

Neither do I. (Actually, you're not going to find that here or anywhere else online—you start worrying about stuff like that and you're ready for the sports wing at the Betty Ford Clinic.) You can, however, find all kinds of interesting statistics in the STATS Sports forum. You can get there with the keyword STATS. The STATS Sports forum is shown in Figure 20.4—it's statistics heaven.

Figure 20.4.

Statistics freaks find a home in STATS Sports.

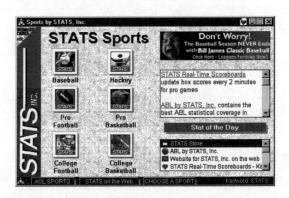

You'll find the most comprehensive statistics available in the online world. However, it only covers professional sports, so don't go looking for the batting averages of the University of Texas baseball team here.

Sports News

Scores and stats may not be enough for you. If you missed a game, you might want to get play-by-play coverage with full color commentary. You can, in Sports News. Click the Top Stories button on the Sports Channel's Main Screen. You'll be zapped into the News Channel's sports department.

You can also click the Top Stories button in any individual sport's Forum, and go right to the coverage of that particular sport. Naturally, the news contents change all the time, but you'll typically find

- [ ] Game stories
- [ ] Previews
- [ ] Feature stories
- [ ] Injury reports
- [ ] Updates on trades and other roster moves

Sports News comes from the same sources as the rest of the news online, principally Reuters and Knight-Ridder news services.

Sporting News

The *Sporting News*, one of America's oldest and most respected sports publications, offers an online edition of the paper on AOL. You can get there from the Sports Channel (you'll need to dig for it) or you can speed right to it with the keyword SPORTING NEWS.

All the *Sporting News'* regular columns, features, and top-notch reporting is available in their forum.

ABC Sports Online

Similarly, ABC Sports offers an online edition, which you can see in Figure 20.5.

Figure 20.5.

Get the latest from ABC Sports Online.

20

Monday Night Football!!

Sports drop-down menu

In ABC Online, you'll get coverage of the latest events being covered at the network, plus special areas for chat, scores, and a chance to go behind-the-scenes at the network.

You can zero in on a favorite sport with the sports drop-down menu shown in Figure 20.5. Just select your favorite sport from the menu, and you'll go right to the ABC Sports area devoted to that sport. One of my personal favorites is the *Monday Night Football* area.

During the football season, the *Monday Night Football* area offers previews, insights from the commentators, plus a lot of great inside scoop for football fans. I won't spoil it by telling you too much here—check it out for yourself.

The Grandstand

In recent years, more and more sports-talk or all-sports radio stations have cropped up around the nation. Why? Because people love to talk sports—*arguing...* I mean, *discussing...* starting lineups, which team is best, and so on.

America Online's Grandstand is perfectly suited for this purpose. To access it, you can click Grandstand on the main Sports Channel window, or you can simply use the keyword GRANDSTAND. You'll open a Grandstand window like the one shown in Figure 20.6.

Figure 20.6.

The Grandstand is like an all-talk sports radio station.

Sports Talk

Who's the best player in baseball? Can the Green Bay Packers build a dynasty? Will Tiger Woods win every major golf tournament he ever plays? These, and many other questions, are asked and answered daily in the Grandstand.

Folks who love live sports chat will find it here. The Grandstand offers chat rooms named for each sport. The boxing chat room, for example, is called *The Squared Circle*.

20

These are some of the liveliest discussions on AOL. In fact, they're usually livelier than the debates on radio, because they bring in people from all over the country.

Fantasy Leagues

Do you think you have the guts and the intelligence to run a sports team just like a real general manager? You can find out in the Grandstand.

Fantasy Leagues, which have grown enormously popular in the last decade, are becoming a favorite online, too. To get involved, or just look around, scroll through the list of forums until you find your fantasy sport. When you find it, double-click its name in the list box. During sign-up periods, you'll also find buttons linking you directly to the Fantasy forum that's currently gearing up—such as the Basketball League button indicated previously in Figure 20.6.

You can see a typical Fantasy League forum in Figure 20.7. This is the basketball forum, because that's the one that's starting up as I'm writing this.

Figure 20.7.

Fantasy Leagues test your sports knowledge.

You draft, trade, use the waiver wire, set lineups, and more, just like the coaches and general managers do in the pros. A small entry fee is charged to your America Online account when you join. At the end of the Fantasy season, prizes are awarded to the winners (usually free online time).

Sports on the Internet

A lot of sports information is available on the Internet. Beyond the thousands of sites devoted to individual sports, there are major sports servers out there that provide constant coverage of all the sports.

We'll look at two of the general sports sites here.

20

TIME SAVER

> If you want to find sites that pertain to a particular sport, try doing a search by that sport's name. The sites I'll describe here are all major sites that cover many, many sports. But if you're looking for information on, say, auto racing, try doing a search using "auto racing" or "NASCAR" as your search criteria.

ESPNet SportsZone

This site is, without a doubt, the #1 sports site on the Internet. It gets more hits than any other site, and there's a reason for it—it offers better content than any other site.

To get there, use this address as a keyword, `http://espnet.sportszone.com`, and you'll go right there. The main ESPNet page is shown in Figure 20.8.

Figure 20.8.

ESPNet is the best sports site on the web.

If you look toward the upper-left of the main page, a constantly rotating scoreboard keeps you updated on all games in progress (it's the blank box under the Take A Tour box in the figure—I caught it as it was changing).

Real sports nuts can click the Add to Desktop button. The scoreboard will remain on your desktop, constantly being updated, even after you've left the Internet—but *only* if you remain connected to AOL. That way, you can go back to writing your chapter and still keep up with the scores (*oops...*I gave away my little secret).

Down the left side are sport names, and each of them has its own page filled with up-to-date news, scores, stats, standings, and more.

COFFEE BREAK

Recently, ESPNet added RealAudio to its scoreboard pages. It lets you actually *listen* to live radio broadcasts of games from around the country—*if* your computer can handle it. In addition to sound equipment, you need to have some extra software, too.

You can get RealAudio, Shockwave, ActiveX, VDOLive, and other essential add-ins from `http://multimedia.aol.com` or keyword `MMSHOWCASE`. Make sure you read the system requirements and installation instructions before you download.

The news on ESPNet is constantly being updated, and ESPNet features great columns and stories. Some material is available only to subscribers, but you can do a lot without joining.

CBS SportsLine

Another outstanding sports site is CBS SportsLine, at `http://www.sportsline.com` (just use the address as a keyword). You'll get great coverage of anything CBS is broadcasting, and more. You get a running "Top News" section down the right side of the page with links to the day's top stories.

Pages are set up for each of the major sports, accessible by clicking any of the sports buttons on the SportsLine title bar. You can also slip into backstage areas where you can get some insight into the men in the truck, the CBS Sports crew. Play around a little and check it out.

Summary

In this hour, you've seen a little of what's available for sports fans on both AOL and the Internet.

Workshop

Use the following workshop to reaffirm the skills you've learned in this hour.

Q&A

Q What about recreational sports? Does AOL have anything to offer in those areas?

A Of course. From the Sports Channel Main Screen, you can click the Outdoor or More Sports buttons to find what you want. You could also use the Sports Channel's Search & Explore button to find your favorite sports online.

20

Q What if I want to find sites devoted to my favorite team?

A You can do an AOL NetFind search for the team's name (for example, "Philadelphia Flyers"), or find the appropriate league's site. They'll have an up-to-date page on each team in the league.

Quiz

Take the following quiz to test your knowledge of sports on America Online and the Internet.

Questions

1. In the Grandstand, I can
   a. Participate in sports discussions
   b. Post messages to sports boards
   c. Play in a fantasy league
   d. All of the above

2. I'll get charged extra if I join a fantasy league on AOL.
   a. True
   b. False

3. ESPNet SportsZone's rotating scoreboard
   a. Can be saved to my hard drive
   b. Can be emailed to a friend
   c. Can be added to my desktop

Answers

1. **d.**
2. **a.**
3. **c.**

Activities

Take some time to explore the Internet and America Online for sports news and information. It's like a never-ending ocean of sports information!

20

PART VI

Your Family and AOL

Hour

Hour 21

Keeping Parental Control

As a parent, you can't control *everything* your child does. You can't watch them 24 hours a day, and children also need to learn some things for themselves—sometimes the hard way.

In the online world, however, parents need to keep as much control as possible, as is appropriate for the age and maturity of the child. Sure, you want your child to learn computer skills, learn to experiment with technology, and learn to learn. But you don't want them to get at some of the material that's out there—the stuff that they're too young to understand, or that's simply inappropriate.

Understanding that parental instinct to protect, AOL offers parents the ability to control how much access their children have to the various parts of the service with Parental Controls.

This hour explains how to use those Parental Controls, one of AOL's most useful features for folks with young kids. Even if you believe your child should be left to his or her own devices online, this is still a good hour to read.

JUST A MINUTE

Don't get the idea that because this hour is all about protecting your kids online, there's nothing fun or safe for them on AOL. AOL has a lot of kid-friendly, wonderful areas. They're covered in the next two hours.

In this hour, you'll learn the following:

- ☐ The Parental Controls basics
- ☐ How to block everything but Kids Only
- ☐ How to use the Chat controls
- ☐ How to use the Instant Message controls
- ☐ How to use the Downloading controls
- ☐ How to use the Newsgroup controls
- ☐ How to use the Mail controls
- ☐ How to use the Web controls

CAUTION

What you *won't* find in this hour is me telling you what is, or isn't, appropriate for the children in your life. That's your decision. Take the information presented here and run with it—or run away from it, if you like.

The Basics of Parental Controls

Before we get into the nitty-gritty of Parental Controls, you need to understand a few basic concepts.

For the Parental Controls to work, your kids need to have their own screen name—whether that's one *each*, or just one for all, that's up to you. If your kids have been using the screen name you created when you first set up your AOL account (your master account screen name), you need to create screen names for your children, and you need to change the password for the master account screen name.

Creating screen names and changing passwords are covered in Hour 14, "Navigating Through America Online *Your* Way." It also covers using AOL 4.0's Switch Screen Name feature, if you're signed on under a screen name other than the master account name.

You can only set and change the Parental Control settings with the master account screen name. If your children have access to that account, and just a little bit of cyber-savvy, they can reset the Parental Controls whenever they like—so keep the password to your master account screen name a secret.

21

TIME SAVER

You can create up to four additional screen names for your account. If all the kids in your home are *about* the same age and level of maturity, you can probably get away with one screen name for all of them. If you've got a range of ages, and maturity levels, you'll probably want to create different screen names for each (or at least each age/maturity level). That way the teens can access material appropriate to their age and interests.

Finally, remember that none of the controls you set is permanent. You can go in and change them at any time if they aren't working out the way you planned. You should also be open to the kids negotiating for more access as they get older, more mature, and more sophisticated in their online usage.

How to Block Everything but the Kids Only Channel

Kids Only, as the name implies, is an AOL Channel designed for kids age 12 and under. You saw it briefly in Hour 2, "Uses for America Online," and you'll see it again in Hour 22, "Letting the Kids in on the Fun." It's a great Channel in which your children will find plenty to keep them entertained.

With Parental Controls, you can limit your child's AOL access to *just* the Kids Only Channel. It's a good idea for very young kids, but keep in mind that it also blocks them from the Research & Learn Channel, which has a lot to offer—with online encyclopedia, dictionaries, and other reference tools.

To get to Parental Controls, click the My AOL button on the toolbar. On the menu that drops down, click Parental Controls. The Parental Controls dialog box opens. Select "set parent controls now" to get to Figure 21.1.

Figure 21.1.

The main Parental Controls dialog box.

Helpful text

Select access level for each screen name

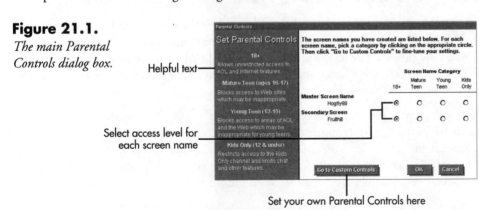

Set your own Parental Controls here

21

For the latest Parental Controls information, read the information in the text box on the left side of the dialog box.

The right side of the Parental Controls dialog box shows the Master account name, and its access level. Any secondary screen names will be listed below the master account name. You can set the access level for each. You have four choices:

- ☐ **18+**—Accounts with 18+ Access are *unrestricted*, except to Internet newsgroups that allow file attachments.
- ☐ **Mature Teen**—These accounts have all the access of 18+ accounts, but they block access to web sites that might be inappropriate for this age group (16–17).
- ☐ **Young Teen Access**—Young Teen Access accounts go anywhere and do anything on AOL, except to Premium Service areas. For the Internet, they're limited to web sites with age-appropriate content for 13–15-year-olds. They're blocked from newsgroups that allow file attachments.
- ☐ **Kids Only Access**—Accounts specified as Kids Only Access accounts are limited to the Kids Only Channel, with select access to age-appropriate web pages (for ages 12 and under). Additionally, Kids Only Access accounts cannot send or receive Instant Messages, cannot enter member-created chat rooms, and can only send and receive text-only email (no pictures embedded, or files attached).

To restrict your child to Kids Only access, click the Kids Only Access check box after the appropriate screen name. While you're at it, you can set the Parental Control level for any other screen names on your account. When you're done, click the OK button. You'll get a message saying your Parental Control settings have been saved. Click OK, and you're done.

You can come back at any time (using the master account name, of course) and alter these settings.

Setting Custom Controls

You may, or may not, like the level of access granted by these arbitrary (if generically fitting) 18+, Mature Teen, Young Teen, and Kids Only Access divisions. Every kid is different, after all, and your preteen may be mature enough to handle Mature Teen Access, or a modified version of it. On the other hand, your 13-year-old may not be mature enough to handle free reign online. That's your call.

You can customize your child's access online by way of the Custom controls. To begin, click the Go to Custom Controls button on the bottom of the Parental Controls dialog box shown earlier in Figure 21.1. The Custom Controls dialog box appears as shown in Figure 21.2. This is Custom Controls central, where you can adjust your child's access to Chat, Instant Messages, Downloading, Newsgroups, Mail, and the web.

21

Figure 21.2.

You can tailor the Parental Controls to suit your child.

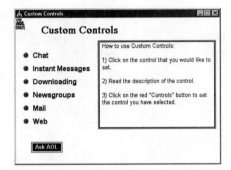

We'll look at the options for each category in a moment. First, this is how the Custom controls work. To begin, click on the category you want to set. The text box to the right of the screen will display information about your options—you should read it; it contains good advice. When you're ready to change the related access options, click the Controls button that appears under the text box—if you're reading about Chat, the button will be Chat Controls; Instant Messages, Instant Message Controls, and so on.

When the particular set of controls opens, you'll either select a screen name *before* the controls appear, or the controls will be like those shown previously in Figure 21.1 (screen names followed by check boxes). There you can set the controls for *all* the screen names on your account at once.

That said, the following sections describe the individual controls.

Chat Controls

Chat is a wonderful thing; however, some chat rooms are just not appropriate for young people. Although you can't block your child's access to a particular chat room, you can block their access to the various *types* of chat rooms. The Chat controls shown in Figure 21.3 let you do just that.

Caution

Most people who chat on AOL are fine, upstanding folks. But, as anywhere, there are probably people online you would rather your kids didn't come in contact with. Remind your children with chat access that, just because it's called a *Teen* chat room, that doesn't mean there's only teens in there. Warn your kids to *never* give out their home address, phone number, or where they go to school. Instill a little healthy skepticism in your kids, so they're cautious of strangers online.

21

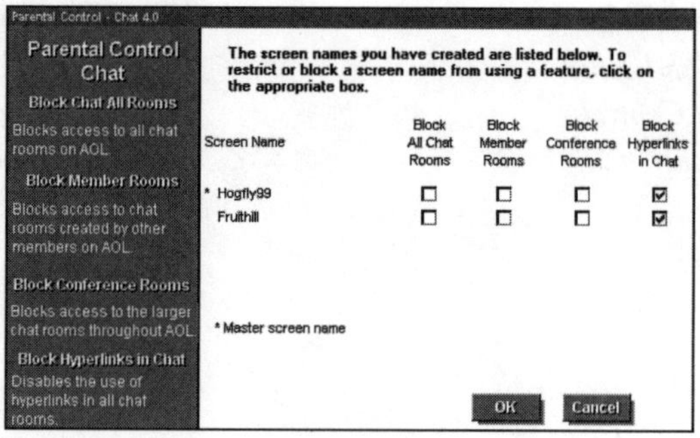

Figure 21.3.

The custom Chat controls.

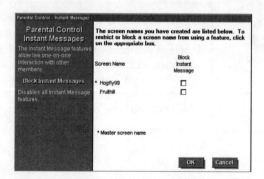

Your chat options include the following:

☐ **Block All Chat Rooms**—Prevents your child from entering *any* chat room in the People Connection.

☐ **Block Member Rooms**—Keeps your child out of member-created chat rooms, but allows them into AOL staff-created chat rooms in the People Connection.

☐ **Block Conference Rooms**—Blocks access to the chat rooms in forums online. Keep in mind that this option will block your child from interactive homework help from teachers in the Research & Learn Channel.

☐ **Block Hyperlinks in Chat**—Keeps your kid from zipping off onto the web from a Favorite Place or Internet address sent into a chat room.

Click the check box beneath the options you want to set, beside the screen name you want to control. When you're done, click OK.

Instant Message Controls

Instant Messages, like most things online, are a lot of fun, but can be misused and abused. I've received some IMs from strangers who would have curled my hair—if I had any. If you care to restrict a child's access to them, the IM Control dialog box is shown in Figure 21.4.

Figure 21.4.

The Instant Message controls.

21

When you restrict a screen name from using Instant Messages, you block that user's ability to send and receive Instant Messages anywhere online, not just in chat rooms.

JUST A MINUTE

IM Phone is a new feature that hasn't been officially added to AOL 4.0. It enables users with sound-capable computers, including a microphone, to send voice messages in IMs. (This *may* be a premium service—that is, costs extra—but it isn't official yet.) Look for IM Phone, and other cool add-ins in later updates to the 4.0 software.

Click the check box beneath the options you want to set, beside the screen name you want to control. When you're done, click OK.

Downloading Controls

Consider blocking your child's access to file downloads for these good reasons: the risk of computer viruses; those Trojan horse password snatching programs; pornography on the Internet.

Your Parental Control options on downloading are shown in Figure 21.5.

Figure 21.5.

The Downloading controls.

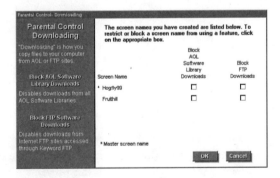

The Downloading options are the following:

☐ **Block AOL Software Library Downloads**—This prevents your child from downloading *anything* from the file libraries on AOL.

☐ **Block FTP Downloads**—Blocks downloads from FTP sites on the Internet—that's where *most* of the viruses and objectionable materials creep in.

Click the check box beneath the options you want to set, beside the screen name you want to control. When you're done, click OK. If you decide to grant your child downloading privileges, be sure to discuss the dangers of downloading files attached to email from strangers, and the risk of downloading a virus.

21

It might be a good idea to have a rule that says the child can't *use* anything he or she has downloaded until an adult has had a chance to look it over—scan it for viruses, or preview document files for content.

Newsgroup Controls

Thousands of newsgroups exist on the Internet, ranging in topic from stamp collecting to sexual fetishes. Unlike the message boards you find on AOL, most newsgroups are not moderated, and can contain *anything.* If you read Hour 10, "Newsgroups and Mailing Lists," you already know that this is one potentially racy aspect of the Internet you'll probably want to restrict.

The Newsgroup controls, shown in Figure 21.6, enable you to restrict a child's access to some, or all, the newsgroups on the Net. This is one of the Parental Controls where you select a screen name *before* you see the controls. You have to repeat the process for any additional screen names you want to restrict.

Figure 21.6.

The Newsgroup controls.

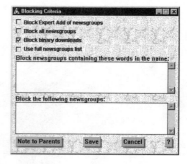

The Newsgroup controls include the following:

- ☐ **Block Expert Add of Newsgroups**—This prevents your child from adding a newsgroup for which they know the full name—if, for example, he hears of a newsgroup from a friend, this prevents him from adding it to his list of newsgroups.

- ☐ **Block All Newsgroups**—The simple, one-click way to cut off all newsgroups. However, it blocks your child from some potentially valuable newsgroups.

- ☐ **Block Binary Downloads**—This blocks downloads of videos, pictures, sounds, and the like. This option is checked by default for all but the master account name.

- ☐ **Use Full Newsgroups List**—This option gives your child access to the *full list of newsgroups*—not just those deemed acceptable by AOL. Click this one with caution.

Below the list of check box options, you'll find two windows in which you can block access to newsgroups whose names contain certain words (that's the top text box), or by typing the full name of the group (in the bottom text box).

A good place to start with this last feature might be to block `alt.binaries.*`, or even just `alt.*`. These are the newsgroups that usually contain illegal software, pornography, or both. The alt newsgroups are known for their bizarre content.

Click the check box beside the options you want to set for this screen name. Enter any words or group names you care to block in the appropriate text boxes. When you're done, click OK.

Mail Controls

Email is a touchy subject—it's a big part of the fun of being online, but its contents (particularly with junk mail) can be problematic for parents with children. You can use the Mail controls shown in Figure 21.7 to block some, or all, of your child's access to email.

As with the newsgroups, you select a screen name before these Mail controls appear. You need to repeat the process for any other screen names you want to control.

Figure 21.7.

The Mail controls.

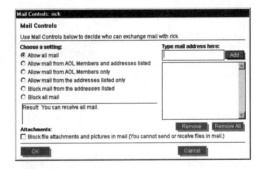

You can select *one* email setting from this list:

- [ ] **Allow All Mail**—Applies no restrictions on email.
- [ ] **Allow Mail from AOL Members and Addresses Listed**—Blocks all mail from the Internet, except for the names you manually enter in the Type Mail Address Here text box. That way your child can receive mail from friends and relatives who aren't AOL members, but have Internet access.
- [ ] **Allow Mail from AOL Members Only**—Blocks all email from the Internet and other online services.
- [ ] **Allow Mail from the Addresses Listed Only**—Blocks all mail from everyone *except* the mail address you enter in the Type Mail Address Here text box.

21

☐ **Block Mail from the Addresses Listed**—Allows mail from anyone *except* the mail address you enter in the Type Mail Address Here text box.

☐ **Block All Mail**—Keeps your child from receiving all email.

You may also click the Block File Attachments and Pictures in Mail check box to prevent your child from sending and receiving mail with files attached, or pictures embedded in the message.

To add a name to the list box at the right of the window, carefully type the email address in the Type Mail Address Here text box, and then click Add. The address will appear in the list box. To remove a name from the list, click on the name to select it, then click the Remove button.

You can completely clear the list of email addresses by clicking the Remove All button.

Make your selection(s), enter the mail addresses you care to block/allow, and click OK.

Web Controls

Parental Controls also gives you the option to customize your child's access to sites on the web, by way of the Web controls in Figure 21.8.

Figure 21.8.

The Web controls.

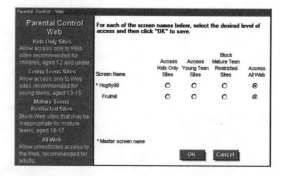

The Web control choices are the following:

☐ **Access Kids Only Sites**—Allows access only to web sites recommended for children, aged 12 and under.

☐ **Access Young Teen Sites**—Allows access only to web sites recommended for young teens, aged 13–15.

☐ **Block Mature Teen Restricted Sites**—Blocks web sites that may be inappropriate for mature teens, aged 16–17.

☐ **Access All Web**—Allows unrestricted access to the web (this option gives the user full access to all web sites, and therefore is recommended for adults only).

JUST A MINUTE

If you're curious, the web sites are checked and rated for appropriateness by Microsystems Software Inc., an Internet rating service.

Click the check box beside the options you want to set for this screen name. When you're finished, click OK.

Summary

In this hour, you've seen the various Parental Controls that you may use to restrict your child's access to material and areas you deem inappropriate for them.

Workshop

Use the following workshop to solidify the skills you've learned in this hour.

Q&A

Q **My 16-year-old is begging me to let her have access to chat rooms, but I'm worried that she's not mature enough. What should I do?**

A Discuss it with your spouse and your daughter, not me. You know your child; I don't.

Q **I know my child knows the password for our master screen name. Do I have to set Parental Control for my screen name just to keep them out of areas I don't want them to go?**

A No, it's better that you change the password for the master screen name. Use the keyword Passwords.

Quiz

Take the following quiz to test your knowledge of Parental Controls.

Questions

1. If I block everything but Kids Only, my child
    a. Won't be able to use America Online
    b. Will still have access to chat rooms
    c. Can only use the Kids Only channel

21

2. You should consider blocking a child's access to Member-created chat rooms because
   a. They're usually unsupervised
   b. They may be naughty
   c. Both of the above
3. When I'm blocking newsgroups, I can
   a. Block newsgroups that contain certain words in the name
   b. Block newsgroups by name
   c. Block all newsgroups
   d. Any of the above

Answers

1. **c.**
2. **c.**
3. **d.**

Activity

If you care to, create screen names for your children. When they have their own screen names, set up the Parental Controls to suit their ages and maturity.

21

Hour 22

Letting the Kids in on
the Fun

We spent the past hour, "Keeping Parental Control," talking about how to keep your kids from getting at some of the material online that isn't appropriate for them. Although you may feel blocking access is both useful and necessary, it does leave a negative sort of aftertaste. Let's get rid of it by examining some of the cool stuff that kids can do online, with little or no parental supervision.

The main focus here will be the Kids Only Channel—the AOL Channel designed *exclusively* for children aged 12 and under. You got a quick peek at it earlier in the book, now it's time to jump in with both feet.

In this hour, you'll learn your way around Kids Only, including:

- ☐ Some stuff for parents to think about
- ☐ Kids Only Central
- ☐ Kids Only Create
- ☐ Kids Only Chat
- ☐ Clubs for kids
- ☐ Kids Only web access

General Considerations for Parents

In Hour 21, you learned how to use the tools AOL has provided to keep your children out of areas on AOL and the Internet that might contain inappropriate material for youngsters. If you skipped Hour 21 because you just can't wait to get your kids online, I recommend that you flip back and read that hour—this one will keep for an hour while you read it.

When Should I Let My Child Go Online?

Kids are all different, so it's dangerous to make generalizations. You know your children best, so you need to make that decision for yourself.

I will say this: The younger the child, the more parental supervision is required. AOL is *not* a baby-sitter any more than a television set is.

No matter what your child's age, when he or she (or even *they*) start using AOL, you need to be there at that computer, helping, explaining, and teaching. After your child is comfortable with the service, you can back off a little—if you're comfortable with that—but be available for questions.

It's a good idea to structure online time—set some rules so the kids know right out of the gate what you expect of them, and what is (and is not) an acceptable use of their online time.

Set Time Limits

Just like video games and television, it's easy for AOL to become an addictive eye candy that keeps your kids inactive, staring at the screen for hours. Scheduling online time, and keeping that schedule, helps avoid that problem. It also avoids sibling arguments over whose turn it is and conflicts between adults and kids, who may end up vying for computer time.

In houses with only one telephone line, it also allows you to schedule breaks between online sessions so you can take, make, and return telephone calls.

TIME SAVER

Actually, it's more of a *mind saver* tip. If the expense of a second, computer-only phone line is too great, you might want to consider getting the Answer Call service offered by your local phone company. It's less expensive than a second line and, when you're online, you can *still* get your telephone messages. Just a thought.

Terms of Service and Kids

Before letting your child use America Online alone—especially if you are going to allow them in chat rooms—make sure to explain the Terms of Service agreement with them.

22

Make sure they understand what is and is not allowed online, because if they violate the TOS, it is you, the primary account holder, who will pay the price.

For example, make sure they understand that abusive behavior, harassment, foul language, and discussion of illegal activities (even in jest) is not allowed. For example, a child who "jokes" about using drugs is akin to "joking" about a bomb while walking through an airport.

Safety Tips

In a similar vein to the TOS and kids, you should sit down with your kids and explain some things about safety—things like:

- [ ] Never give out personal information online—no full names, address, telephone numbers, passwords, or school name.
- [ ] Never download files attached to email without asking permission first.
- [ ] If a child receives mail or an Instant Message that makes him or her uncomfortable, or asks too many personal questions, he or she should call an adult.
- [ ] Always ask permission before downloading a file.
- [ ] Always ask permission before entering a contest, or filling out an information form online.
- [ ] When in doubt, *ask*.

Kids Only Central

Kids Only (shown in Figure 22.1) is a unique area online. It's like all of AOL has been squeezed down to kid size, and painted in bright primary colors. To get there, you have the usual options—click the Kids Only button on the Channels screen, or on the left side of any Channel's Main Screen; select it from the toolbar's Channels menu; or use the keyword KIDS ONLY.

Figure 22.1.

Kids Only doesn't look like the rest of America Online.

Department buttons

News & Weather   Features

You'll notice that the Kids Only Main Screen has the usual assortment of department buttons and featured areas as any other Channel—it's just…loud.

On your first venture into Kids Only, you might want to stop in at Kids Only Central first. It's a little like the main hall at school, only you don't need a hall pass to walk through. It's a central gathering place where kids can talk, share ideas, and then zip off to do whatever else they want in Kids Only.

To get to Kids Only Central, click the Central button on the Kids Only main screen. You'll get a window like the one shown in Figure 22.2.

Figure 22.2.

Kids Only Central offers a little of everything.

Kids Only Central is dominated by two features, the triangular department buttons on the left, and the Everything list box on the right. Everything is aptly named: You'll pretty much find everything there is to do in Kids Only.

Some of the highlights include the following:

- [ ] **Cartoon Network World**—Exciting stuff from the cable cartoon giant, and a personal favorite.

- [ ] **DC Comics**—Keep up with Superman, Batman, Wonder Woman, and the rest of the DC panoply of superheroes.

- [ ] **Kids' WB**—The online home of the WB Network's kids programming. You'll find Pinky and the Brain plotting to take over the world, not to mention those wacky Warners—Yakko, Wakko, and Dot.

- [ ] **Highlights for Children**—The venerable magazine's online edition. Take a nostalgia break and visit it yourself—it's just like you remember it, only online.

- [ ] **Nickelodeon Online**—The cable network for kids comes to life—find out what Tommy Pickles and the rest of the *Rugrats* are up to today.

Also in Central, you can Speak Out! on various issues—everything from whether you like cats or dogs best, or whether there's life on other planets. When I visited today, the topic *du jour* was *Do you believe in ghosts?*

22

22

You'll usually see one of the Speak Out! responses posted right in Kids Only Central, along with the screen name of the kid who provided the insight. That's *got* to be a kick and a half for the kids whose answers show up there.

TIME SAVER

> You'll find time-saving indexes, like the Everything list, all over Kids Only. Each of the other lists is geared to the topic of the forum you found it in. In Kids Only Create, for instance, the list only takes you to areas that encourage kids to create something.

Kids Only Create

Kids Only Create is outstanding in both quality and quantity. It's like a great big, kid-sized To Do list, presenting all sorts of creative ideas and projects. Best of all, kids are encouraged to share their creations with others online, by uploading copies of their work that others can see and download themselves.

The coolest of the Create areas is called Blackberry Creek (keyword BLACKBERRY). You can take a gander at it in Figure 22.3.

Figure 22.3.
Blackberry Creek is a creative haven for kids.

Here, your child can submit stories, drawings and other creations, or check out what other kids have done. Additionally, you'll find party ideas, scripts for plays and movies, more polls you can take, chat rooms, and more.

Kids Only Chat

Chat is probably the one area kids like the most, but it's also the one area parents are most concerned about. We have enough trouble keeping track of the neighborhood kids our children play with. Trying to keep track of the kids they know online (from across the country, and around the world) is *way* harder.

If you decide to let your kids chat, here are some things you (and your child) should know:

- [ ] Grown-ups can't participate in Kids Only chats, except as observers. Parents are encouraged to observe, however—and it's a good idea. It'll keep you informed on what your kid actually *does* while online.
- [ ] All chat rooms within Kids Only are age-specific. Make sure your child goes into the rooms appropriate for his or her age.
- [ ] Many Kids Only chat rooms are supervised by Kids Only personnel—you'll recognize them by the KO at the start of their screen names.
- [ ] Make sure your children know to *never* give out their password, phone number, address, or even the name of their school, to anyone, even their best friend—either online or off.

There's even a kid-sized version of the Guide Pager called *Guidepager for Kids*. It's a button on the bottom of all chat windows in Kids Only. It opens the *very* easy to use I Need Help! dialog box shown in Figure 22.4.

Figure 22.4.
I Need Help!

The child clicks the appropriate help button, and answers a couple of questions (like the name of the room the bad thing is happening in) and the information will go right to an AOL Guide.

Clubs for Kids

Kids love to join clubs, and they love to make up their own clubs—and make up rules for the club, don't forget them. Kids Only is full of great clubs for the kids to join. To find out about them, click the Clubs button on the Kids Only main screen, you'll open the window shown in Figure 22.5

22

Figure 22.5.
*Kids can join several
cool clubs.*

Each club has different things to offer, but most have newsletters, members-only chat room meetings, bulletin boards, games, contests, and more.

Some of the clubs your kid can join include the following:

☐ Art Shop
☐ Comics by Kids
☐ The Hangout
☐ Pixels Art Gallery
☐ Scrap Books
☐ Story Library
☐ Win Big

Kids and the World Wide Web

The great thing about Kids Only is that it offers kids their own, simplified web browser to access cool stuff on the Internet (see Figure 22.6). The great thing for *parents* about that browser is that it can only access web sites with content appropriate for kids ages 12 and under.

To get at the browser, click the Web button on the Kids Only main screen. When it opens, click the Random button and you'll be taken to a random (get it?) site from those available for kids. You can then browse around from that page, clicking links and going where you will, or you can just click Random again and let luck or fate lay a web page on you.

The page you see in Figure 22.6 is an Internet version of the *Mad Libs* books we used to get when I was a kid—where you'd ask a friend to pick a noun, a verb, an adjective, and so on, and plug them into a story with goofy results.

Figure 22.6.

The Kids Only WEB browser has simplified controls even a grown-up can use.

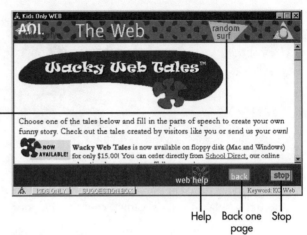

Random browse —

Help   Back one   Stop
        page

JUST A MINUTE

If you want to give your kids access to the web *without* limiting them to Kids Only, you can still restrict their access to inappropriate materials with (all together now) the Parental Controls, which were explained in the past hour.

Kids Only Games

One of the *most* popular areas in Kids Only is the Game area, shown in Figure 22.7. Here kids can play games with each other, read information about their favorite video games, and even download games they can play on their computers when they aren't online.

Figure 22.7.

Games!

22

The list box at the right of the Kids Only Game screen is full of links to games kids can play online, right *now*. The Game Grabber gives them the opportunity to download PC- and Mac-specific game software from the area's file libraries—kids, make sure you ask permission before you download or install any software.

Summary

In this hour, you have learned about the wide variety of stuff your kids can do online, particularly in the Kids Only Channel.

Workshop

Use the following workshop to solidify the skills you learned in this hour.

Q&A

Q My teenager spends hour after hour talking in the chat rooms. Should I be concerned?

A Yes. While there is nothing wrong with chatting online, when it starts to replace real-life conversations with friends, outdoor activities, or schoolwork, it's a problem.

Q I saw a Homework Help button on the Kids Only main screen, but you didn't say anything about it. What's up with that?

A Homework help is covered in the next hour, "Getting Help with Schoolwork." I didn't want to mix work and play.

Quiz

Take the following quiz to test your knowledge of this hour.

Questions

1. If my child violates the Terms of Service:

    a. The child can have his or her account canceled

    b. My entire account can be canceled

    c. Nothing can happen because he or she is a minor

2. If my child encounters a TOS violation in a chat room, he should:

    a. Get out of that room

    b. Notify AOL using Guidepager for Kids

    c. Both of the above

3. Compared to America Online, the Internet:

    a. Is harder to control

    b. Is easier to control

    c. Is impossible to control

Answers

1. **b.**

2. **c.**

3. **c.** You can't control the Internet, you can only control your child's access to it with AOL's Parental Controls web, newsgroups, and downloading/FTP options.

Activity

Spend some time with your kids exploring some of the wild, wonderful, wacky, and other adjectives that start with W, things available in Kids Only.

22

Hour 23

Getting Help with Schoolwork

In the past hour, you learned about all the fun stuff for kids on AOL. At this point, the kids in your life probably think you're the most wonderful parent in the world to have shown them all that cool stuff.

Time to break the *bad* news to them: AOL can help them do their homework, too. Depending on the kid, that's the best, or worst news you can give them.

Seriously, some great are tools available to help kids of all ages with their homework—and it's not just for children. Anyone, from first grade to post-graduate students, will find academic nirvana online. You can even take a class or two, right online, from the comfort of your home. The courses are even *accredited*.

In this hour, you'll learn how to

- ☐ Get homework help
- ☐ Take classes online
- ☐ Prepare for college
- ☐ Locate resources for teachers

☐ Find reference materials

☐ Find other educational resources (including some for *parents*)

Getting Help with Homework

You've been there: Your son is looking at you, expecting you to explain (preferably *solve*) his algebra problem. To *you*, the problem looks like: X = a couple of squiggles and an x a curlicue to the eighth power.

What do you do? Do you:

a. Tell him "You'll never learn how to do this if you don't figure it out on your own."

b. Admit: "Hey, I couldn't do this stuff in school, I'm sure as heck not gonna do it *now.*"

c. Fall on the floor and fake a coma until the kid gives up and asks his mother.

d. None of the above.

Of course, the correct answer is C. No, no. No, it's not. It's D. What you really want to do is sit the kid down at the computer, tell him to log onto AOL, and get help from a professional. (If you usually resort to answer C, maybe *you* should get a little professional help, too. Just a thought.)

Kids Only—Homework Help

In AOL's Homework Help area, your child can find the answer by himself or, when all else fails, can even email a real teacher and get the help they need to get the assignment done.

To get started, you go back to the Kids Only Channel, last seen in Hour 22, in Figure 22.1. When you get to Kids Only, click the Homework Help button. That opens the Homework Help window shown in Figure 23.1.

Figure 23.1.
Homework Help.

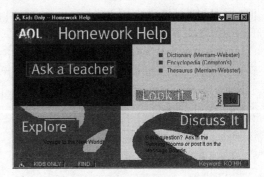

Four ways your child can find the answers he or she needs are the following:

☐ **Look It Up**—This takes you to all of AOL's online reference materials, including dictionaries, an encyclopedia, and other reference works.

☐ **Ask a Teacher**—Opens the Teacher Pager window shown in Figure 23.2. Type your question in the large text box, then click the subject area of your question, and off it goes to a teacher in that subject.

CAUTION

> It can take up to 48 hours to get a response to your Teacher Pager message, so *never* wait until the last minute to use Ask A Teacher. If you need an answer *right now,* use one of the other homework help resources.

Figure 23.2.
The Teacher Pager.

Type your question here

Send it to the appropriate subject area here

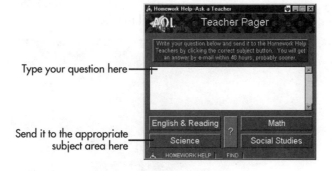

☐ **Discuss It**—Takes you to a set of chat areas on specific subjects. Pop into the appropriate room and see who's around to help.

☐ **Explore**—Gives you access to special academically oriented online activities—it may not help with *tonight's* homework, but it's a great way for kids to explore all the educational resources online.

Naturally, Kids Only Homework Help is geared toward the same ages (12 and under) as the rest of Kids Only. If you've got older students in the house (like yourself, maybe) there are more advanced versions of help available.

Ask-A-Teacher—The High School and College Editions

You can ask a teacher questions at *any* educational level. You can use the keyword ASK-A-TEACHER, and you'll go to the Ask-A-Teacher area in AOL's Research & Learn Channel (see Figure 23.3).

Figure 23.3.

You can Ask-A-Teacher at any level of education.

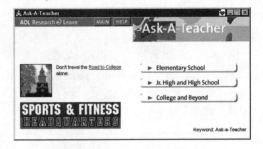

When you get there, click the button for your academic level. Elementary School takes you to the Teacher Pager you saw in the last section in Figure 23.2. The Jr. High and High School button opens the Ask-A-Teacher dialog box shown in Figure 23.4. The College and Beyond button opens a screen similar to the one shown here, but with access to college level materials and teacher.

Figure 23.4.

The Junior High and High School version of Ask-A-Teacher.

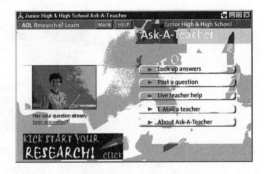

The set of buttons shown in the figure should sound familiar—they're similar to those offered in the Kids Only Homework Help area:

☐ **Look Up Answers**—Takes you to online research materials.

☐ **Post a Question**—Gives you access to message boards—where you can post your question and wait for a response—or browse around and see if your question has already been asked and answered.

☐ **Live Teacher Help**—Chat rooms on a variety of academic subjects, with teachers just itching to help you out.

☐ **E-mail a Teacher**—The grown-up version of Teacher Pager.

☐ **About Ask-A-Teacher**—Explains the area, how it works, and how to use it to your best advantage.

23

Taking Classes Online

It's tough, with the pressures of everyday life, to find time to take a personal enrichment course, a class to help you on the job, or just to learn something new. AOL can help. With the Online Campus (part of the Research & Learn Channel) you can select any of the dozens of classes available.

You can see the Online Campus in Figure 23.5, or you can go there yourself with the keyword CAMPUS.

Figure 23.5.

AOL's Online Campus (keyword CAMPUS*).*

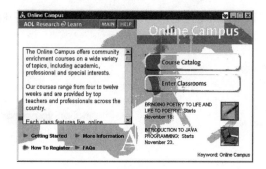

23

A large number of classes are offered by the University of California, and their classes are all accredited—that means the credits from them are accepted at *most* universities nationwide. If you're not into the accreditation thing, there are also some great classes you can take for the sheer joy of learning.

The course subjects offered include:

- ☐ Arts
- ☐ Business/Professional Studies
- ☐ Computing
- ☐ English and Writing
- ☐ Hobbies and Special Interests
- ☐ Humanities
- ☐ Languages
- ☐ Mathematics
- ☐ Religion and Spirituality
- ☐ Science and Nature

You might want to check out the course catalog (just click the Course Catalog button), or check out the information files on Getting Started, More Information, How to Register, or the FAQs.

FAQ—Online abbreviation for Frequently Asked Questions. To say it, just say the letters: F-A-Q. An FAQ is a list of commonly asked questions, and their answers. When you find an FAQ, you should read it—if you're at all curious about the subject matter.

Keep in mind that you *are* taking an actual class, from professional educators, so there are *expenses* involved—the cost of the course, your online time, and any books or other materials required.

Preparing for College

If you, or one of your kids, is getting ready to take the plunge into higher education, AOL has some resources that can help.

JUST A MINUTE

> You might want to check out *The Complete Idiot's Guide to Getting Into College* for more help with getting ready for college. It's a handy reference with all the information you need to start your search, whether you're planning way in advance, or jumping in at the last minute.

You'll find one of the best college planning resources in the Research & Learn Channel: The College Board (keyword COLLEGE BOARD), shown in Figure 23.6.

Figure 23.6.
The College Board—have a sharpened #2 pencil ready.

College Board is a nonprofit association of universities and colleges and is a great resource for information on majors, financial aid, and much more. The highlight of the area, in my humble opinion anyway, is the College Handbook search tool.

You can use the Handbook to find schools that offer specific programs (or combinations of programs) that interest you. For example, if you need a school that offers majors in microbiology, East Indian Studies, *and* Sports Management, the College Handbook search

23

tool will help you find it. You can see the Handbook Search window in Figure 23.7—it looks and works like all the other search tools you've used online.

Figure 23.7.

The College Handbook Search lets you search for colleges by name or course offerings.

Select a search type

Enter a key word or phrase here

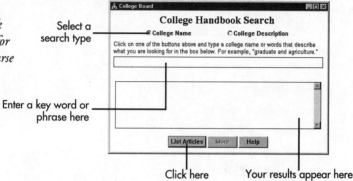

Click here   Your results appear here

After the Handbook returns a list of the schools that suit your needs, double-click an entry in the list to read more about that school. You can even save individual articles to your hard drive (select Save from the File menu), or print out a copy (click Print on the toolbar).

There's a lot more to the College Board area—parents will especially like the financial aid area. If you're headed to college, you really should check it out.

Resources for Teachers

Even teachers need a little help from time to time, and America Online has several areas that can be of help to education professionals. From continuing education for teachers, to helpful hints on preparing lesson plans, there are several areas that can meet teachers' needs.

To locate the resources *you* need, use the keyword EDUCATION. You'll go to the Education forum in the Research & Learn Channel. In the Education Resources list box, locate Resources for Educators and double-click it. You'll open the Resources for Educators dialog box as shown in Figure 23.8.

Figure 23.8.

Resources for Educators.

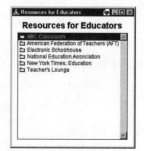

JUST A MINUTE

Everybody loves teachers, even the folks at AOL. Teachers who are members of the National Education Association are eligible for discounts on their AOL bill. Use the keyword NEA to find out more about the NEA discount.

The resources you'll find there include the following:

- ☐ ABC Classroom
- ☐ American Federation of Teachers (AFT)
- ☐ The Electronic Schoolhouse
- ☐ National Education Association
- ☐ *New York Times* Education
- ☐ The Teachers Lounge

Stop in and compare notes with teachers from all across America.

For parents of students in kindergarten through 12th grade, you'll find your own set of resources in the Education list box, just double-click Resources for Parents K-12.

Help from TV

Television has long been associated with education. From *ABC Afterschool Specials*, to the programming on PBS, and more recently, cable TV's Cable in the Classroom service, teachers have a lot of television resources to draw from. Now these television resources have moved into cyberspace.

Several television networks offer educational resources in their AOL forums, or on the web, including

- ☐ ABC Classroom (keyword ABC CLASSROOM)
- ☐ Cartoon Network (keyword CNW)
- ☐ CSPAN Classroom (keyword CSPAN)
- ☐ CNN Interactive (keyword WWW.CNN.COM)
- ☐ Discovery (keyword WWW.DISCOVERY.COM)
- ☐ National Public Radio (keyword NPR)
- ☐ The Learning Channel (keyword WWW.DISCOVERY.COM)

Okay, so National Public Radio isn't a *television* network. So shoot me.

23

Reference Materials on America Online

America Online's Research & Learn Channel is chock full of reference materials for use by students and anyone who needs to find some information. They are *constantly* updated, so there's never any worry about getting old, out-of-date information.

Figure 23.9 shows the Research & Learn main screen, including buttons for all the references online.

Figure 23.9.

There's plenty of reference material available on AOL.

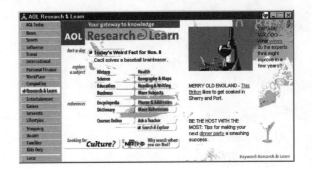

These are the buttons you can use:

☐ **Encyclopedia**—For access to Compton's Encyclopedia.

☐ **Dictionary**—To use Merriam-Webster's Dictionary, or other specialty dictionaries, online.

☐ **Phone & Address**—Takes you to the online versions of the White and Yellow page phone directories, among others.

☐ **More References**—Gives you even *more* reference choices.

Other Educational Resources

AOL has a huge assortment of educational resources online—way too many to list individually. Here's a cross-section of some of the other learning tools online. You can start here, then browse your way through the rest:

☐ Princeton Review (keyword PRINCETON REVIEW)

☐ Scientific American Online (keyword SCIAM)

☐ The White House (keyword WHITE HOUSE)

☐ Smithsonian Online (keyword SMITHSONIAN)

While you're exploring, don't forget about the big, wide, information-rich world of the Internet and World Wide Web.

Summary

In this hour, you learned about the various educational resources available online, particularly Homework Help for students of all ages, and some resources for teachers.

Workshop

Use the following workshop to solidify the skills you learned in this hour.

Q&A

Q Do the individual member schools of the College Board offer information about themselves?

A Yes. If you want specific information about a particular college or university, double-click its name, and you'll get course, financial aid, and an abundance of other information about that school.

Q Should I be concerned about my child using the Teacher Pager too much?

A That depends on your child. You should encourage your child to use Look It Up first and to only call in a teacher if they can't find the answer for themselves. Remember, it can take up to 48 hours to get a reply to a Teacher Page.

Quiz

Take the following quiz to test your knowledge of the educational opportunities available on America Online.

Questions

1. Educational tools can be found in:

    a. Only the Research & Learn Channel

    b. Lots of channels, but particularly Research & Learn and Kids Only

    c. There are no education resources on AOL

2. Homework Help in Kids Only is designed for

    a. Children of all ages

    b. Younger children (typically pre–high school)

    c. High school and college-age students

3. Online reference tools are great because

    a. They are easily accessible

    b. They are always up-to-date

    c. Both of the above

    d. None of the above

23

Answers

1. **b.**
2. **b.**
3. **c.**

Activity

Explore the education resources discussed here. Start with the Research & Learn Channel, then set off on your own to explore the other educational resources scattered throughout AOL. There are tons of great resources for educational purposes, both for you and your children.

23

PART
VI

Hour 24

The Family Vacation

I've been working too hard. Too many meetings, too many late nights, and my pager has been beeping so much that its batteries are running low. Worse, all that work has taken me away from my family.

I need to relax, refocus, take some time with the family to just plain have some fun. We need a vacation. What a coincidence that the final hour of this book is on using AOL to plan a family getaway.

AOL offers a lot of different resources for people planning a trip—whether it's a family vacation or business trip. With AOL, you can book airline reservations, hotels, car rentals, and even figure out what to do after you arrive at your destination.

In this hour, you will learn the basics of planning your trip online. You'll also learn about America Online's many sources of information that will help you plan an exciting itinerary of things to do when you arrive. Included in this hour are

☐ Finding information on domestic vacation spots

☐ Finding information on international destinations

☐ How to use the Independent Traveler

☐ How to use the Traveler's Corner

☐ How to use Preview Travel to book trips

Let's get started, and before you know it, you'll be packing your bags and heading for the door.

Finding Vacation Spots

To plan a trip, you need a destination. Well, most people have a good idea of *where* they want to go—the Bahamas, Alaska, or Hong Kong all make exciting destinations. Whether you're in the mood for international travel, or something a little more domestic, you can use AOL to help you find the perfect destination.

After choosing a vacation spot, you can then use AOL to help you plan the attractions you'd like to visit while there.

For travel within the United States, there's no better starting place than the Local Channel, also known as Digital Cities.

Digital Cities

The Digital Cities are jam-packed with useful information for vacation planning. You can use it to get the scoop on more than two dozen domestic destinations.

To get to Digital Cities, click the Local button on the main Channels window, or the main screen of any other Channel. You can also select Local from the Channels menu on the toolbar. When you arrive, you'll see the familiar U.S. map that you've seen in other hours (such as Hour 2, "Uses for America Online"). Click the name of the city you'd like to learn about, and a Digital City dialog box appears as shown in Figure 24.1.

JUST A MINUTE

Digital City Houston, shown in Figure 24.1 looks an awful lot like a web page—because it *is* a web page. The Digital Cities, as of this writing are at about a 50/50 split between web pages and AOL Forums. Nothing to worry about, just be aware of the sort of page you're looking at. Digital City web pages work like all the web pages you've seen, and the same is true for the forums.

Look for more and more of AOL's content to come from web pages as the boundary between "online service" and "the Internet" becomes even more blurred.

Figure 24.1 shows the Digital City Houston, Texas. Like all Digital Cities, Houston offers a number of things for you to consider while planning your vacation. You can check out a city's:

☐ **Entertainment information**—Find out about restaurants, movie theaters, theme parks, sports teams, and other entertaining things to do on your vacation.

☐ **Cultural details**—Learn the location of the closest art and history museums, theaters, concert halls, and opera houses.

☐ **Historical sites**—See what places of historical interest are near your destination, then find out about the sites themselves—plan a little sightseeing by site-seeing. You can see some of the historic sites around Houston listed in Figure 24.2.

☐ **News and weather**—Get forecasts to help you determine the best time of year to visit your city of choice.

Figure 24.1.

A Digital City can help in vacation planning. This is Digital Houston, Texas.

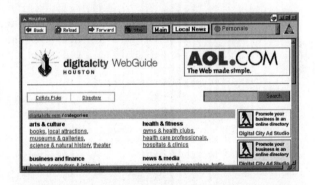

Figure 24.2.

Historic sites can be found with the click of a mouse.

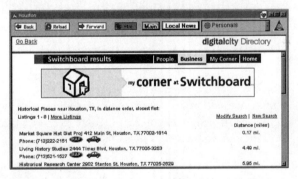

International Destinations

Domestic travel may not be what you crave in a vacation. You can do some homework on exotic, international locations in the International Channel. To get there, click the International button on the main Channels window or the main screen of any other Channel. You can also select International from the Channels menu on the toolbar. When the International Channel's main screen opens, it will look something like Figure 24.3.

Figure 24.3.

The International Channel is a great resource for travelers.

Click a continent to go there online

To get information about your destination country (or countries), you can click a continent on the map to open the related forum (with lists of the countries on that continent). Double-click a country to find out all about it.

For the geographically impaired (like me), you can also click Country Information on the International Channel's main screen. Country Information is a search tool that lets you search for a country by name or browse for a country by continent. Either way, you'll be swimming in information in short order.

Message boards and chat rooms are also available in many of the forums in the International Channel. You can use them to get firsthand accounts of what other folks have seen and done in your potential vacation spot—and what troubles they may have had, so the same thing doesn't happen to you.

The Travel Channel

After spending a little time in the International and Local Channels, you probably have one or more destinations in mind for your trip—you may have a whole itinerary worked out. Now all you need to do is book some airline and hotel reservations, and you'll be set. For that, you'll want to pop into the Travel Channel.

To get to the Travel Channel, click the Travel button on the main Channels window, or the main screen of any other Channel. You can also select Travel from the Channels menu on the toolbar. The main Travel screen (shown in Figure 24.4) opens right up.

The Travel Channel is completely devoted to helping you have the best trip possible. You can book your own flights, hotel reservations, car reservations, and get helpful tips to get you where you're going (and back) with a minimum of fuss.

You'll find even *more* suggestions for places to go (click Where to Go What to Do); money-saving tips and trips (click Travel Bargains), and even help for the business person (click Business Travel).

24

Figure 24.4.
*The Travel Channel is
your starting point.*

Farefinder

Most people don't have an unlimited budget to spend on a trip. Sometimes you need a vacation, but are afraid you can't afford one. As shown in Figure 24.5, Farefinder is a must-visit spot for the budget-conscious. It's an easy way to find *all* the lowest airfares from a city near you.

Figure 24.5.
*Simply select a departure
city and get huge lists of
bargain airfares courtesy
of Farefinder.*

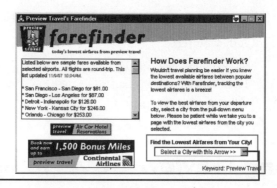

Select a departure city here

To use farefinder, just select your city (or a city near you) from the drop-down menu in the lower-right corner. Wait a moment or two, and a list of the day's lowest airfares to popular destinations will open on your screen. If one of the bargain fares suits your needs, you can click it to go to Preview Travel to book that flight.

Travel Talk

Travel Talk is a chat area devoted to (you guessed it) talking about travel. To get there, click Messages & Chat on the Travel Channel's main screen.

Travel Talk is probably one of the rarer finds online: a useful, even practical chat room, because the people who visit here can be a great help to you when planning your vacation.

Independent Traveler

The Independent Traveler is a crazy quilt of travel resources, including articles from travel writers, tips and tricks from travel veterans, and more (see Figure 24.6). To go to Independent Traveler, click Resource Center on the Travel Channel main screen. You can also use the keyword TRAVELER.

Figure 24.6.

The Independent Traveler Resource Center is worth the trip.

This is just a sampling of the kinds of tips, tricks, and information you'll find waiting for you:

☐ Airfare Secrets

☐ Guidebook Guide

☐ Health, Safety, & Insurance

☐ Lodging Tips & Tricks

☐ Seniors, Students, Women Travelers

Using Preview Travel to Book Your Trip

All the planning is finished. You know where you're going and you know what you want to do when you get there. All you need now are airline reservations, hotel reservations, and maybe a rental car. It's time to head for preview travel, shown in Figure 24.7.

Figure 24.7.

Travel on your own terms with preview travel.

24

Before you can book a flight through preview travel, you need to create a Travel Profile for yourself (and your family). To begin, click the Book Travel Here button on the right side of the window.

If you don't have a Travel Profile already set up, you'll need to create one—it's a simple, step-by-step, fill-in-the-blank process. You'll be asked the usual questions like *"what's your name?"* and *"where do you live?"*.

CAUTION

> The first thing you're asked to do when you create a Travel Profile, is enter a username and password to protect your personal information. Don't forget what you entered! It will make it tough when you want to come back to book another trip at a later date.

You'll be asked to select the airlines you prefer to use. This is for folks in one of those frequent flyer programs, so they can fly the airlines that reward them. If you're not a frequent flyer, don't worry about it. Select No Preference. When the time comes to actually search for flights, you'll be able search all available airlines, not just the two you can enter here.

After your profile is set up, you'll move right to Itinerary Planning. You'll be asked how many passengers (including yourself) you're booking tickets for. Enter the number, then click Continue. The Itinerary Planning dialog box opens as shown in Figure 24.8.

Figure 24.8.

Begin planning your itinerary here.

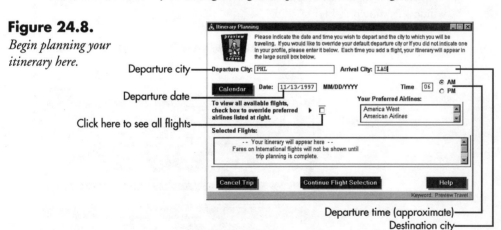

You'll see your departure city in the appropriate box, because you entered it in your profile. It's time to start the reservations process.

Book Airline Reservations

1. Enter the city you'll be flying into to start your trip in the Arrival City box. It will turn into the three-letter code for that city's airport, so if you know it, save time and enter that. In Figure 24.8, I've entered LAS for Las Vegas.

2. Enter the date of departure. You can highlight the date in the box and type in the correct one, or click the Calendar button.

3. Enter the approximate time you would like to depart, making sure to click the correct AM/PM button. You'll get a selection of flights both before and after that hour.

4. If you only want to query the two airlines you selected in your profile, skip ahead to step 5. If want to query *all* airlines, click the check box below the date.

5. Click the Continue Flight Selection button. After a short wait, a list of possible flights pops up. Click the flight you want, and then click the To Select Flight From Above, Highlight Flight and Click Here button (see Figure 24.9).

6. Your selected flight moves to the bottom pane of the window. You can repeat the process to add a leg to your trip (for a multi-city vacation), or you can click the Round Trip button to book a return flight. Because this is just practice, click Round Trip.

7. Repeat steps 2–5, then click Flight Selection Complete.

8. Your selected flights are displayed in the bottom box of the Flight Selection window as shown in Figure 24.9.

Figure 24.9.

Your itinerary is ready.

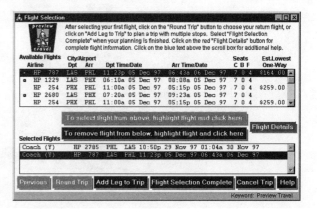

Consider yourself done, for the sake of this exercise. Click the Cancel Trip button (unless you're *really* planning a trip, of course). You'll be asked to confirm the cancellation, click Cancel Trip again, and you'll go back to preview travel.

24

Had you completed the process, you would have clicked the Flight Selection Complete button, and finished up your reservation with the opportunity to check for lower fares, to book hotel and car reservations, and to round out your travel plans. Naturally, you would have had to *pay* for all of it, too—but with your newly learned travel savvy, it would have been *much* less expensive than you'd ever dreamed.

Summary

In this hour, you've learned about many of the travel planning resources available online.

Workshop

24

Use the following workshop to solidify the skills you've learned in this hour.

Q&A

Q When I went in to make hotel reservations, the window changed. It looked like I was on the Internet. Could that be true?

A Yes. AOL's fully integrated Internet access enables you to move seamlessly between AOL and the Internet. You probably ended up at the reservations web site for the hotel you chose.

Q Here I am, using my credit card online again. Is it safe?

A America Online has a secure server that enables you to input your credit card data and send it without it being intercepted.

Quiz

Take the following quiz to test your knowledge of travel resources on America Online.

Questions

1. I can find out more about a particular city
   a. In the Local Channel
   b. In the International Channel
   c. In the Travel Channel
   d. All of the above

2. I can book reservations
   a. With preview travel
   b. In Digital City
   c. I can't book reservations online

3. Having a Travel Profile enables me to

    a. Learn more about a destination

    b. Travel overseas

    c. Book reservations online

Answers

1. Trick question—it depends on the city in question. A U.S. city may be found in the Local Channel. International cities in the International Channel, and popular travel destinations in the Travel Channel.

2. **a.**

3. **c.**

Activity

If you have the need, go ahead and create a Travel Profile and research some flights, either with preview travel, or the farefinder.

PART
VII

Appendixes

Appendix

Appendix A

Installing AOL 4.0 on a Macintosh-Compatible Computer

System Requirements

To use AOL 4.0 on your Mac-compatible computer, you need to make sure your system can handle this new, spiffy version. You need to have:

- ☐ **A modem**—A 28.8bps (bits per second), or faster, modem is recommended, but it should at least be a 14.4bps modem.

- ☐ **A telephone line**—To connect to your modem so the software can connect to AOL.

- ☐ **15–20MB of free space on your hard drive**—You'll need that just to install the software.

- ☐ **A CD-ROM drive**—Because AOL 4.0 won't fit on a floppy disk, it comes on a CD-ROM. Unless you download it directly from AOL (see the "Download It" section, coming up shortly), you'll need a CD-ROM drive to install the software.

☐ **A 68030 processor**—AOL recommends a 68040 or better processor (meaning any PowerPC processor).

☐ **A monitor**—Capable of displaying at least 256 colors, or shades of gray, with a resolution of 640×480.

☐ **8MB of physical RAM**—16MB of physical RAM is strongly recommended. With only 8MB of RAM, you will need to turn on Virtual Memory, or install RAMDoubler.

Installation

Before you install the software, make sure you have no other applications running—particularly screen savers or virus detection programs. They can mess up the installation process. When everything else is shut down, you're ready to start.

To begin installing AOL 4.0 on your Macintosh computer, pop the AOL CD in your CD-ROM drive. When the CD's icon appears on your desktop, double-click the icon to open its window (it may open all on its own).

Locate the Install AOL 4.0 icon in the CD's window, then double-click it to launch the Installer.

The first thing you'll see is a Welcome screen that gives you the option of reading or printing a Quick Reference Guide. If you want to print the Guide, click Print Now. If not, click Continue. You also have a Save As option that enables you to save the information in a text file on your hard drive.

When you click Continue, a standard Macintosh installation dialog box appears as shown in Figure A.1.

Figure A.1.
The Macintosh Install dialog box.

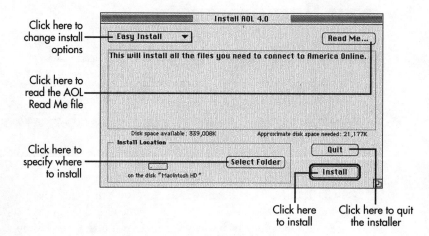

A

The default installation option is Easy Install. This is the best option for all but the most experienced AOL users, and even for most of *them.*

If you'd like the AOL software installed in a particular folder on your hard drive, click the Select Folder button. It gives you an open-type dialog box that you can use to select the folder in which you want your copy of AOL installed. Click the folder's name to select it, then click Select. You'll return to the Installer.

When you're ready to proceed, click the Install button. You'll be warned that the installation requires that your Mac be restarted. Click Continue. The installation will start, and you'll see a status display telling you how much stuff is left to be copied onto your hard drive.

After all the software has been copied to your hard drive, the installer will ask you two questions about how you'll be using AOL and the Internet. The first appears in a screen as shown in Figure 1.5. It wants to know if AOL will be your only access to the Internet.

If you already have access to the Internet through an Internet service provider or through a network connection at work, click No. If not, click Yes.

JUST A MINUTE

> If you don't know what it means, you probably don't have an Internet service provider. Just click Yes and get on with your life. If you're wrong, you can always change it later.

Finally, an alert appears to remind you that you must restart your Mac before you can use the AOL 4.0 software. Click Restart. Your Mac will go through its startup routine, and when you return to the Mac desktop you'll have a brand new America Online 4.0 window open, with the AOL application icon inside.

You're finished. Congratulations. You can skip back to Hour 1, "Installing America Online and Signing Up" and complete the set-up process so you can sign on to AOL.

Appendix B

When Things Go Wrong

When you get right down to it, America Online really is just another piece of software on your computer—meaning that, sometimes it gets messed up. In fact, because you're dealing with a modem, telephone lines, an intermediary connection at your local access number, *and* AOL's computers, there are even more opportunities for things to go wrong.

The best advice I can give is "don't panic." Nothing can go so horribly wrong that your computer will explode or you'll inadvertently launch a nuclear missile strike.

Where Things Go Wrong

Typically, there are only three places where AOL can give you trouble. Knowing where they are, and what sort of things can go wrong at each, is the first step in tracking down and dealing with whatever trouble you're having. The three places where things can go wrong are

☐ **Your Computer**—Either trouble with your computer and modem, or trouble with the AOL software installed on your system. Usually, if you can't even get your system to dial in to the local access number, the problem is with your system.

☐ **Local Access Number**—If your software starts up, and dials the local access number, but can't connect, then the problem is usually with the local access number (although there's still a chance your system is the culprit).

☐ **AOL**—When your software starts fine and connects to the local access number without a hitch, but then you can't get connected to AOL (or things are behaving badly while you're online), the odds are that something is going wrong with AOL. However, it could *still* be your computer, or the local access number.

When you run into a problem, note where the problem happens and at what stage of the connection process.

When things go wrong before you connect, the problem is yours and yours alone: Check your modem, modem configuration, software installation, and phone line connection.

When things go wrong *while* you're connecting, try an alternative local access number if available.

After you've connected to AOL, and things start to go wrong (and we're talking *wrong*, not that you don't know how to do something), chances are good that the problem is beyond your control. You may want to try to connect again, and see if the problem goes away, or sign off and try again in a few minutes.

Saying "when things go wrong" or "when there's a problem" is vague at best. The following lists a dozen or so things that most often go wrong, their usual causes, and what you can do about them:

☐ **Software Won't Launch**—When your AOL software won't start, or freezes while starting, chances are that the software was incorrectly installed, something vital was accidentally deleted, or it was damaged by some unknown computer burp. Your best bet is to reinstall your software.

☐ **Modem Problems**—If your software starts up, but gives you error messages about your modem (`AOL can't initialize your modem`, `Modem won't accept commands`, or even `AOL can't locate your modem`), first check the obvious stuff. Is your modem plugged in, turned on, and connected to the phone line?

If all that seems to be fine, try shutting the modem off (if it's an external model) and restarting your system. Try to connect again. If you still can't get AOL to use your modem, try using your modem with generic communications software, or another online service if you're a member. If you can call out and connect to another service, the problem is with your AOL modem setup. If you can't connect to *anything* via your modem, the modem is the problem. Check your manual, or call the manufacturer's technical support number.

☐ **No Dial Tone**—When you try to dial in to your local access number, but you get an alert that there's no dial tone, chances are your modem isn't connected to the phone line. Check to make sure the cord is plugged into the correct jack on the modem, *and* into the wall jack. Pick up your phone and see if there's a dial tone. There could be trouble with the line.

If you have AnswerCall, the broken dial tone you get when you have messages waiting confuses the heck out of your modem—check your messages and try again.

☐ **Access Number Is Busy**—It happens. Your only option is to try other access numbers, or keep trying the ones you have until you get through. Be patient.

☐ **No Answer**—Sometimes the local access number doesn't answer. Try, try again—a couple of times, at least. If there's still no answer, try a different access number, or wait 30 minutes and try again.

☐ **No Carrier**—You'll see this alert part way through the connection process (or after you've been unceremoniously dropped from the service). One of the intermediate computers burped and lost you. Try connecting again, or connect with a different access number.

☐ **Final Connection to AOL**—Sometimes the connection process will fail while the status display says `Requesting Network Attention` or `Checking Password`. Try again. If it *keeps* happening, there may be trouble with your access number (try another) or AOL is busy and can't squeeze you in (try again later).

☐ **AOL Is Slow**—Sometimes you connect to AOL, but everything is running slow, like molasses in January. You can't do much about that—that's usually heavy traffic online, or at your local access number. You can stay online and cope with it, if you're the patient sort, or you can sign off and immediately try to connect again. Sometimes that fixes it. Sometimes it's just best to sign off and wait for online traffic to die down—20 minutes or so.

☐ **You've Been Disconnected**—If AOL's computers are bogged down with requests (and *anything* you do online involves a request to AOL's computer) you may find yourself suddenly disconnected with an error message saying `Host failed to respond` or something similar. Try again.

If you get disconnected without any such error message, the problem may be with your local access number (try another), or you forgot to disable Call Waiting (check your setup).

☐ **Trouble Downloading Files**—If you can't seem to get AOL to finish a download—either singly, or a group of files with the Download Manager, the problem is often heavy online traffic. Try using Automatic AOL (covered in Hour 6, "Automatic AOL") to download in the wee hours of the morning.

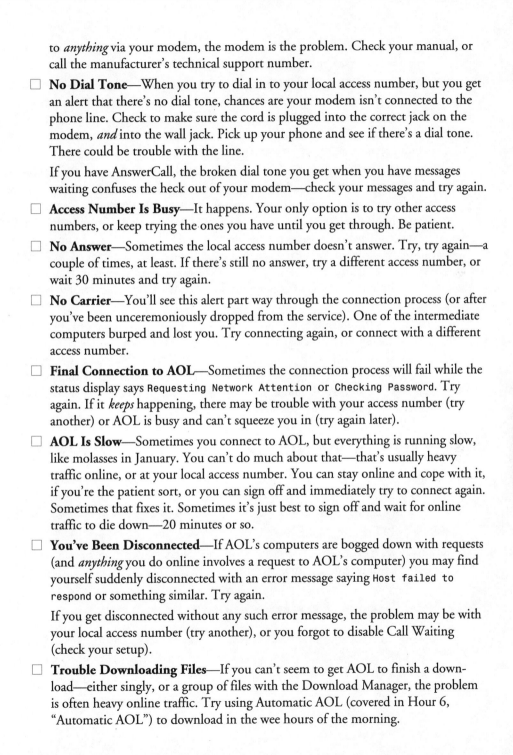

B

If you *consistently* have trouble with downloads, use the suggestions from the *You've Been Disconnected* bulleted item earlier in this list.

- ☐ **Downloaded Files Won't Open**—After downloading a file, if you get an error message that the file is damaged when you try to open it, check to be sure your screen saver is disabled—screen savers often misinterpret downloads as idle time and start up, often damaging the chunk of file currently being transferred. Turn your screen saver off, and try the download again.

- ☐ **Mac Users**—The most frequent source of Macintosh problems is the dreaded extension conflict—something in your Extensions Folder doesn't like something else in there. Use the Extension Manager to disable all but the most essential extensions (especially your modem driver, AOL Link, and AOL Scheduler extensions) and see if that solves the problem. If it *does*, keep adding one new extension until the problem reappears. When it does, the last extension added is probably the culprit. See if you can live without it, or create a set of Extensions without it for AOL sessions only—you'll then need to remember to switch extension sets, and restart your Mac, before and after using AOL.

- ☐ **Windows 95 Sounds Vanish**—Why it happens, I'm not quite sure, but it does. You suddenly stop hearing: *Welcome! You've Got Mail!* The problem is that Windows has lost track of the sound files. Click the Start menu, point at Settings, then click Control Panel. When the Control Panel opens, double-click the Sound icon, and reselect your AOL sounds for Welcome, Mail, and the rest. The original sound files are located in your AOL folder.

What to Do When Things Go Wrong

Nothing is completely foolproof—and I'm the fool that's proven it, time and time again. New and unusual things may go wrong for you, and go spectacularly wrong. The savvy computer user learns not to panic, and how to get help right away. I can't help with the panic, but I can show you how to get help on the double.

Three basic ways exist to get help from America Online: while you're online; while you're offline; and by calling tech support.

Getting Help Online

You're signed on to AOL and something wonky happens (that's a technical word, "wonky," use it to impress your friends). Something isn't working right, or you can't figure out how to use a certain feature. Don't panic.

On your AOL menu, you'll see a menu labeled Help. Click it. The first item on that menu is Member Services Online Help. Click that, too. You'll go right to Member Services, shown in Figure B.1.

TIME SAVER

The Help menu can also take you to specific help areas while you're online. You can get help with Parental Controls, Keywords, Accounts and Billing, and AOL Access Phone Numbers. Just select the appropriate item from your Help menu while signed on to AOL.

Figure B.1.

Member Services, your one-stop help shop.

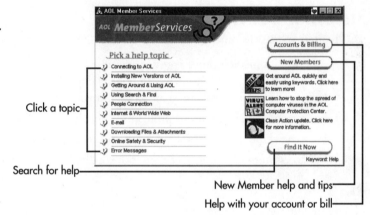

Click a topic ─

Search for help ─

New Member help and tips ─
Help with your account or bill ─

Click a help topic on the left of the Member Services screen, and you'll be given a similar window with topics on the left, and a list box of helpful text files to the right. Click a topic, then double-click a help file in the text box.

Another helpful resource is the Members Helping Members message boards, where you can post a question and other AOL Members will help you out. Members Helping Members is available from any of the topic screens, or from the New Members area.

If you can't find the information you need, you can try to search for it, with the Find It Now button on the main Member Services window, or you can click the Ask The Staff button on any of the topic windows. It will lead you to Member Help Interactive, which is live, one-on-one online help from an AOL technician in a mini-chat room.

Getting Offline Help

Generally, if you can get online, you should, because there are more resources available to you there. But if you can't get online, or if getting online is the problem you're having, then offline help is the way to go.

To open Offline Help, launch your AOL software. When the Sign On screen appears, click the Help menu, and select Offline Help. You'll open the kind of help files standard for your computer. For Windows and Windows 95, that means the kind of indexed help files you find in other Windows applications. For Mac users, it means Apple Guide help.

Calling America Online

Like all software and computer companies, AOL maintains customer service lines you can call and ask a real live person questions by phone. They also maintain a fax service and a good old-fashioned computer bulletin board.

Customer Service

AOL offers several customer service lines, specifically:

- [ ] America Online Solution Express is available at 1-800-827-6364. This is an automated line, but it's available 24 hours a day. During most of the day, you *do* have the option of speaking to an actual human being.
- [ ] For screen name or password problems, call: 1-888-265-8004.
- [ ] For general questions or problems, call: 1-888-265-8006.
- [ ] For access number problems or questions, call: 1-888-265-8009.

BBS

If you are somewhat computer savvy and have used a computer bulletin board service (BBS), you can connect to AOL's BBS at 1-800-827-5808. You'll need to use a generic communications program (one probably came with your modem), and the software should be set to the standard 8-N-1 settings.

On the BBS you'll find technical help, current versions of the AOL software you can download, and other helpful tips and information. Naturally, the problem you're having can't affect your computer's modem—you'll need it to connect to the bulletin board.

FAXLink

AOL's FAXLink service is available at 1-800-827-5551. With FAXLink, you call and request information by way of the number pad on your touch-tone telephone. The information you request is then faxed to you shortly after you hang up.

To use FAXLink, your fax modem can't be the problem—you'll need it to receive the faxes, unless you have a regular fax machine as well.

Between the online, offline, and telephone support you can get, and this book, there shouldn't be a problem so calamitous that *someone* can't help you with it. Just stay calm, keep breathing, and remember: In case of a water landing, your seat cushion can be used as a floatation device.

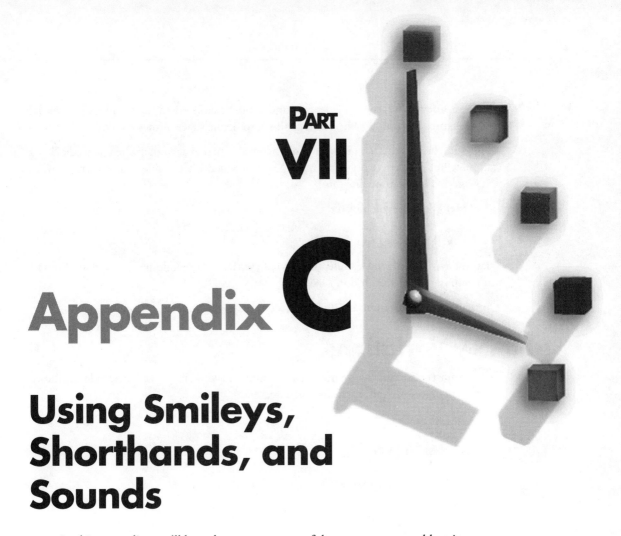

Appendix C

Using Smileys, Shorthands, and Sounds

In this appendix, you'll learn how to use some of the more common abbreviations and funny faces used in chat rooms online.

These People Have a Punctuation Problem!

I remember the first time I was ever in a chat room—it was back in the day before America Online was America Online. I was talking to someone in a chat room and they ended every sentence they typed with the strangest punctuation. Stuff like:

:-)

I thought, *jeez, what a crummy typist.* Turned out, I was a crummy chatter.

If you turn this book so the right parenthesis)is toward the bottom of the page, you'll see that the bizarre set of punctuation marks make a *smiley* face.

> **New Term**   **Smiley**—A face made from punctuation marks, used to communicate facial expression online, where you can't see someone's face as they speak.

Smileys are the way chatters get around not being able to see each other when they talk. They can point out the fact that you're making a joke, when it's possible to misinterpret what you've said. They're used like this:

Me: Well, see you all later!

You: Not if I see you first! ;-)

That smiley is a wink and a smile, used to tell me that you're kidding—otherwise, I might think you're mad at me, or don't like me.

There are a *lot* of variations on the two basic smileys you've seen.

Smiley Variations

The two most commonly used smileys are the smile and wink. Plenty of other smileys indicate all kinds of emotions and reactions. Such as:

:-o   Minor shock.

:-O   Major shock.

=8-O   Call a paramedic.

:-x   My lips are sealed.

0:-)   I'm angelic—usually used when you *really* mean:

}:->   I'm a devil.

:-(A frown.

:-| Neutral.

:-/   Chagrin.

:-P   Sticking my tongue out at you.

:-D   A *really* big smile.

:-*   A kiss.

C

Some folks create smileys that look like themselves (well, as much as you can look like a set of punctuation marks). Drew Carey might use one like:

[B-)x

The [for his flat top. The B for his glasses, the nose and smile as usual, and the x for his bow tie.

Non-face Fun

Another set of symbols is used online, particularly in hosted rooms, that might throw you for a moment. They use the keyboard symbols to draw other things, like (my favorites):

C[_]   A cup of coffee.

===[}   Throwing a pie.

@----}—   A long-stemmed rose.

{}   A hug.

{{{}}}   A BIG hug.

To deliver either of the hugs properly, you put the screen name of the person you're hugging between the brackets: **{{{PIV!}}}**.

There are others, but you won't have too much trouble figuring them out—folks tend to indicate what they are, like this:

Piv: Throwing a banana cream pie at **You2**.

PIV: =======[}

It can be fun, if you're in the right mood. Silly as all get out, if you're not.

Shorthands

A shorthand is an abbreviation for a commonly used expression. They save time, because you don't have to type out the whole phrase—which is really handy if you're not that great of a typist to begin with.

These are some of the ones you'll see used most often online:

LOL   Laughing Out Loud

ROFL Rolling On the Floor Laughing

BTW By The Way

GMTA Great Minds Think Alike

AFK Away From Keyboard—to let folks know you're leaving your computer for a moment. When you return, you use:

BAK Back At Keyboard

IMHO In My Humble Opinion

IMNSHO In My Not So Humble Opinion

DL/Dling Download or Downloading

UL/Uling Upload or Uploading

<g> Grin

<G> Big grin

<EG> Big *evil* grin

JUST A MINUTE

If someone uses a smiley, symbol, or other abbreviation that you don't understand, just ask what it means. People don't mind explaining. The easiest way to ask is to repeat what they said followed by a couple of question marks, like this: **ROFLMAO???** Someone will come back with a translation.

TIME SAVER

If you'd like to learn more about smileys and shorthands, use the keyword SMILEYS to visit an online forum devoted to the fine art of expressing yourself with punctuation.

Using Chat Room Sounds

You may be startled sometime in a chat room when your computer pipes up "Welcome!" or some such AOL sound you normally only hear in other areas online. That's because you can get AOL to play a sound on *everyone's computer in the chat room.* It's very cool. There are a couple of conditions, however:

☐ Your computer must be sound capable. All Macs are, and any PC with a sound card installed can make the sounds.

☐ You must have the sound file installed on your computer to hear it.

☐ You must type the command into the chat text box exactly right, or it won't work.

TIME SAVER

On a PC the sound files (with the file extension .WAV) should be in your AOL folder. With Windows 95, the sounds can also be in the Media folder, inside your Windows folder.

On a Mac, the sound files (sometimes with the .SND file extension) should be in your System Suitcase, inside your System folder.

Send a Sound In a Chat Room

To Do

Just for giggles, get to a chat room and use this line of chat to send a sound into the chat room:

{S soundname

For example, if you wanted to use AOL's "Welcome" sound, you'd do this:

1. Click to place your cursor in the chat text box.

2. Type: **{S welcome**

3. Click **Send**.

When your chat hits the chat room, you should hear the same AOL "Welcome!" you hear when you sign on.

Hundreds of thousands of chat room sounds are flying around online. You can acquire them a number of ways:

☐ **Ask for them on email**—If someone sends a sound into a chat room that you don't have, ask them to email it to you. Make sure you get the correct type of sound for your computer.

☐ **Browse for them**—Most forums that have software libraries and chat rooms, also have collections of sound files you can download.

☐ **Search for them**—Hour 5, "Dowloading Files and Searching Databases," explains how to search for software and other stuff online.

A lot of ways exist to communicate in a chat room that don't involve typing your everyday sentence. With a little practice, you'll be up to speed in no time flat.

INDEX

MACMILLAN COMPUTER PUBLISHING USA

A VIACOM COMPANY

Technical ---- Support

If you need assistance with the information provided by Macmillan Computer Publishing, please access the information available on our web site at **http://www.mcp.com/feedback.** Our most Frequently Asked Questions are answered there. If you do not find the answers to your questions on our web site, you may contact Macmillan User Services at **(317) 581-3833** or email us at **support@mcp.com**.